WRITING WARS

THE NEW AMERICAN CANON

The Iowa Series in
Contemporary Literature and Culture

Samuel Cohen, series editor

WRITING WARS

AUTHORSHIP AND
AMERICAN WAR FICTION,
WWI TO PRESENT

David F. Eisler

UNIVERSITY OF IOWA PRESS | IOWA CITY

University of Iowa Press, Iowa City 52242
Copyright © 2022 by David F. Eisler
uipress.uiowa.edu

ISBN 978-1-60938-865-2 (pbk)
ISBN 978-1-60938-866-9 (ebk)

Printed in the United States of America

Design and typesetting by April Leidig

No part of this book may be reproduced or used in any form or by
any means without permission in writing from the publisher. All reasonable
steps have been taken to contact copyright holders of material used in this
book. The publisher would be pleased to make suitable arrangements
with any whom it has not been possible to reach.

Printed on acid-free paper

Cataloging-in-Publication data is on file
with the Library of Congress.

CONTENTS

Preface vii

Introduction 1

ONE

"Stick to Her Own Farms and Farmer Folk":
World War I and the Origins of Combat Gnosticism
21

TWO

"Tell It Like It Was":
World War II and the Institutional Curation of Memory
45

THREE

"You Had to Be There":
Vietnam and the Veteran's Consolidation of Authority
65

FOUR

"You Don't Have to Be a Veteran":
The All-Volunteer Force and the Dispersion of Authority
83

FIVE

"The New Battle":
The Civil-Military Gap and the Shock of Coming Home
109

SIX

"The Other Side of COIN":
Counterinsurgency and the Ethics of Memory
137

SEVEN

"You Volunteered to Get Screwed":
Public Trust and the Literary Representation
of the Professional Military
163

APPENDIX

The American Novels of Iraq and
Afghanistan through 2020
187

Acknowledgments 191

Notes 193

Bibliography 231

Index 243

PREFACE

I ALWAYS THOUGHT I would write a novel when I came home from war. After joining the army as a commissioned officer in 2007, I deployed to Iraq in the summer of 2008 and then to Afghanistan in 2010. Like other literary-minded veterans, I had read Ernest Hemingway and Tim O'Brien and I knew that the veteran-turned-author was a well-trodden path. I even wrote a blog during both of my deployments, thinking that perhaps I would eventually turn it into something bigger and more meaningful.

Instead, I wrote this book, the culmination of thinking about war writing and civil-military relations for more than a decade. Even though I left active duty in 2012, I remained connected to the military in a variety of ways. I went to graduate school on the post-9/11 GI Bill, studying international security policy and meeting other fellow veterans who became close friends. We shared our frustration with the lack of attention our wars were getting from the rest of the country, a frustration that I had felt even before I had served on active duty when, on the day I received my undergraduate degree from Cornell University in May 2007, a classmate's mother expressed shock at my decision to join the army during a time of war. ("Why would you want to do that?" she said). That feeling of detachment left me with a bitter taste as well as a hope that someday I could find a way to bridge the divide.

At its core, this book is exactly that: the embodiment of hope and the excitement of discovery that there is, in fact, a more vibrant and engaged discussion about these wars taking place in the pages of American fiction. Despite my own initial reluctance to read the novels and short stories about the conflicts in which I had served, confronting them created an unexpected spark of insight when I noticed how many authors had never served in the military themselves. This surprised me—as I'm sure it will surprise others—and that observation grew into a series of questions about the connections between civil-military relations and American war fiction.

I come to this project foremost as a scholar, though, and my own first-hand experiences are relevant only in that they made me curious about the subject matter. Like the chorus of voices that appear in the later pages of this book, I also believe that war is too important to be left to the purview of veterans alone.

WRITING WARS

INTRODUCTION

Who writes novels about war? For nearly a century after World War I, the answer was simple: soldiers who had been there. The assumption that a person must have experienced war in the flesh in order to write about it in fiction was taken for granted by writers, reviewers, critics, and even scholars. The veteran-author's authority was rarely challenged, having become embedded into the fabric of the genre's conventions. If there were war stories to tell, veterans would tell them.

It might have come as a surprise, then, when army veteran–turned–author Matt Gallagher published an article in 2016 titled "You Don't Have to Be a Veteran to Write about War" on the same day that *Youngblood*, his own novel about the Iraq War, came out. He wrote of an "ugly undercurrent of thought in this part of the writing world — usually unspoken but ever pervasive — that one shouldn't write about war unless one participated in it as a combatant or otherwise survived its destruction." He called this a "silly idea," pointing to the power of fiction to create worlds from the imagination regardless of who the author is or what experience they have. Writing is writing, and "an author adept at the craft doesn't need to have experienced combat directly to bring readers to war."[1]

Viewed within the literary historical context of American war fiction, Gallagher's article was a curious marketing strategy to attract readers to his own war novel. Since the Civil War, veterans have relied on military credentials as a testament to their narrative authority, arguing that they had shouldered the burden of experience and thus had earned the right to write about it. But for a nation whose most recent encounter with sustained conflict on home soil ended in 1865, the introduction of geographic distance between the battlefield and what become known as the "home front" spilled into the field of cultural production. American civilians, safely ensconced between two oceans, were spared the horrors and devastation of bombs and bullets, allowing veterans-turned-authors to enter the literary field with a ready-made banner of symbolic capital that publishers gladly waved to a readership eager for the truth of what it must have been like "over there," whether

Introduction

"there" happened to be the battlefields of Europe, the Pacific, Korea, Vietnam, or the Greater Middle East.[2] This trend began after World War I and eventually became enshrined in the American cultural landscape—a "war at a distance" mentality that views wartime service with a combination of respectful fear and reluctant awe.

As war became something that happened "over there," the veteran's authority found new expression within the literary field, and veteran-authors emerged as a special class of writers who came to dominate the creation, production, and reception of literary works about war and conflict. During this time, a new American war fiction genre was built on the philosophy that personal experience, narrative authenticity, and literary authority were inexorably linked and mutually dependent, making the genre the providence of veteran-authors—nearly all of whom were men—and excluding the voices of women and nonveterans at their expense. After World War I, the respected novelist Willa Cather, whose previous work had focused on the American frontier at the end of the nineteenth century, was heavily criticized for daring to write about a soldier who joins the Allied Expeditionary Force to fight in France, prompting one especially negative reviewer to say, "The pity is that Miss Cather did not know war for the big bowwow stuff that it is and stick to her own farms and farmer folk." Meanwhile, the works of John Dos Passos and, later, Ernest Hemingway were hailed as authentic war stories because they had driven ambulances near the front.

The veteran's symbolic capital became part and parcel of the nascent creative writing institutions that formed across the country after World War II, especially the famous Iowa and Stanford workshops. These programs packed literary-minded veterans into classrooms and taught them to "write what you know," leading to an institutional curation of memory that reinforced an aesthetic sensibility that prized personal experience as the source of narrative authenticity. Wallace Stegner, founder of the program at Stanford, was happy to have war veterans in his classes rather than the "green nineteen and twenty-year-olds" he was used to at Harvard.[3] These veterans looked to Hemingway for guidance on writing about war, something Hemingway believed "was one of the major subjects and certainly one of the hardest to write truly of," making those without war experience jealous because it was "something quite irreplaceable that they had missed."[4] Many

Introduction

of the veterans who graduated from Iowa and Stanford in those years went on to fill the academic ranks as professors of literature and creative writing, shaping American literary institutions for decades to come.

By the end of the Vietnam War, the saying went that "you had to be there" if you wanted to understand the war, let alone write about it. One Vietnam veteran even published an article in which he argued that the purpose of a war story "is not to enlighten but to exclude; its message is not its content but putting the listener in his place. I suffered; I was there. You were not. Only those facts matter. Everything else is beyond words to tell."[5] Veterans, it seemed, completely owned the experience of war and were in no hurry to let others into their world.

But cracks have formed in the genre's foundation, and the literary house built on the authority of experience has become outdated and unstable. A simple accounting of published works since 2001 reveals that the veteran-author's near monopoly over the literary representation of conflict in American memory culture, so dominant for nearly one hundred years, has all but vanished. Gallagher's plea to the literary community that the subject of war does not belong to veterans alone seems to have found a receptive audience: of the fifty-nine authors who have published novels and story collections about the conflicts in Iraq and Afghanistan as of 2020, fewer than half (twenty-three) have been veterans, a distribution of war fiction authorship unseen for a century.[6] To understand why, we have to look beyond the literary field and go back nearly fifty years to a political decision about military personnel policy whose ramifications rippled into the field of cultural production, transforming the foundational characteristics—authorship, content, and form—of the American war fiction genre.

W riting Wars reveals a surprising and unexpected connection between civil-military relations and American literature. It tells the story of how veteran-authors came to monopolize the cultural authority over the literary representation of war in the twentieth century, and how they have ceded that authority for the conflicts in Iraq and Afghanistan in response to changes in the relationship between the military and American society. As the American population has become disconnected from the

Introduction

consequences of overseas conflicts since the end of conscription and the shift to an all-volunteer force, veteran-authors have sought ways to unburden themselves from the sole responsibility to interpret these conflicts in fiction.

The forging of American identity as a nation begins with an act of violence that echoes through the ages of the country's existence and continues today. The catastrophic wars of the early twentieth century wreaked havoc across much of the world, but the United States was largely spared the worst of their consequences. Placed in comparison with other major belligerents, the United States not only avoided the large-scale destruction of its national territory and the deaths of a significant portion of its civilian population, but it emerged from the wars in a more dominant geopolitical position than almost any of its rivals. This difference in national experience left the United States as "the only advanced country that still glorifies and exalts the military, a sentiment familiar in Europe before 1945 but quite unknown today," in the words of historian Tony Judt.[7] For a nation founded in the flames of crashing cannons and musket fire, war takes on a different symbolic meaning than it does for nations whose countrysides still bear the scars of battle.

Over the course of the twentieth century, the term "American wars" became synonymous with "foreign wars," and Americans' geographic separation from distant battlefields influenced not only the political calculations with respect to future conflict but also its cultural associations. Historian Mary Dudziak writes that "the principal character of American civilians' relationship to war death in the 20th century was distance from the carnage."[8] She refers to the process as the "cultural distance from war death," arguing that this distance "characterizes contemporary American war politics." In contrast to much of the commentary on American civil-military relations, Dudziak believes that "the most important divide is not between civilians and their soldiers but civilian distance from the broader experience of war and war's effects."[9]

American civil-military relations took a major turn in 1973 when, during the last throes of American involvement in Vietnam, the military abolished the draft as a means to compel citizens to serve in uniform during times of war and began to rely entirely on volunteer, career soldiers. Over time, this arrangement has resulted in a separation between the military and American society, leading to what analysts, scholars, and commentators

Introduction

have called the "civil-military gap."[10] The burden of the wars in Iraq and Afghanistan—the first sustained conflicts in American history to be fought entirely by a professional, volunteer military—has been borne by a small fraction of the population while little has been asked of the rest of the country: no restrictions, no supply rations, no additional taxes, no conscription. While some scholars argue that the significance of this civil-military gap has been overblown, others point to a society in which citizens can spend their entire lives blissfully uncaring and untouched by the causes and consequences of their nation's conflicts, providing a permissive environment for the United States' increased reliance on force as a mechanism in foreign policy. Secure in the belief that they won't be drafted to fight in a war or taxed to fund it, most Americans have become insulated from the consequences of waging a war on foreign territory.

With an all-volunteer military, though, accepting the premise that only veterans can understand the truth of war also means that only those who choose to serve are saddled with the burden of war's interpretation. Against the backdrop of the civil-military gap, I will argue that the volunteer veterans of Iraq and Afghanistan have rejected their own authority as the sole gatekeepers of war representations in American memory culture. They have looked for ways to rid themselves of this responsibility, such as downplaying the importance of personal experience as essential for narrative authenticity, writing as much about the domestic home front as they do about the combat zone, and writing more frequently from the perspective of non-American characters. Each of these trends represents a major shift away from the rhetorical and narrative conventions of the genre, especially as compared with the works that have come to define the fictional response to the Vietnam War. The result has been a dispersion of the veteran-author's authority—a way to share the burden of war with the rest of the American population.

The connection between civil-military relations and American war fiction begins with a field that describes the structural relationship between the military, policymakers, and society. American civil-military relations have been a subject of academic interest since Samuel Huntington and Morris Janowitz published the field's canonical texts in the late 1950s and early 1960s.[11] While Huntington was concerned with how to maintain

Introduction

civilian control of the military in a democratic state without compromising the military's ability to defend against external threats, Janowitz argued that sustaining democratic values within the military institution and encouraging civic participation within society were the primary policy objectives.[12] Both of them, however, recognized that cultural representations of the military were worth paying attention to as a kind of civil-military relationship barometer, though neither took the analysis much further than a few cursory observations.

Over time, the field of civil-military relations has grown beyond questions of military effectiveness and absorbed other elements, including the idea of a civil-military gap. Since the Vietnam War and the abolition of conscription, political science researchers have examined both the theoretical and the practical consequences of the gap, with a particular focus on the role of the military in American society and the growing abdication of civic responsibility that became an unintended consequence of the all-volunteer force. To date, though, these scholars have rarely examined literature and authorship as a component of American civil-military relations, nor have literary scholars devoted significant attention to the broader implications of literary authority as applied to fiction about war.

While most scholars and policy analysts tend to accept that there is a gap between the military and American society, there is some disagreement on its magnitude and importance. Serious discussion about the civil-military relationship predates the terrorist attacks of September 11, 2001; journalist Thomas Ricks wrote an article for *The Atlantic* in 1997 titled "The Widening Gap between Military and Society" that became one of the first in-depth commentaries on what has become a familiar theme.[13] A 2003 article by army colonel Richard Hooker (prior to the sustained deployments to Iraq and Afghanistan that were to come) noted that "the dominant academic critique takes several forms, charging that the military has become increasingly estranged from the society it serves," but concluded that "the dynamic tension which exists in civil-military relations today, while in many cases suboptimal and unpleasant, is far from dangerous. . . . Modern U.S. civil-military relations remain sound, enduring, and stable."[14] Similarly, a 2016 collection of essays edited by former secretary of defense James Mattis and research analyst Kori Schake took the view that "the relationship between America's military and its civilian society is fundamentally strong

Introduction

and healthy."[15] Historian and retired army officer Andrew Bacevich's body of work suggests otherwise, pointing to the increased willingness of American politicians to support and defend a state of perpetual war without fear that they will be held accountable by concerned citizens who want a voice in how their military is employed.[16] Other scholars have questioned the health and stability of the all-volunteer force in general.[17]

For those who do believe that the gap has important consequences, civil-military relations theory has suggested that the responsibility to bridge the divide broadly falls on the military.[18] In that sense, it is unsurprising that war veterans would wish to tell their stories to fellow citizens as acts of communicative memory, functionalizing them as what memory studies scholar Astrid Erll calls "collective texts" that help form and shape the meaning of the war experience in historical memory.[19] This has become something of an American literary tradition, and a parade of literature has followed every American war for the last century. Many writers have attempted to follow in Hemingway's footsteps and seek out war experience as a surefire path to literary fame and notoriety (a practice that Eric Bennett brilliantly satirizes in his 2015 novel *A Big Enough Lie*). Norman Mailer, for example, whose 1948 debut novel *The Naked and the Dead* became an instant bestseller and one of the genre's early classics, even wrote that "in the forty-eight hours after Pearl Harbor, while worthy young men were wondering where they could be of aid to the war effort, and practical young men were deciding which branch of service was the surest for landing a safe commission, I was worrying darkly whether it would be more likely that a great war novel would be written about Europe or the Pacific."[20]

Within the field of cultural production, and literary fiction in particular, the war novel takes on a mysterious aura of untouchability unlike almost any other subject, where even the authority to write about it is a matter of heated debate. "Who owns the story," as Roxana Robinson wrote for the *New York Times*, "the person who lives it or the person who writes it?" Robinson's novel *Sparta* followed a young marine officer struggling with post-traumatic stress after a tour in Iraq. "Most comments I've received from veterans have been positive," she continued,

> but during a radio interview someone wrote in by email: This woman has never been in combat and knows nothing about it. He was both

right and wrong: I've never been in combat, but, actually, I do know something about it. I've learned about it, not by being there, but in another way that writers learn: by paying attention.[21]

The question of "the right to write" (fittingly the title of Robinson's article) has a history within literary criticism, though most scholarship has tacitly accepted the veteran's authority over the literary representation of war even while reflexively commenting on its apparent limitations. In a 2018 book designed as an introduction to American war literature, Jennifer Haytock points out that "one of the primary contested points about war literature is the question of who has the credibility to write it." She continues:

> combatants frequently claim the exclusive authority to speak about war. Many readers and scholars privilege texts by soldiers and veterans because these individuals offer first-hand reports by those who were there. Indeed, much powerful writing has come from combatants who offer detailed accounts of what they saw, did, and felt. While most people think first of soldiers when they think of individuals at war, many participants are non-combatants: they are support staff, nurses, refugees, reporters, and more. They too can and do offer first-hand accounts of their experience of war.[22]

Haytock's attempt to broaden the authority to write about war beyond the combatant nonetheless rests on the argument that noncombatants can also write "first-hand accounts," implicitly excluding the *nonwitness* account from consideration. She then concludes that authenticity is a crucial element of war writing, asking two important questions: "to what extent do we value war stories based on the experiences of their author, and to what extent do we acknowledge an artist's ability to imagine events and emotions?" After all, literary fiction is intended to be the realm of the imagination, so imposing the artificial constraints of mimetic realism for war as a subject goes against the very spirit of fiction.

From this perspective, the war veteran's story derives its cultural authority from its proximity to lived experience. Haytock herself sets war apart as a subject for literature—at least in the American context—because the *experience* of war is presumed to be unlike anything the typical reader could imagine. War is "is a matter of life and death for its participants and requires

Introduction

the complicity of the citizens on whose behalf it is fought, so getting it right matters."[23] In another book on the literary representation of war, Kate McLoughlin similarly lists "credibility" as one of war literature's most important factors. "Who tells of war?" she then asks, followed by, "What factors enhance the telling (opportunity and authority seem to be basic requirements) and how are they acquired and conveyed?"[24] Her answer is clear:

> First-hand experience . . . is indeed the crucial ingredient of authority, legitimacy and credibility in war reporting. The eye-witness offers the epistemological guarantee *you can believe it because I saw it happen.*[25] [italics in original]

The notion that only veterans get to write about war often finds its way into academic debates as well. A reviewer of Stacey Peebles's 2011 book, *Welcome to the Suck: Narrating the American Soldier's Experience in Iraq*, stated that "Soldiers—and combat veterans in particular—often chafe when civilians try to speak about war. There are dues to be paid before one can speak about the experience of combat, so the story goes, and those who haven't experienced the hardship haven't the right to describe the experience."[26] Although the reviewer's tone comes across as skeptical ("so the story goes"), he then marvels that Peebles "steps bravely across the line dividing civilians from the military to analyze war texts from the Gulf War to the just-ended War in Iraq." The reviewer seems to assume that even a civilian academic must tread carefully when writing critically about war.

That personal experience was a prerequisite for knowledge and understanding is the heart of Paul Fussell's *The Great War and Modern Memory* (1975), a work of literary and cultural history whose influence on war literature and criticism has been unparalleled in the decades since its publication. *The Great War and Modern Memory* was the thread that tied together America's three major wars of the twentieth century to that point—Fussell was a decorated World War II combat veteran, writing about World War I literature, just as the Vietnam War was limping to its conclusion. The book went beyond proposing and inaugurating a canon of World War I literature, though, instead transforming into a kind of literary litmus test for a work's authenticity. Fussell drew a sharp division between what those who served on the First World War's front lines had experienced and what those who didn't were capable of understanding, and his exaltation of soldiers' writings channeled

Introduction

its analysis into a cultural authority of war literature that, wittingly or not, ensured that the veteran-author would ascend to a position of dominance within the genre. Perhaps it was Fussell's own status as a combat veteran that made his arguments resistant to the many critiques that have faulted him for ignoring women and nonveteran writers as well as the flaws in his lionization of experience as the sole conduit to representing war. The most important of these critiques came in 1999 from James Campbell, who coined the term "combat gnosticism" to describe the ideology in which war experience is seen as a kind of knowledge that is incommunicable to the uninitiated.[27] Subsequent studies of war literature critical of the authority of experience have zeroed in on combat gnosticism as the focal point of their attack, though *Writing Wars* broadens this criticism by contextualizing the veteran-author's narrative authority alongside developments in American civil-military relations.[28]

Despite the critical focus on the ideology of combat gnosticism in the twentieth century, the line of thought that links personal experience and narrative authority has its origins in the evolution of war and memory culture since the mid-eighteenth and early nineteenth centuries. Historian Yuval Noah Harari uses the term "flesh-witness" to describe how the physical, bodily experience of war acquired a revelatory status that became a privileged source of knowledge and authority according to Romantic notions of the sublime.[29] In Harari's view, the authority ascribed to the flesh-witness comes from conceiving of the experience as something transcendental, creating a division between storyteller and listener that merely emphasizes the listener's ignorance. This notion would prove to be a powerful tool in the hands of Vietnam War veterans looking to regain control of a cultural narrative that had largely turned against them during the United States' involvement in the conflict.

As it happened, the Vietnam War veteran's narrative authority was cemented even before the conflict was over. Protest and cultural movements against the war in the United States ensured that there was a distinct rhetorical marker between Vietnam and "the World," as so many veterans called it, with American society becoming the indirect antagonist to those who had been sent overseas. The rhetorical characterization of the war as a unique event in American history encouraged a clear dividing line drawn between those who were there and those who weren't, and the imaginative

Introduction

representations of the war were ceded almost exclusively to those veterans who believed they had a stake in the way the war would be remembered. Despite publishers' initial reluctance to reopen recent wounds once the war was over, output eventually soared to more than six hundred novels, the vast majority of which were written by male combat veterans.[30]

In general, the literary response to the Vietnam War became synonymous with a handful of big names: Tim O'Brien, Michael Herr, Larry Heinemann, Robert Olen Butler, Jim Webb. Their works dominated the cultural landscape and early reimaginations of the war. But in 1985, Bobbie Ann Mason—a writer with no connection to the war or the military—published the novel *In Country* about a girl whose father was killed in Vietnam before she was born. Although Mason was initially hesitant to tackle the subject, a moving experience at the Vietnam Veterans Memorial led her to believe that the war did not just belong to those who had fought there, but that it was "every American's story."[31] The novel was widely praised, though some reviewers couldn't help but notice that Mason was not how they pictured the typical war fiction writer—the first line of the *Kirkus* review said, "How ironic—or maybe not—that one of the so-far best, most affecting Vietnam novels ever should come from a woman."[32] That the reviewer felt compelled to comment on Mason's gender is just one aspect of male combat veterans' influence within the genre.

While Mason's novel appeared ten years after the fall of Saigon, the lag between the war's actions and the publication of novels written by authors with no direct connection to them has all but evaporated for the conflicts in Iraq and Afghanistan. Something has happened within the field of literary production that has led to more published war novels written by authors with no personal experience in the wars. Perhaps publishers—those with the ultimate authority over which works enter the literary arena—no longer believe that war novels require the easy stamp of "authenticity" that comes with a veteran's voice, or that the distinction between a veteran and nonveteran author does not matter as much for marketability. As I will argue, this pluralization of authorship goes hand in hand with a collapsing of the temporal distance between the conflicts as current events and their revision and reinterpretation as history; the wars are so far from the average American's daily lives that they might as well be history, and authors see these wars as a subject begging for literary investigation. To borrow Bobbie Ann Mason's

Introduction

words, contemporary writers—veterans and nonveterans alike—have embraced the idea that these wars are "every American's subject." And while the resulting stack of novels is a mixed bag of critical perspectives, with some more skeptical of the military than others, each work nonetheless contributes to a broader understanding of these conflicts and their global ramifications.

What's happening in the war fiction genre also runs counter to many of the prevailing norms and trends in American literature, where the notion of "speaking for others" has encountered increasing resistance.[33] Since the 1960s, questions of cultural identity have led to a more diverse notion of literary authorship, encouraging writers from historically marginalized communities to tell their own stories.[34] In recent years, a greater appreciation for the inequalities in the publishing industry has also led to a recognition that a concept like authenticity cannot be separated from the structural imbalances placed in the way of nonmajority writers seeking to capture that nonmajority experience in fiction.[35] When a writer crosses this line, accusations of cultural appropriation are sure to follow, as they did in droves, for example, when American author Jeanine Cummins published her novel *American Dirt* (2020) about the experience of a Mexican family attempting to flee to the United States.[36] Having long watched others speak for them, minority groups now more frequently assert their right to speak for themselves.

The one exception to this trend has been contemporary veteran writers. While military service is not equivalent to ethnicity or race, Mark McGurl's history of postwar creative writing programs includes veterans as part of the trend toward high cultural pluralism and technomodernism in which "veteranness" became a unique cultural identifier that functioned in similar manner.[37] Today, veteran writers are not only claiming that personal experience is not a prerequisite to write authentic war fiction, they are also communicating a more cosmopolitan understanding of these wars by broadening their narratives to include the perspectives of those who have typically been excluded from American interpretations.

Critics who still see the shadows of imperialism in contemporary war fiction tend to point at the continued influence of university creative writing programs on American literature as well as the abundance of nonprofit writing workshops that cater specifically to veterans of Afghanistan and Iraq.[38]

Introduction

Joseph Darda, for one, refers to a "new generation of MFA-trained veteran-writers" whose works reflect a "narrative of white humanitarian sacrifice" based on the high cultural pluralist values of the workshop classroom.[39] Yet the charge that "nearly all recent war writing has been cultivated in the hothouse of creative-writing programs," as Sam Sacks wrote in 2015,[40] has not been matched by the data: of the twenty-three veteran-authors of contemporary war novels that I have identified in this project, only twelve have MFA degrees (fourteen of the remaining thirty-six nonveteran authors have MFAs). While creative writing programs continue to play an important role in shaping the American literary field, their effect on contemporary war fiction has been overblown in critiques that also miss the way veteran-authors have taken a more universalist approach in their work.

In fact, the consequences of American interventions in Iraq and Afghanistan for the people who experienced them as something other than an American soldier is a common motif in novels written by veterans. These works stand in stark contrast to the arguably self-absorbed and nationalist fictional responses to World War I and World War II that were preoccupied with American-centric narratives and themes, characteristics that were then taken to the extreme after the Vietnam War where a denial of the "Other's" humanity was a literary resort to reassert control over national shame. While we might expect this kind of writing to continue in response to the ethically questionable wars in Afghanistan and Iraq, this has not been the case. The fictional response to these conflicts has been far more concerned with the moral and ethical questions that writers tended to ignore after the so-called "good war."

By avoiding the standard form of American war fiction, these veteran-authors relinquish their own authority as narrators of the contemporary war experience by implicitly calling the centrality of the American veteran's experience into question. Unlike the dispersion of authority that comes from forces inside and outside the literary field and has changed the proportion of contemporary war fiction authorship — that is, the ascription of "authenticity" and importance of personal experience — the trend of veteran-authors writing from non-American perspectives is driven by these authors' own narrative choices and strategies. Whereas literary authorship is a function of multiple variables within the field of production — market trends, agent and editor preferences, reader tastes, and so on—a novel's characters come from the author's own decisions. These narrative choices therefore form an accurate reflection of the story that the author deems important to tell.

In addition to including non-American characters who are complex and well-rounded, these novels also tend to tell more complicated stories about the Americans who fought in these wars. There are no saints among the volunteers. The authors of these characters are not interested in hero worship or civilian platitudes; rather, they explore the ugly side of serving as an instrument of state violence. These novels explicitly reject the nationalistic, American-centric narrative as a sufficient approach for the literary representation of the wars in Iraq and Afghanistan. Most of them come close to what Viet Thanh Nguyen calls the "ethics of recognition" by depicting the complex moral choices that both American and non-American characters make, often pulled into war's cycles of violence while trying to preserve some semblance of their own goodness. This is especially true for many non-American characters, some of whom are directly responsible for the deaths of other people—including Americans—but nonetheless retain elements of their humanity that may have gone unrecognized or undistinguished if contemporary veteran-authors merely mimicked their authorial predecessors after the Vietnam War.

That is not to say that these are the only kinds of narratives coming out of these wars, but reading them alongside many of the early works about Vietnam suggests that today's authors are seeking a greater sense of empathy with war fiction's traditional Other. The brutality of Vietnam War fiction, and in particular the dehumanization of Vietnamese civilians, is designed to shock the reader and present the unfiltered horrors of that war's experience. Yet there tends to be a lack of moral reckoning with those actions and an undeserved clarity of rightful purpose that is, I believe, correctly missing from contemporary war fiction. Although the dominant mode of today's war fiction is cynicism, there is a moral ambiguity and complexity rooted in the way we have come to think about these "forever wars" and our role in precipitating them as American citizens, whether in uniform or not.

Although the trend of veteran-authors writing from non-American perspectives is a step in the right direction toward less narcissistic conventions within the war fiction genre, we can't ignore questions of cultural appro-

Introduction

priation. A more critical view could argue that these novels still represent just another side of the imperialist coin, robbing those whose lives were destroyed by these wars of the ability to tell their own stories. Issues of cultural appropriation and "speaking for the other" are justifiably important and worthy of debate and discussion, but a singular focus on them obscures the crucial role of narrative choice within literary texts. There is still value in approaching the fictional response to a conflict from a national perspective, analyzing how American authors have depicted non-American characters in their literary representations of war. At the broadest level, ethical questions about representation as they relate to memory culture ask who *should* be represented in war fiction and *how* should they be represented. Authors *choose* what they wish to represent, and tracing changes in those choices at the level of a fictional response (that is, the set of texts that respond to a historical event) can yield insights into shifting dynamics within a national memory culture.

American authors who write from Iraqi or Afghan perspectives thus face a paradox: writing strictly from their own perspective risks the marginalization of others by foregrounding the American experience as the most deserving of remembrance, while including non-American perspectives risks appropriating their voices and thereby controlling the narrative without their participation. Ironically, the veteran-authors who make this narrative choice are using the cultural authority accrued through their experience as well as the moral authority of the volunteer military to attack the very system that granted them the cultural capital to do so. Apart from having served overseas and, perhaps, spending more time personally with the local people, these authors have no better claim to represent the voice of the Other than a nonveteran author who simply wishes to empathize with that perspective. Yet the authority of their experience somehow lends the narrative a level of credibility that functions differently from that of the author who has no personal experience with the conflict. Thus, questions of narrative authority are not limited to soldier versus civilian, but also American soldier and American civilian versus the others. The very existence of this discussion shows how veteran-authors who volunteered to serve have sought to share both the experiential and the moral burden of these wars with the rest of American society.

Introduction

The purpose of this book is to show how the changing relationship between the military and American society influenced the production of war fiction in the twentieth and twenty-first centuries, with a particular focus on the timeframe between Vietnam and the conflicts in Iraq and Afghanistan. Although there was a significant literary response to the Civil War in the second half of the nineteenth and into the early twentieth century, the cultural conditions of a conflict fought on American soil differ from the overseas wars that followed, so I have excluded works published before World War I. My approach to these questions has been to compare the fictional responses to these conflicts, using the transition to an all-volunteer force as an inflection point to see how the cultural production of war fiction has changed over the last fifty years. Because the main argument of this book deals with the interplay between authors and the literary field, I have also excluded works that have been independently published rather than the traditional path through an imprint at a publishing house.

The first three chapters describe how, between World War I and Vietnam, veterans accumulated the cultural authority over the literary representation of war in American memory culture. Beginning with chapter 4, I examine three ways in which veteran-authors have since ceded their authority following the end of the draft and the creation of an all-volunteer force. Chapter 4 links the surprising prevalence of nonveteran authors of contemporary war novels to the state of American civil-military relations and the dispersion of the veteran's authority. I argue that the civil-military gap has accelerated the process in memory culture whereby current events become subsumed by the historical, transitioning from "happening" to "history" and shifting the source of narrative authenticity, as perceived within the field of reception, from extratextual to intratextual. Today, nonveterans are writing "historical" novels about these conflicts at a time far earlier than previously seen in literary history. And veterans, far from attempting to leverage their status as volunteers to reclaim their authority, have actively argued that personal experience is not necessary to write about war, doing so as a way to share the experiential and interpretive burden of the conflicts with the disconnected population.

In considering these works as historical novels, I am following Birgit Däwes, who has argued convincingly that novels dealing with the Septem-

Introduction

ber 11, 2001, terrorist attacks should be approached as "contemporary historical fiction" in that "they not only represent, in much detail, the events themselves, but they will them with precisely the narratives of 'social and human motives' that [Georg] Lukács emphasizes in his 1962 study."[41] In her case, the 9/11 novel as a literary genre represents the fictional response to a single event, whereas war fiction represents the fictional response to a series of distinct but conceptually related events (that is, wars) spread over time. It is telling that the fictional response to 9/11 has not emphasized the authority of personal experience in a way that had become common in the war fiction genre. Only a small number of people directly experienced the attacks (whether in New York City or Washington, DC), but the entire country and much of the world witnessed them in essentially real-time via broadcast television. The plurality of that experience and its place in American memory seems to negate any unique claims to authority over the literary representation of the attacks in fiction; no literary critic has argued that "you had to be there" on 9/11 in order to write about that day in fiction.

Once we move away from the novel as a cultural object and begin to look at the texts themselves, we can see distinct shifts in how contemporary authors have chosen to represent war in literary fiction. Chapter 5 shows how the civil-military gap has combined with the nature of counterinsurgency warfare in Iraq and Afghanistan to make *coming home* the defining experience of contemporary war rather than the experience of battlefield violence. For the fictional response to Vietnam, particularly the early phase of fiction through about 1990, most narratives focused on the suffering of the individual American soldier in combat and the transformation from innocent civilian to traumatized veteran. These stories are set in combat zones and focalized through an American point of view. While there were some novels about Vietnam interested in the aftermath of war, combat and killing were the true stars of the majority of these works.

With the fiction of Iraq and Afghanistan, though, that is no longer the case. In a narrative reversal of the content from Vietnam, only a handful of the dozens of contemporary war novels actually stay in country, and even those that do seem to have an eye on what comes after. Many of these novels focus on the "invisible wounds of war"—also known as post-traumatic stress and moral injury—a theme that examines war's psychological, rather than physical, toll by showing characters who struggle to deal with the

Introduction

consequences of what they saw and did after they return home. While these issues have always been part of the war experience, the psychological and moral aspects of the veteran's homecoming have become a staple of contemporary war fiction—whether authored by veterans or nonveterans—perhaps stemming from the psychological tension between volunteering to serve and the reality of that service. This shift in narrative focus from the physical dangers of combat to the psychological challenges of reintegration fits the pattern of veterans ceding authority over the literary representation of war; no special knowledge or experiential revelation is needed to see and write about the social conditions between the military and American society.

The form of these works has also changed, and in chapter 6 I show how veteran-authors have found another way to share the experiential and moral burdens of the conflicts with the rest of the population, namely by adopting narrative strategies that include focalizing through non-American characters in their novels. The veterans who served in Iraq and Afghanistan and returned to write novels about their experiences have written from these perspectives at a rate far higher than their counterparts from the Vietnam War, a war whose fiction is to a large extent characterized by a thematic dehumanization of the Vietnamese people. Novels such as Benjamin Buchholz's *One Hundred and One Nights* (2011), Michael Pitre's *Fives and Twenty-Fives* (2014), Elliot Ackerman's *Green on Blue* (2015), Roy Scranton's *War Porn* (2016), and Brian Van Reet's *Spoils* (2017) all include at least one non-American character as a focalizer. These novels introduce moral complexity by rendering the consequences of these wars through characters on all sides of the conflict. To do so is to present the full nature of the conflicts, rather than one-sided memories and interpretations.

In the final chapter, I explore a paradox of civil-military relations when it comes to the literary representation of the professional military. The image of the American veteran in contemporary fiction has been overwhelmingly negative at a time when public trust in the military as an institution remains high. Collectively, contemporary war novels paint a picture of a legion of traumatized veterans who only volunteered for military service because they had no other choice. Such portrayals largely exacerbate the social gap that characterizes the relationship between the military and society. Despite the progressive influence that the dispersion of the veteran-author's

Introduction

cultural authority has had on the war fiction genre—broadening its authorship, reducing the dominance of the male perspective, the addition of well-developed non-American characters—the literary representation of the professional military may do more harm than good to the civil-military relationship by reinforcing cultural stereotypes about broken, traumatized veterans who only volunteered to serve because they had no other choice and deserved everything that happened to them because, as one character says to his veteran son, they "volunteered to get screwed."

CHAPTER ONE

"Stick to Her Own Farms and Farmer Folk"

World War I and the Origins of Combat Gnosticism

In a 1999 essay about the poets and poetry of the First World War, James Campbell coined the term "combat gnosticism" in order to critique the ideology that exalted war and combat as "a qualitatively separate order of experience that is difficult if not impossible to communicate to any who have not under gone an identical experience."[1] Campbell contended that this ideology "has served both to limit severely the canon of texts that mainstream First World War criticism has seen as legitimate war writing and has simultaneously promoted war literature's status as a discrete body of work with almost no relation to non-war writing." Paul Fussell, whose 1975 book *The Great War and Modern Memory* became the standard text on the canon of First World War writing, bore the brunt of this criticism, mostly because he dismissed nearly all noncombatants and women from his analysis, and because he wrote things like this:

> Even if those at home had wanted to know the realities of the war, they couldn't have without experiencing them: its conditions were too novel, its industrialized ghastliness too unprecedented. The war would have been simply unbelievable.[2]

Fussell's belief that only those who had seen war could truly understand it led to Campbell's criticism of a literary field that viewed "war experience as a kind of gnosis, a secret knowledge which only an initiated elite knows." This philosophy served to authenticate combat literature written by those who had experienced war while denigrating most writing by women and nonveteran authors, elevating personal experience with the subject matter over literary aesthetics as markers of authenticity. No idea would have a greater influence on shaping the narrative and rhetorical characteristics of what critics, readers, and even authors would come to expect from the war fiction genre for the rest of the century.

CHAPTER ONE

Even though more than twenty years have passed since Campbell's essay, the debate surrounding the ideology of combat gnosticism persists in contemporary fiction as well as literary criticism. Kate McLoughlin, in her 2011 book, *Authoring War: The Literary Representation of War from the Iliad to Iraq*, responds directly to Campbell's argument, saying that "though Campbell is right to find fault with a critical tendency that erects a canon of war writing on the basis of combat knowledge, there is no getting around the fact that battle is a unique order of experience, able to confer particular authority on those who have undergone and seek to represent it."[3] Jennifer Haytock, in her 2018 *Introduction to American War Literature*, treads carefully around the question of narrative ownership while separating war writing from other kinds of literature, suggesting that studying war literature "comes with unique minefields." Emphasizing the "high stakes of war" and noting that "many veterans, writers or not, feel strongly that those who have not been to war cannot understand it and find attempts do so to be insulting and fruitless," Haytock concedes the point: "One must, I believe, respect this position."[4]

Similar perspectives can be inferred in reviews of contemporary war novels and interviews with their authors, where questions of autobiographical influence often overshadow poetic artistry and aesthetic style. Following in Campbell's footsteps, David Buchanan spends an entire chapter of his book *Going Scapegoat: Post-9/11 War Literature, Language and Culture* (2016) attacking "the fetishization of experience" in the literary representation of war. Buchanan argues that "the power of combat gnosticism" is that "it drowns out everything else by a manipulation of authority, one conferred by the dubious term 'combat' while the epistemology it puts forward as superlative is no less suspicious than the loudest and unadorned pro-war propaganda."[5] He then goes after Fussell and the works of his "disciples" such as Samuel Hynes's *The Soldiers' Tale: Bearing Witness to Modern War* (1997), Ty Hawkins's *Reading Vietnam amid the War on Terror* (2012), Wallis Sanborn's *The American Novel of War* (2012), and George Packer's 2014 essay for the *New Yorker*, "Home Fires." Each of these authors, in Buchanan's view, promulgates Fussell's philosophy that personal experience in war is a prerequisite for understanding and writing about it.

Paul Fussell has remained the scapegoat for the ideology of combat gnosticism because his work had the greatest influence over the last four

"Stick to Her Own Farms and Farmer Folk"

decades. Other critics, both before and after Campbell, took Fussell to task for ignoring the contributions of women writers to World War I literature, and Fussell's name is inescapable whenever debates about authorship and war writing surface, as they still do today, often rechristened with phrases like "the authority of experience" or "the anxiety of authenticity."[6] But the ideology behind combat gnosticism did not originate with Fussell, and the literary field did not always conflate experience with authority. After the Civil War and the birth of American literary realism, the concept of authenticity took root in conversations about authors such as Ambrose Bierce, a Union Army veteran turned author, and Stephen Crane, whose The Red Badge of Courage (1895) became the most lauded novel of the war despite his having been born six years after Robert E. Lee's surrender at Appomattox Court House.

It was after the First World War (but more than a half century before The Great War and Modern Memory) that the American critical response to two novels — John Dos Passos's Three Soldiers (1921) and Willa Cather's One of Ours (1922) — set the tone for the rest of the decade and paved the way for the "disillusioned" literature, written by combat veterans, that has become synonymous with the literary memory of the war. Dos Passos, as the first American veteran of the war to write a novel that broke free of previous genre conventions, represented a new kind of writer (the "veteran-author") whose subject was a new kind of war. Critics adapted to the new literary reality, and authenticity became the dominant theme of aesthetic appreciation. Without obvious tools to assess a concept like authenticity, personal experience with the subject became an easy reference point, and the literary critics of the era judged Cather's novel harshly against these new standards. These critics, who supported Dos Passos's version of the war over Cather's, wielded more cultural authority than either the amateur readers who made One of Ours a bestseller or the literary institution that awarded Cather the Pulitzer Prize in 1923. The preeminence afforded to an author's personal experience as a writer of war fiction — the seed of the idea that Campbell would later christen as combat gnosticism — would become embedded into this new genre, influencing the next generation of writers and literary critics who would build their arguments on the foundations laid at the beginning of the 1920s.

CHAPTER ONE

American War Fiction, 1914–1920

Despite the emphasis on what literary historians have dubbed the "war books boom" of 1929, the Great War in Europe was a frequent subject of American fiction between 1914 and 1920 (figure 1). In the early years, before the United States had even entered the conflict, more than two dozen novels were published that included the war as a central element of the story.[7] At first, writers fit the war into preexisting literary structures and genres, treating the war as *a* subject but not *the* subject. Before there were the more famous novels of "disillusionment" written by the likes of Dos Passos, Ernest Hemingway, E. E. Cummings, and Thomas Boyd, there were dozens of romance novels, potboilers, melodramas, detective novels, spy thrillers, and works of patriotic propaganda. All told, between 1914 and 1920, 133 American authors — 52 women and 81 men — published 164 war novels.[8] Although this initial wave of cultural production has been essentially forgotten today, there were so many books coming out about the war that popular literary magazines like *The Bookman* dedicated entire sections to describing the market's most recent editions, even publishing a parallel bestseller list specifically for war books.

Many of these early novels tended to highlight soldiers' heroism while downplaying the horrors of the trenches. American readers devoured fiction in those years, but their appetite did not crave the verisimilitude of battlefield violence. This continued a trend that began after the Civil War, where literary attempts to capture the savagery of warfare were met with resistance by a publishing industry and readership that preferred sentimentality. Market demand for heroic action-adventure stories carried over to the early novels of the First World War, which were "imbued with the mystique of violence which vicariously exalts death in battle into a self-evident virtue."[9] While some of this may have been the result of the Committee on Public Information's strict controls and censorship of war-related content, a detachment from the historical reality of the trenches in these works gave later writers something to rebel against.[10]

Few authors of these novels had seen the war firsthand; of the 133 American authors who published war novels between 1914 and 1920, only seventeen had personally experienced the war in some capacity.[11] Ten had served in the military, and seven had experienced the war either as journalists or

"Stick to Her Own Farms and Farmer Folk"

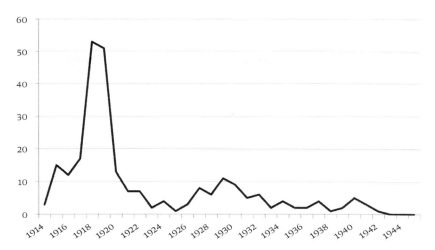

FIGURE 1. American novels published about World War I between 1914 and 1945. Data based on works found in Philip Hager and Desmond Taylor, *The Novels of World War I: An Annotated Bibliography* (New York: Garland Publishing, 1981) and the author's original ethnographic research.

as civilians, such as Frances Wilson Huard, an American woman who lived in France during the war and published two novellas under the title *Lilies, White and Red* in 1919. (Huard had also written a bestselling memoir about the war in 1916.)[12] If an author with personal experience published a novel about the war, it was more of a novelty than an expectation of authenticity; literary critics focused far more on the novel's style and content than the author's biography.

Some examples illuminate the critical environment of the time. Frederick Palmer, a seasoned foreign correspondent commissioned into the army to cover the war in Europe, was the first American veteran to publish a novel about the war. Palmer's 1916 novel *The Old Blood* told the story of an American visiting distant relatives in England and France when the war breaks out. The *New York Times* ran a review under the title "Frederick Palmer's Wartime Romance," noting that "It is a story about the war that is full of vivid glimpses of wartime scenes and events, swift character sketches, illuminating flashes of French ardor and of German discipline. It is a human story, written out of a wide knowledge, and with an admirable perspective."[13] The *Independent* called the novel "A Hospital Romance" and also nodded to Palmer's time spent in the trenches. The reviewer was disappointed, however, since *The Old Blood* "does not describe the movements and combats of great armies or surging souls of the nations; it is a personal romance from start to finish."[14] Another review in the *New Republic* said, "Aside from a welcome authenticity in detail, the first two-thirds of the book slowly unfold a rather inconsequential and sentimental story, told in an undistinguished style that just escapes being clumsy."[15] None of Palmer's critics, it seems, was willing to cut him any literary slack simply because he had been there.

Women were writing fiction about the war as well. Grace Livingston Hill-Lutz and Mary Roberts Rinehart wrote popular spy novels. Mary Shipman Andrews wrote patriotic novellas. In the same year as Palmer's *The Old Blood*, Margaret Pollock Sherwood, a professor of English literature at Wellesley College just outside Boston, published *The Worn Doorstep*, an epistolary novel about an American woman living in England who dedicates herself to helping Belgian refugees after her fiancé is killed in France at the beginning of the war.[16] A reviewer in the *Sewanee Review* calls the novel "a simple, touching revelation of a keenly sensitive, sympathetic soul, told with kindly humor, delicacy."[17] Sherwood also received a positive review in *The Nation*.[18] Neither reviewer questioned her authority to write the novel, nor did they feel compelled to mention her gender.

The tension between experience, gender, and the traditional ways of reading war fiction came together with Ellen La Motte's *Backwash of War*, a collection of vignettes about serving in a frontline field hospital based on La Motte's own experiences as a volunteer nurse. Initially published in 1916, the novel received generally favorable reviews but was quickly censored and only reissued nearly twenty years later.[19] The content of the reviews, however, shows how literary critics still concerned themselves primarily with elements of style, technique, and affect rather than the "authenticity" of the text. The review in *Publishers' Weekly* says that "it isn't a great book, though it is sincere and in places intensely dramatic and, if for no other reason than its sheer horror, never unarresting." The reviewer notes that La Motte had been "stationed at a French hospital some ten kilometers behind the first line in Northern France" before observing that "she doesn't use pretty or conventional words to describe it."[20]

"Stick to Her Own Farms and Farmer Folk"

Edith Wharton's work generated a similar response. Already a celebrated writer who lived in Paris during the war, Wharton published *The Marne* in 1918 about a young American boy who falls in love with France and yearns to join the war effort. Too young to fight when the Germans invade during his family's annual summer vacation in 1914, he returns to America, eventually making his way back as an ambulance driver during the Marne's second battle three years later. The *New York Times* called the novel "beautifully written," and "the best description we have seen yet of the attitude of certain classes toward the war. . . . Always a critic of life, Mrs. Wharton has never written a broader, keener criticism than this, her first long story of the war."[21] A reviewer in *Publishers' Weekly* called *The Marne* "A Clear-Cut Gem of War Fiction."[22]

Or consider Temple Bailey, who, like Willa Cather, had already published several novels and had a good reputation as a writer when her novel *The Tin Soldier* was published late in 1918 and became a bestseller the following year, rising to the number eight spot in the *Publishers' Weekly* tabulation of the years' bestselling novels. The *New York Times* review of the book doesn't mention Bailey's biographical details at all.[23] A few other periodicals published short reviews as well, all focused on story and content. The American Library Association's *Booklist* said the novel was "too long and too sentimental, but full of good principles."[24] *The Outlook* summarized it as "a simple and wholesome story of a young man who feels that certain obligations of honor prevent him from entering the war, and of the girl who helps him to bear the suffering and humiliation that follow."[25] The *Wisconsin Library Bulletin* had another one-paragraph review, saying that the story was "quite sentimental, harmless, and will be liked by young girls."[26] *Publishers' Weekly* had a longer review that even applauds her decision to write about the war: "It is safe to prophesy that *The Tin Soldier* will equal if not exceed in popularity Miss Bailey's earlier novels; it abounds in the same optimism; it is up to the minute in setting and theme; and it has agreeably presented romance to suit all ages."[27] A longer review essay in *The Nation* was the only one that comes close to criticizing her biography: "We need not doubt that the author . . . quite believes in her own belief in the shopworn romantic pretenses upon which her fiction is based. Or rather, let us say, she succeeds in not even suspecting them of being either pretenses or shopworn." But again, the reviewer takes aim mostly at the novel's plot, not the details of

CHAPTER ONE

the creator: "Our criticism of this kind of fiction is not that its basic ideas of love and sacrifice are unsound, but that it uses them cheaply and falsely for the gilding and propping of the most ramshackle and romantic contraptions."[28] Whether Bailey had the authority to write the novel never came into question.

Soon thereafter, though, literary magazines heralded the death of war books. In a January 1920 quarterly survey of Americans' current taste in fiction, a columnist for *The Bookman* puts it bluntly:

> What kind of novels are people in general wanting at this particular moment? Well, to put it negatively, the tendency just now is first of all away from war fiction. Our story-tellers have by this got their early impressions and reactions pretty well off their chests. We were glad to have the record of them. But on the whole they turned out to be a bit monotonous. . . . The time will come when the story-tellers will get their second wind and second thought. Out of all the sifted facts and varying impressions and balanced testimony of the earlier war-writing, some novelist will rise to mold for posterity a really masterful interpretation. Meanwhile, as I have said, the tendency of novel-readers is away from the new war novels, and toward either 'non-fiction' or other kinds of fiction.[29]

The author notes that Bailey's *The Tin Soldier* had been an exception to this general movement away from war fiction, while he criticizes its sentimentality and indirectly summarizing the thematic approach of many war novels up to that point: "You may call it pap or soothing syrup, but there are times when it is better to be soothed than, as the English say, to be poked in the eye with a burnt stick."

American war novels between the beginning of the war and shortly after the armistice, almost all of which were written by authors who had no military experience whatsoever, were largely sentimental romances and heroic action-adventure stories that stuck to the conventions of their existing genres, and they were judged by the same aesthetic standards rather than scrutinized for evidence of their authenticity. This practice would change almost overnight, though, with the publication of *Three Soldiers* in 1921.

"Stick to Her Own Farms and Farmer Folk"

A New Kind of Author, a New Kind of Novel: Dos Passos and *Three Soldiers*

By the early 1920s, two incongruent perspectives of the war's collective memory were clashing in the pages of American fiction: the war had either been noble, fought for a necessary cause and imbued with meaning and purpose in service of global democracy, or it had been a senseless slaughter.[30] The critical, institutional, and public reception of two novels — John Dos Passos's *Three Soldiers* (1921) and Willa Cather's *One of Ours* (1922) — illustrates the tension between these two views, a tension that Steven Trout has called a "flashpoint" of collective memory, or a moment "when the schism between two or more versions of the Great War suddenly came into stark relief."[31] Dos Passos and Cather were each lauded and faulted for the image of the war they presented in their novels. Soldiers who had served in the war recognized something of their own experiences in both — *Three Soldiers* was either too negative and pessimistic about life in the army, or it perfectly captured the military's totalitarian tendencies to stamp out individuality; *One of Ours* was either too cheerful and romantic, or it accurately captured the doughboys' patriotic spirit. In both cases, there was something for everyone. A century later, though, *Three Soldiers* still stands as one of the genre's most influential early texts, while *One of Ours* has never fully recovered from its initial negative reception despite later attempts to rehabilitate its image as a war novel.

John Dos Passos had begun gathering material for a novel while he was still overseas. Like Ernest Hemingway, Dos Passos had volunteered to serve as an ambulance driver during the war and spent time in Italy and France. He wrote his first novel, *One Man's Initiation — 1917* (later republished in 1945 with the title *First Encounter*), during and immediately following his service in Europe. It was published in 1920 but sold poorly and, according to a number of critics, offered little more than an autobiographical recreation of Dos Passos's war experiences with a different name substituted for his own.[32] A year later, he published *Three Soldiers*, turning him into a literary celebrity at the age of twenty-five.[33] The novel was reviewed in dozens of newspapers and literary magazines across the country. "Not since Stephen Crane's *The Red Badge of Courage* had an American novel stirred such heated debate," according to Barry Maine in the introduction to a volume of collected reviews of Dos Passos's work by his contemporaries.[34]

The novel presents the interwoven stories of three young men serving in the American army just after the United States' entry into the war—John Andrews, a Harvard-trained composer from New York who enlists to lose himself in the anonymous columns of foot-soldiers but quickly regrets his decision; Dan Fuselli, a clerk from San Francisco who believes he can use the army to climb professional and social ladders; and Chris Chrisfield, a farmer from Indiana who reveals himself to harbor a deep-seated anger in search of an outlet. Throughout the novel's six parts (titled with impersonal images of industrialized production: "Making the Mould," "The Metal Cools," "Machines," "Rust," "The World Outside," and "Under the Wheels"), the military is depicted as a totalitarian institution that will indiscriminately crush the ambition of anyone within its ranks. Although Dos Passos writes from the point of view of all three characters, he spends the most time with Andrews, a character widely acknowledged as autobiographical.[35] In imagery typical of the novel's themes, we first meet Andrews during a medical screening where he "stood tamely being prodded and measured, feeling like a prize horse at a fair" (19). Dos Passos constantly emphasizes the military's dehumanizing tendencies, having Andrews refer to the life of a lower enlisted soldier as akin to "slavery" multiple times throughout the novel. In merely one example of many such appraisals of the novel's content, Owen Gilman notes that "each of the three major characters in the novel—Fuselli, Chrisfield, and Andrews—suffers personally from his involvement in the war,"[36] though Andrews comes across as the individual with the most talent and potential and, as a result, the one who suffers the most at the hands of the military machine. "Fuselli believed and the army broke him. Chrisfield hated and the army broke him. Andrews rebelled and the army broke him," as one of the novel's contemporary reviewers wrote.[37]

Three Soldiers marked a turning point in the fledgling war fiction genre. Compared with the novels about World War I that preceded his, Dos Passos offered a far bleaker tale of the war and, even more cynically, the military itself, and his skeptical novel stood out against the earlier fiction that treated the war as a heroic adventure. Only a few years earlier, owing to the Committee on Public Information's strict censorship program, a novel like *Three Soldiers* would have been unthinkable.[38] "This is the kind of book that

"Stick to Her Own Farms and Farmer Folk"

anyone would have been arrested for writing while the war was yet in progress," military veteran and author Coningsby Dawson wrote angrily in the *New York Times*.[39] Literary critic H. L. Mencken wrote something similar, but his tongue-in-cheek phrasing reflects his pleasure that such a book was now possible: "Published three years ago, or even two years ago, John Dos Passos' *Three Soldiers* would have been suppressed out of hand, and the author hurried to Leavenworth or Atlanta, with a Federal judge bawling obscene farewells to him from the bench."[40] One reviewer in the pages of *Vanity Fair* called Dos Passos "a genius," saying that "If it were only that *Three Soldiers* is the first complete and competent novel of the American army it would deserve great praise, but it is more than that, for, in Mr. Dos Passos' hands, the army becomes a symbol of all the systems by which men attempt to crush their fellows and add to the already unbearable agony of life."[41]

But Dos Passos's view of the American military and the senselessness of the war itself earned him a number of responses from critics whose personal blend of patriotism could not accommodate the sourness of disillusionment, and it was here that his own experiential authority came under the microscope. The *New York Times Book Review* ran two front-page reviews of *Three Soldiers*, both negative. The first, with the title "Insulting the Army," was written by Coningsby Dawson, an American who had served with the Canadian Army during the war and had written his own high-spirited war novels. Dawson found Dos Passos's relentlessly negative portrayal of the military distasteful and unpatriotic. "It is either a base libel or a hideous truth," Dawson wrote, adding, "You must be either for it or against it." Dawson believed that "the spirit of the book is all wrong," and that "Mr. John Dos Passos seems to have either imagined or remembered every exceptional example of abuse of authority on the part of subordinates, and has pasted them together into a moving picture which he labels a novel." He neatly summarizes the patriotic viewpoint on the war and its sacrificial cause, saying that the novel "is a dastardly denial of the splendid chivalry which carried many a youth to a soldier's death with the sure knowledge in his soul that he was a liberator."[42]

Dawson admitted that his experience with the Canadians likely differed from that of his American counterparts and invited anyone with an American perspective to evaluate the novel. A week later, the newspaper ran a cover story on its book review pages by Harold Norman Denny, a journalist

CHAPTER ONE

who had enlisted in the infantry and was wounded during the American campaign for the Argonne Forest in 1918.[43] His review of *Three Soldiers* comes across as conflicted. Though he praises the novel as "brilliantly written," he takes aim at Dos Passos's military experience, drawing a distinct line between someone who may have been overseas and someone who truly experienced the war. "The man who has been under fire will recognize that Mr. Dos Passos must have been in uniform, but he will see also long before he finishes this embittered diatribe that he was not in the fighting." Primed to attack Dos Passos as a "slacker," Denny concedes his surprise that Dos Passos's service record "was really quite credible. But his record at the same time confirms the conviction that he was not of the line."[44] That is, not a frontline combat infantry soldier. In a phrase that echoes Dawson's review, Denny argues that "to prove his thesis Mr. Dos Passos has combed the army for every rotten incident that happened, could have happened, or could be imagined as having happened, and welded it into a compelling narrative." And, while Denny grants Dos Passos his experience as an ambulance driver, he dismisses it as incomparable with that of the frontline infantry, arguing that "the offense of the book is that Mr. Dos Passos does not know what he is talking about. He was a non-combatant."

Denny even goes as far as allowing that Dos Passos was *near* the action, that he likely "heard shells burst not far away," that "he can honestly assert that he was under fire," but that these experiences are not enough. In an emotionally charged rebuke of Dos Passos's authority, Denny contends that

> Mr. Dos Passos has never felt that sinking of his heart, with its thrill, too, which comes to an infantryman as he steps up to an ammunition cart and hangs his bandoliers of extra cartridges on his shoulders, and knows then that he is about to go into action; Mr. Dos Passos has never walked across a wheat field, with his nearest neighbor five paces away, and tried to look nonchalant as machine-gun bullets buzzed past him; Mr. Dos Passos has never laid quivering for hours under a barrage, sweating and dribbling into his gas mask, with 1.55s jolting him from the ground and covering him with clods, with shrapnel yelling and "pchinging" overhead, and with tortured, shattered boys about him, boys he has come to love, begging and sobbing for stretcher bearers or just silently dying. Mr. Dos Passos has never done

"Stick to Her Own Farms and Farmer Folk"

these things, and yet he pictures the men who have as mean, driven cowards.

Denny faults him for little details, too, mistakes that "cause those who were there to smile," such as having one of his characters pull the string of a grenade when "even an ambulance driver should know, however, that no American grenade had a string." Overall, Denny finds the novel "glaringly untrue" because his characters are all "vicious or contemptible" and anyone who reads the novel "would never guess that there was any other kind of men in the army." He continues — in what we can see as an early expression of combat gnosticism — that "there is hardly a glimmer of the real American soldier in all his four-hundred pages. No non-combatant ever could know the American soldier, and when Mr. Dos Passos wrote his book, though he wrote it skillfully, he spoke of things he knew nothing about."

The reviews by Dawson and Denny were echoed by other amateur readers who felt compelled to voice their displeasure at what they believed to be Dos Passos's unfair and unrealistic portrayal of army life in France during the war, a portrayal that likely drew from Dos Passos's feelings of marginality or inadequacy as an ambulance driver in a war effort that favored combat soldiers.[45] Yet neither Dawson nor Denny were professional literary critics operating within the literary field; they were outsiders whose criticism of the novel was based on the authority of their own war experience. One reviewer who had a foot in both worlds was Sidney Howard, a young writer who had served in an ambulance unit and then as a pilot during the war and would later become known as a prizewinning playwright and screenwriter.[46] When *Three Soldiers* was published, Howard was on staff at *Life* magazine, and he wrote a review of the novel a few weeks after Dawson and Denny, calling *Three Soldiers* "the first living account of our supreme, incredible adventure in humanity, the American Expeditionary Forces," while acknowledging that "it is evidently a very personal book, deeply concerned with its author's own experience, a bitter book written of days bitterly remembered." Like Dawson and Denny, Howard invokes his own experience to appraise the novel's authenticity: "As Mr. Dos Passos builds his colossus of stupidity and power, we who knew it for ourselves, who were there and were desperate or scornful or cynical beneath it, must recognize it for what it was and own that he has built honestly." Howard falls on the side of the novel's reception that saw *Three*

Soldiers as an antidote for the overblown patriotic fervor that characterized the earlier American novels about the war, complaining that "We have been drugged with much poppycock about the glory of the trenches. Coningsby Dawson who denounces Mr. Dos Passos for insulting the army, is responsible himself for much of the drugging." Although Howard, like Denny, takes issue with some of the characterizaions of the army in the novel, he allows Dos Passos the freedom to "write a book of the army as he knew it and as he felt it."[47]

The question of authenticity—argued on both sides within the pages of newspapers and literary periodicals—became the central theme of the novel's reception. In contrast to the reviews of the many war novels published between 1914 and 1920 that focused on textual aesthetics and poetic artistry, Dos Passos's reviewers concerned themselves entirely with the novel's content.[48] Yet that content was wrapped in an additional layer of authenticity because of Dos Passos's status as a veteran of the war, whether his combat bona fides satisfied people like Harold Denny or not.

Amid this mixed critical reception, *Three Soldiers* sold well but failed to become a bestseller despite the buzz within the literary community.[49] Just as the article from *The Bookman* had predicted in 1920, readers were tired of books about the war, and Dos Passos's novel was preaching an antiwar stance to a public already grown tired of war stories and eager to move on.[50] But that was exactly the message that resonated with the critics whose opinions carried the most weight within the literary field. H. L. Mencken, arguably one of the most influential critics in the years after the war, reviewed the novel twice in *The Smart Set*, the literary magazine he edited. More glowing reviews came from Heywood Broun in *The Bookman* and Henry Seidel Canby in the *New York Evening Post Book Review*. These critics, with their established cultural authority and symbolic capital, lauded the novel and cemented its reputation, ensuring that John Dos Passos would be considered a major American author.

A critical shift was slowly unfolding that placed the war novel in a different category from traditional fiction, one in which style and language could become subordinate to narrative content; only five years earlier, as mentioned in the previous section, reviewers had labeled Frederick Palmer's *The Old Blood* as "a rather inconsequential and sentimental story, told

"Stick to Her Own Farms and Farmer Folk"

in an undistinguished style that just escapes being clumsy."[51] Now, novels written by former soldiers would be picked apart for their autobiographical details, becoming "novels of witness and testimony," as William Matsen dubbed them in *The Great War and the American Novel*, whose most important element was the "mimetic recreation of their personal experience in narrative."[52]

Three Soldiers would soon be viewed as a "transitional work in the evolution of American war fiction from near-journalistic accounts of witness and testimony to the more finely crafted works of fiction written in the late 1920s and early 1930s," and it was this interpretation of the novel's achievements, aided by the early critics who showered it with praise for having so aptly captured their own sentiments on the war's futility, that solidified its long-term reputation and influence on the next generation of writers.[53] In 1966, one literary scholar wrote that "*Three Soldiers* was the original example, in subject and tone, of the American war novel as thereafter developed by Hemingway, William March, Hersey, Mailer and James Jones."[54] Four years later, Wayne Miller wrote that *Three Soldiers* "breaks new ground, and, in effect, establishes the form that most of the novels occasioned by World War II and the Korean War would take. . . . His concentration on an American unit, representative of various ethnic groups and social strata within United States culture at large, becomes standard for an avalanche of novels out of two wars."[55] Jeffrey Walsh later commented that "Dos Passos became the first important novelist after Stephen Crane to treat war as a major fictional theme, and his tutelage of American war writers may be fairly likened to that of [Henri] Barbusse upon Europeans. . . . In *Three Soldiers* the reader encounters for the first time in American fiction a radical note of protest against the army's bureaucratic and hierarchical organization."[56] And, as recently as 2018, Jennifer Haytock acknowledges that "*Three Soldiers* portrays a world in which the individual exists only as part of a vast machine that, in a naturalist vein, shapes all individual choices and in which the bureaucratic military crushes individuality. For this reason, this novel and Dos Passos's later work proved highly influential for writers of World War II."[57] Time and again, scholars and critics would reaffirm the novel's position as the original twentieth-century war novel.

The legacy of *Three Soldiers* is undeniable, its influence on the genre unquestionable. But *Three Soldiers*, so different as it was from the war writing

CHAPTER ONE

that came before, also provided a convenient reference point to measure the "literary fracture" between the two generations of writers that straddled the years of the war.[58] Celebrated older writers like William Dean Howells and Henry James—who renounced his American citizenship in 1915 as a protest against his birth country's refusal to enter the war—"lost a good deal of their appeal and their credibility."[59] Dos Passos became the vanguard of the new generation of veteran-authors and their critical champions who carried their disillusionment with them from the battlefield to the page, intending to place many of the old literary masters out to pasture and drive away what they saw as the outdated, romantic view of war that claimed so many lives and desolated large swaths of western European land. One of the authors who would soon find herself in these critical crosshairs was Willa Cather.

A Respected Novelist Confronts an Evolving Genre: Willa Cather's *One of Ours*

Willa Cather had already published four novels by the time she found her creative process consumed by the Great War. At forty-nine years old, Cather was of a different generation than the young Dos Passos, known for her stylistic depictions of American prairie life in a trilogy of highly regarded novels: *O Pioneers!* (1913), *The Song of the Lark* (1915), and *My Ántonia* (1918). When the armistice came and the war ended, Cather already enjoyed a reputation as a celebrated American writer of midwestern fiction.[60]

Like many of her fellow American citizens, Cather's life was personally touched by the war when, in May 1918, her cousin Grosvenor Cather (known as G.P.) was killed at the battle of Cantigny. G.P.'s death haunted Cather and invaded her writing. In a letter to friend and fellow author Dorothy Canfield Fisher, Cather recalls how she learned of her cousin's death while reading the newspaper at the beauty parlor. From that moment on, "he was in my mind," she wrote, "but he was in my mind so much that I couldn't get through him to other things. . . . [S]ome of me was buried with him in France, and some of him was left alive in me. . . . It was just to escape from him and his kind that I wrote at all."[61]

That summer, while staying with her aunt and uncle and reading her cousin's wartime letters, Cather decided to turn G.P.'s story into her next

"Stick to Her Own Farms and Farmer Folk"

novel. She immersed herself in the project, going beyond her cousin's letters by reading other books about the war, interviewing veterans at home and in the hospital, and even traveling to the French battlefields in 1920 to photograph her cousin's gravesite and get a personal feel for the terrain.[62] She spent four years writing, revising, and painstakingly checking the historical details of a work that she "knew she would have to capture with absolute plausibility or risk offending Army veterans and offering an easy target to book reviewers."[63]

The resulting novel was *One of Ours*, a work that would become "among the most controversial American novels of the 1920s."[64] Cather's literary artistry took the biographical details of her cousin's life and transformed them into something far more subtle and complicated in Claude Wheeler, the novel's protagonist. Claude is a rural Nebraskan who becomes dissatisfied with the banality of farming and marriage and seeks a greater sense of meaning and purpose when he volunteers for the army after the United States enters the war. When he arrives in France, he is captivated by the country and its people as well as the thrill of leading soldiers in battle and is later killed while rallying his men in a desperate defense against a German attack.

The novel was published in September 1922, just under a year after *Three Soldiers*. It became an instant bestseller and generated a great deal of critical interest, far more than any of her previous works.[65] In fact, *One of Ours* was reviewed far more extensively than *Three Soldiers* had been, and many of the same critics who reviewed *Three Soldiers* later wrote about *One of Ours*.[66] Of all the war fiction written in the 1920s — including Hemingway's *A Farewell to Arms* (1929) — *One of Ours* remained on the weekly bestseller lists the longest.[67]

Cather's portrayal of Claude and the sense of fulfillment he gets from the war formed the basis of readers' interpretations, from the professional critics who published reviews in literary magazines to "ordinary members of the so-called reading public who purchased the book and then wrote directly to Cather."[68] The response was as broad then as it remains today, with some readers applauding the ironic construction of Claude's point of view to reveal the truth of the war's horrors, while others — many of whom were veterans of the war — praised her authentic portrayal of army life in France. Cather even received a letter from the mother of a fallen soldier from Colorado who found the ending, written from the perspective of Claude's mother

CHAPTER ONE

after learning of his death, poignant and accurate: "The last ten pages of your book were written especially for the mothers, and as one of them I thank you. We know—but I cannot understand how you do."[69]

The novel's critical attention would prove to be its downfall, though, at least in terms of its longevity and reputation within the war fiction genre as well as among Cather's own works.[70] Critics read Cather as belonging to the pre–Dos Passos form of genre fiction that took the war's objectives and conduct at face value. They rejected what they read as a naïve perspective of the war as seen through the eyes of the novel's protagonist. Even though the positive reviews outnumbered the negative ones, Cather's critics in the 1920s—notably Heywood Broun, H. L. Mencken, Sinclair Lewis, Henry Seidel Canby, and Sidney Howard (all of whom had reviewed *Three Soldiers*, except Lewis)—were some of the most influential men of letters at the time, and their reading of the novel as the antithesis of *Three Soldiers* turned Cather into the target that she had feared becoming from the beginning. Cather's detractors focused on her lack of military credentials, ironically mirroring the same type of criticism that veterans like Coningsby Dawson and Harold Denny had leveled at Dos Passos. For many of these critics, though, Cather's lack of personal experience in the war meant that she did not, or could not, know what she was talking about. In one of the most infamous anecdotes of author gossip in literary history, Ernest Hemingway sneered at Cather in a letter to fellow author and critic Edmund Wilson, claiming that she had "Catherized" the description of battle scenes in the second half of the novel from what she had seen in recent films. "Poor woman," Hemingway scoffed, "she had to get her war experience somewhere."[71] Even though Cather had died long before Hemingway's letters were published, his words stung like none other, especially as they have been quoted nearly every time their names are mentioned together.[72]

Authenticity and experience became a running theme in the critical reception of the novel, just as they had been with *Three Soldiers*, though Cather's case had the added element of her gender. Mencken and Lewis (both of whom had previously praised Cather's work) published reviews that focused on the novel's latter chapters and their depiction of the French battlefields. Mencken, like Hemingway, found the combat scenes in the novel's final chapter to be plucked from a "Hollywood movie-lot," adding that "there is a lyrical nonsensicality in it that often grows half pathetic; it is precious near

"Stick to Her Own Farms and Farmer Folk"

the war of the standard model of the lady novelist."[73] Lewis took issue with Cather's decision to send her protagonist to war in the first place, saying that "she might as well have pushed him down a well,"[74] since, in his view, the war's narrative function seemed to be to resolve Claude's issues at home, namely his existential angst and domestic discontent. Lewis continues:

> Such things do happen; people with problems fairly explosive with vexatious interest do go off to war—and do fall down wells—but the error is to believe they thereby become more dramatic. . . . [T]ruth does guide the first part of the book, but she disastrously loses it in a romance of violinists gallantly turned soldiers, of self-sacrificing sergeants, sallies at midnight, and all the commonplaces of ordinary war novels.[75]

For the big names in literary criticism such as Mencken and Lewis, Dos Passos had struck the right chord with *Three Soldiers*, and they couldn't help but compare Cather's latest novel with what they had viewed as a groundbreaking work in the genre, especially as the two novels were published so close together and differed so significantly in tone. Mencken does this explicitly in his review. In criticizing *One of Ours*, Mencken says that

> what spoils the story is simply that a year or so ago a young soldier named John Dos Passos printed a novel called *Three Soldiers*. Until *Three Soldiers* is forgotten and fancy achieves its inevitable victory over fact, no war story can be written in the United States without challenging comparison with it—and no story that is less meticulously true will stand up to it.[76]

Mencken may have been projecting his own truth—he was famously against American entry into the war—onto Dos Passos's fiction, though. In fact, few of the reviewers who praised *Three Soldiers* or criticized *One of Ours* were in the position to critique the authenticity of the combat scenes based on their own knowledge and experience. One exception was Sidney Howard, the wartime ambulance driver and aviator who by that time had been promoted to *Life* magazine's literary editor and wrote one of the more scathing reviews of Cather's novel. With the patronizing title "Miss Cather Goes to War," Howard proceeds to put the novel in what he believes its rightful place:

CHAPTER ONE

While Claude — so the hero is named — sticks to his own western lands, the thing is above reproach. . . . All of him, all of his family and associates and locale is perfect because Miss Cather has written them as only she can write such matters. The washing of a car, the minister's elbows at the table, a first dress suit, an electric separator, a train hands' restaurant — these are the elements for her uniquely sensitive authority.[77]

For Howard, the parts of the novel that deal with the war are merely a "potpourri of soldier yarns and impressions of Rheims two years after, amalgamated into a 'Saturday Evening Post' version of *Three Soldiers* and about as true to the actuality of warfare as propaganda for the bonus."[78] He ends his review with a comment that encapsulates the viewpoint that would come to define the genre's growing gender divide:

It seems to me a book to show what a woman can write supremely well and what she cannot write at all. . . . The pity is that Miss Cather did not know war for the big bowwow stuff that it is and stick to her own farms and farmer folk.[79]

Howard's review — as well as the misogynist undertones in the reviews of Mencken and Lewis — began pushing the message that women had no business writing about war. Reading her novel as a straightforward tale of heroism and sacrifice (and missing the ironic subtext of the novel's conclusion), Cather's critics contended that a woman could not possibly have the proper perspective to write authentically about the war in the way that the veteran-author Dos Passos had. This view would shackle the novel's commercial success with the burden of masculine expectations and, in the long run, drown it in a sea of relative obscurity.[80] Despite Cather's care in producing what she believed was an authentic story about the war based on research that she had hoped to convert into narrative authority, the long-term reputation of *One of Ours* was doomed by a few thousand words published in a handful of literary magazines that would guide the next generation of critics, men who took to authors like Dos Passos, Thomas Boyd, William March, and, later, Ernest Hemingway at least partly because of the authenticity and narrative authority ascribed to their works due to their status as war veterans. The critics then pointed to that authority as evidence that their view of the war

"Stick to Her Own Farms and Farmer Folk"

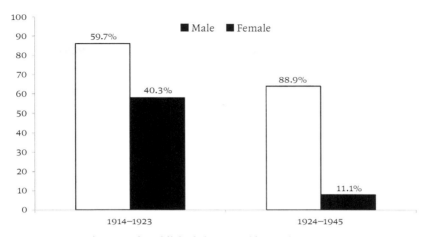

FIGURE 2. American novels published about World War I between 1914 and 1945 according to the author's gender.

was the correct one, while the more positive perspectives of other veteran writers like Coningsby Dawson and Harold Denny were disregarded. Cather, who could not claim the authority of experience and whose novel was read against the disillusionment of Dos Passos and the steady stream of veteran-authored novels that followed, never had a chance.

Critical Consequences for the Genre

After *One of Ours*, the ratio of war novels published by women plummeted (figure 2). Between 1914 and 1923—the year Cather received the Pulitzer Prize—the proportion of women who published war novels was more than forty percent (58 of 144 authors). After 1923 and until the end of the Second World War, that proportion dropped to a mere eleven percent (8 of 72 authors). War fiction had become a men's domain and would stay that way for the next ninety years.

In the aftermath of Dos Passos's and Cather's reception, authenticity and mimetic realism became the staples of a new genre of American war fiction. When it came to Cather, the next generation of critics would pick up where Mencken, Lewis, Howard, and others had left off. In a 1933 essay bearing the title "The Case against Willa Cather," literary critic Granville Hicks (who was a teenager during the war) called Cather's view of the war in *One of Ours* "romantic and naïve."[81] Stanley Cooperman, in his influential 1966 study *World War I and the American Novel*, refers to Claude Wheeler as a "war lover" for his idealistic views and argues that Cather had an "inability to deal with army and combat realities far removed from her own experience."[82] Cooperman, like H. L. Mencken and Sinclair Lewis before him, was another critic who had never served in the military but nonetheless felt compelled to adjudicate the authenticity of Cather's war scenes:

> Miss Cather, of course, knew very little about the war she was describing; her picture postcard trenches, her pretty villages, her 'mushroom-picking expeditions' had little to do with the impact of actual war experience. . . . That technological combat shattered rather than fulfilled is something Miss Cather could not be expected to grasp in 1922, when the nature and impact of such combat was only vaguely understood by most Americans.[83]

That Claude Wheeler felt invigorated by the war and his participation in it is clear from the text. Willa Cather's view as an author is less so. Yet this identification of Cather's perspective as identical to Claude's — put forward in nearly all of the novel's early reviews — has dominated the critical interpretation ever since. Since 1975, a number of scholars have offered alternate interpretations that alleged more distance between Cather and Claude, beginning with David Stouck's *Willa Cather's Imagination*, in which Stouck reads the novel as a satirical sendup of "both the shallow values of contemporary Middle America *and* the delusions of its protagonist."[84] A more subtle interpretation, championed by several scholars beginning in the 1980s, was that Cather's depiction of Claude as a gung-ho, idealistic patriot was meant as an ironic critique of those who glamorized war and combat.[85] Even with these more nuanced reinterpretations, "opinion on the novel remains as starkly divided as the opposing trenches on the Western Front."[86] For example, James Dawes calls Claude's death "absurdly heroic" in his 2002 book *The Language of War* and argues that his mother "takes grim satisfaction in his death" as depicted in the novel's final pages.[87] The debate continues even today, as Jennifer Haytock seems to favor the ironic interpretation of the novel while Kimberly Licursi still reads Cather as "part of an older generation of writers who believed the war was morally significant while Hemingway represented a group of more modern, disaffected writers who believed the war had no redeeming value."[88]

Future scholarship about World War I in American fiction would casually brush aside the literary works of women writers: "A number of American women wrote of the war with varying degrees of success. All are outside the mainstream of the World War I novel, primarily because of their general lack of intimate knowledge with the conflict," Wayne Miller wrote in 1970, devoting only a single paragraph to women writers in an entire chapter about First World War fiction. He mentions Edith Wharton's *A Son at the Front* as "more concerned with the psychological relations between father and son and with life in Paris than with the war itself," while Cather's *One of Ours* is "really more concerned with the moral and cultural desolation of the American midwest" than, apparently, with European battlefields.[89] And in their 1981 annotated bibliography of First World War fiction, Philip Hager and Desmond Taylor seem to contradict so much of the early criticism leveled at Cather while simultaneously placing the novel outside the canon: "Although the war scenes are vivid and based on authentic knowledge of the war, the great conflict serves more as the process to reveal the solution for the personal problems of Claude."[90] Why these authors were willing to grant Cather an authenticity that her contemporaries believed she lacked suggests that the standards of authenticity may change as time removes the immediacy of the event and its fictional treatment.

The competing visions for the war's collective memory continued well into the 1940s. That the literary memory of the war today is almost totally consumed by the novels of disillusionment is, in fact, a testament to the cultural authority of a handful of critics in the 1920s whose elevation of Dos Passos, a literary newcomer who had served in the war, over Cather, a respected novelist confined to the "home front," rippled into future generations' criticism. As a result, the authority of the author's personal experience with the subject matter became one of the basic forms of a literary work's critical reception—a writer who had not seen war but nonetheless chose to write about it could be sure that this lack of experience would be mentioned, despite the canonization of a novel like Crane's *The Red Badge of Courage*.

Understanding the origins of combat gnosticism enables us to deconstruct the conditions that allowed the authority of experience to shape the war fiction genre for decades. Removing the "anxiety of authenticity" is the first step toward a new concept of narrative authority, one that does not rely on personal experience as the primary marker of authenticity. Today, just over a century after the publication of *Three Soldiers* and the birth of a new kind of war fiction genre, cracks are forming in the foundations of combat gnosticism. Although *One of Ours* could not survive its critical onslaught at the time of its publication or in the years after, Cather's process of treating the war as a subject bigger than battle would resurface in novels by Bobbie Ann Mason after Vietnam as well as with writers like Ben Fountain, Helen Benedict, Roxana Robinson, Cara Hoffman, and many others during the wars in Iraq and Afghanistan.[91] These trends suggest that the publishing industry may no longer view war experience as a "secret knowledge" belonging to an initiated few—as Campbell argued in response to Paul Fussell—but that war experience belongs to anyone who wishes to imagine it and its consequences for all of American society.

Although Dos Passos had offered the opening salvo in the new way of writing war fiction, his reign would be short. By the end of the 1920s and into the 1930s, Ernest Hemingway would eclipse Dos Passos as the quintessential veteran-author in the inchoate canon of American war fiction (despite Hemingway's own dubious authority as a veteran).[92] Hemingway's success, beginning with *The Sun Also Rises* in 1926 and followed by *A Farewell to Arms* in 1929, cemented his status as a major American author whose views on war and war literature would come to shape the next generation of writers unlike anyone before or since. Alongside Hemingway, the issues of authority and authenticity that had come to define the reception history of Cather and Dos Passos would form the basis of the genre's conventions following World War II.

CHAPTER TWO

"Tell It Like It Was"

World War II and the Institutional Curation of Memory

Not long after returning home from the European battlefields of World War II, army veteran James Byron Hall found himself holding back tears in a university classroom. It wasn't memories of the war that got to him, though — Hall, alongside many other veterans, was a student in one of the earliest creative writing classes at the newly formed Iowa Writers' Workshop, where he found the criticism of his poems and short stories at the hands of his peers and instructor (the celebrated poet Robert Lowell) more harrowing than his time in combat. But Hall persevered, earning his master's degree and later PhD from Iowa before beginning an academic career at Cornell University. Over the next fifteen years, Hall was instrumental in expanding West Coast creative writing institutions beyond Wallace Stegner at Stanford, founding programs at the University of Oregon, the University of California–Irvine, as well as a new arts college at the University of California–Santa Cruz.[1]

One of Hall's students at Oregon was Ken Kesey, best known for his 1960 novel *One Flew over the Cuckoo's Nest*. Kesey later recalled how Hall's teaching "unlocked for me the door to the resounding hall of real literature." And how did Hall do that? With a single line from a short story by an author who, by that time, had become a household name for war writing — Ernest Hemingway's "Soldier's Home."[2]

A World War II veteran teaching a Hemingway text in a university classroom is a crowning example of how the authority of experience over the literary representation of war became embedded in the institution and instruction of creative writing programs after World War II. A confluence of factors — from workshop curriculum and the outsized influence of Ernest Hemingway to the careers of the graduates themselves — helped World War II veterans build on the cultural authority that their predecessors began to amass in the 1920s at the hands of the critics who exalted them. Many

45

CHAPTER TWO

of these veterans would graduate from programs such as Iowa and Stanford to become professors of literature and creative writing, teaching Hemingway's stories and shaping the postwar literary institutions for the next twenty years.

As with the end of the First World War, the end of the Second World War ushered in a new era of cultural production as authors sought explanations and understanding in fiction that the real world failed to offer. The American soldiers sent to fight on the beaches and in the jungles of the Pacific, the deserts of North Africa, or the farm fields of Europe had all been schooled in the reality of what was waiting for them by their parents' generation and the protest literature of the 1920s and 1930s. The literary objective for many of these veterans-turned-authors was to convey what they had seen to a population now drunk on victory but unacquainted with its costs in human lives beyond the names and numbers reported in the local newspaper. Although the justness and morality of the war was rarely questioned, many veterans who had experienced the brutality of combat and technological warfare shunned such positivity and took a more bitter view. One way to temper the euphoria of victory in the hopes that the nation would not forget William Tecumseh Sherman's famous Civil War dictum that "war is hell" was to leverage the authority of experience to write realistic depictions of what the frontline combat soldier had endured.

Unlike the American literature of World War I, which spawned numerous monographs and book-length critical assessments, World War II has been viewed less as a singular literary event and more as a convenient historical dividing line for American literary history.[3] Yet despite the even greater scale of organized death, destruction, and technological progress, World War II was less of a shock to the world's collective consciousness and more of an expected, if disappointing, sequel. The effect on postwar American memory culture was a fictional response grounded in reportorial realism and enhanced by an institutional emphasis on craft and technique. American novels about the war in the 1940s and 1950s tended to foreground the individual's experience and avoid larger questions of historical forces and geopolitics. The essence of the experience for these writers was the day-to-day grit and grind, not some greater truth about war or humanity.

The major literary development in the first decades after the war was not in style but rather the way the authority of experience became embedded in the emergent creative writing institutions. Building on the foundations of the American fictional response to World War I, veteran-authors who returned from the battlefields of Europe and the Pacific saturated the literary landscape with more than two thousand novels between 1945 and 1965, leaving little room for other voices. Continuing the trend that had begun with the previous war, literary aesthetics focused on personal experience as the defining element of narrative authenticity, an idea that would find a home in the philosophy of postwar creative writing workshops as well as reinforcement from the words and cultural influence of a single writer, Ernest Hemingway.

The Big X: The Presence of Veterans in Postwar Literary Institutions

The year is 1996, and Elizabeth Tallent would have you "imagine a classroom crowded with clean-shaven young soldiers newly returned from a war." In this imaginative exercise it is the fall of 1945, and Tallent puts you in the shoes of Wallace Stegner, the founder of Stanford University's creative writing program. Tallent, who was appointed director of the program in 1994, asks you to "Imagine these young men unable to slouch or sprawl, as your writing students always have before, but sitting in straight, starchily attentive ranks because military discipline has owned them for so long, and is reluctant to let go. Moreover, they don't know who they will be when it does let go. Imagine reading their eyes for proof of damage."[4]

She speaks of Stegner's classroom as "haunted by reality, by a lot of realities," the specter of the recent past looming heavily over the shoulders of the men seated at the desks awaiting his instruction. The first story Stegner read for his new creative writing class at Stanford was Eugene Burdick's "Rest Camp on Maui." Burdick was a navy veteran, and his story impressed Stegner to the point that he was inspired to create a program of writing instruction specifically aimed at returning veterans. "Most writers," Stegner would write in a 1950 article, "are not ready to say anything publicly until they are crowding thirty." He contrasts the typical student—"too immature to know his own mind or have enough experience in the world to know where he stands in it"—with the military veterans, who "came mature and experienced and serious; they had something to think with and something to feel with and something to say; the qualities they possessed were the qualities necessary for any real and fruitful collaboration between teacher and student of writing."[5] As a teacher, Stegner valued students "whose minds are adult and whose experience is fairly wide" as the basis for encouraging and guiding literary talent and ambition. In his unpublished autobiography, Stegner reminisced about teaching veterans in the later 1940s: "Instead of green nineteen and twenty-year-olds, my classes were full of mature, experienced, highly-motivated men and women with hard experience, serious minds, and an urge to catch up lost time. . . . Teaching had never been, and has not been since the pure pleasure that it was in those years."[6]

These veterans, riding the wave of homegrown patriotic victory and supported by the recent GI Bill legislation that would finance their university education, brought their experiences with them to the classroom, perhaps intending to emulate Dos Passos, Boyd, Cummings, Hemingway, and other forebears of fiction from the First World War. "What his students could make of what they had seen," Tallent writes with the benefit of a half century of hindsight, "was un-knowable, a great big X, enigma, mystery, yet Stegner trusted it."[7]

What Stegner trusted was the process of extracting these veterans' war experiences and transforming them into narrative prose. That these veterans had stories to tell was never a question; the outpouring of cultural production that came after the First World War had laid the foundation for a genre to which the new crop of veterans could turn for inspiration and literary guidance. American society had welcomed its returning war veterans with open arms and a wealth of new opportunities to reintegrate into the country. The GI Bill aimed to provide a path to a college education, and, at the same time, newly developed creative writing programs were popping up and looking to court students. Trading rifles for pens and paper, veterans made up the majority of the creative writing students at Stanford and Iowa, two of the most important institutions at the time. In Iowa, workshops took place in "military-style Quonset huts set up along the Iowa River" until 1966.[8] Mark McGurl writes of the "grizzled student-veterans" who, released from the captivity of institutional uniformity enforced by the military, "were now converting that uniformity back into expressive individuality."[9] Creative writing classrooms broke down the conformity of the uniform to find the kernel of truth in each individual's perspective. Under the creative writing program's tutelage, veterans were encouraged to turn to their war experience for inspiration. And, at least in Stegner's view, they were successful. "Stegner was impressed with the unusual authority and maturity with which the veterans packed into his classroom in the late 1940s could respond to the call to 'write what you know,'" McGurl writes, "and they became the measure by which subsequent generations of creative writing students at Stanford seemed to him to pale in comparison."[10]

"Write what you know" was the pithy mantra that shaped the aesthetic sensibility of American literary culture after World War II, placing an explicit premium on personal experience as a source of narrative authenticity and driving the entire field toward a certain type of realism as a mode of representation that can be summarized by the widely used term "authenticity." As with the critical reception of Dos Passos and Cather after the First World War, the focus on authenticity as an integral element of creative writing became intimately linked with the writer's personal memory and experience. Stegner was teaching his students to "write what you know" while he was still at Harvard in 1940,[11] but it wasn't until he brought it to the postwar classroom that it became part of the institutional philosophy of creative writing. McGurl writes that "the injunction to 'write what you know' [was] woven deep into the fabric of creative writing instruction from the outset." He continues:

> Titled toward a crudely empiricist conception of knowledge as that which the author has directly observed, this injunction was nonetheless served up with the subjectivist proviso that it should be the observer-experiencer himself who, interacting with his object, is the true subject and end of the composition.[12]

If we replace McGurl's "observer-experiencer" with "veteran-author," it is no wonder that so much war fiction is written (and read) as autobiographical. Between the First and the Second World Wars, the kinds of knowledge gained from war experience began to be interpreted more directly as unique or revelatory in nature. The veteran-author, in most cases unschooled in the technical arts of fiction writing until after the war, came instead with a mountain of memories that could be mined for good material. They were amateur writers, but their experiences were interpreted as something extraordinary—in the most literal sense—within the context of American society. They knew what they saw, and the classroom could teach them the rest. Further, the logical complement to write what you know—*don't write what you don't know*—supported the same view of authenticity and war writing that had prevailed in the 1920s. Whereas the original vision came from literary critics, this next incantation of the same ideology became the "official" doctrine of the creative writing institution with its incorporation into the classroom's program of instruction. Thus, with direct, truly subjective observation serving as the source of authorial knowledge, the next generation of veteran-authors were armed with a privileged form of authenticity as they grappled for a place among the sources of postwar memory formation.

In McGurl's model of "autopoetics," three primary values combine to form the building blocks of creative writing: experience, creativity, and craft. McGurl associates the value of experience with both authenticity and memory, summed together as "write what you know." Authenticity and memory both have layers as well; personal memory combines with the technical craft of fiction writing to, in theory, produce an authentic depiction of some lived experience. This form of self-expression necessarily relies on realism as a mode of representation, and ties closely with Astrid Erll's version of the "experiential" mode within the rhetoric of collective memory, passing on a fictionalized version of the author's lived experience.[13] Alex Vernon refers to this as the "*being there* reportorial style in fiction" that, by World War II, "had become the convention of war literature."[14] He goes on:

> For new writers returned from war, to write what they knew—the details and discourse of soldiering—they adopted the factual, reportorial mode. The need to write about war with this kind of verisimilitude is motivated not only by the amateur author's limited literary experience and talents, but it also is motivated by the author's desire to prove his authenticity—essentially to testify—by the new expectation for authentic depictions of battle and its attendant experiences.[15]

Vernon touches an important point by observing the veterans' "need" to write and to "testify" about their experiences with as much authenticity as possible. Jennifer Haytock, too, refers to the "obligation" that so many of these veteran-writers felt to "tell what they had seen and done, to educate their readers in an immersive, factual experience about war."[16] For the student-veterans attending creative writing workshops, coupling the

"Tell It Like It Was"

pedagogical charge to "write what you know" with the need to recount their experiences as accurately as possible transformed the aesthetic objective of war fiction into "tell it like it was," a phrase that implicitly contained the veteran-author's authority to write and interpret the war experience as well as the assumption of authenticity that came with the veteran's voice.

The combination of the expanding creative writing institutions with the veterans' reception in American society allowed those who served overseas to build a literary identity around their wartime experience. The early history of the "program era" shows how veteran-authors came to the postwar classroom and created a separate class of high-cultural pluralist writing that departed from ethnic or regional identity—characteristics that create long-term conditions for personal identification—and instead focused on the outsized influence of a single set of experiences overseas during the war. War experience, unlike one's ethnicity or regional culture, is a shock to a person's system, something that interrupts the individual's identity formation and inserts a series of extraordinary experiences. The experiences of only a few years (or even less, in many cases) are so outside the boundaries of the typical life in Western civilization that they produce enough material for novel after novel. This, McGurl writes, led to "the emergence of a virtual cultural identity emanating from an authoritative experience of war."[17] Unlike other forms of racial and ethnic identity, though, the veteran's cultural identity is based on a single experience rather than a lifetime. The same cultural forces in the classroom that led Sandra Cisneros to brand herself as a Chicana writer or encouraged Flannery O'Connor to embrace her "southernness" also nudged military veterans to see themselves first and foremost as representatives of the nation's wartime experience—as battle and combat personified and transferred to the page.

Although the presence of World War II veterans in postwar creative writing workshops at Iowa and Stanford has become a well-known fact of literary history, there is an important follow-up question missing from the story: What happened to them? What effect did they have on the development of the American literary institutions in later decades? While scholars have often noted that the early years of creative writing workshops at universities like Stanford and Iowa were packed with veterans financed by

CHAPTER TWO

the GI Bill, their influence on the field after graduation has never been fully appreciated. To find out, I went through the list of Stanford's Stegner Fellowship recipients and Iowa Writers' Workshop graduates from 1945 through 1955 and, where possible, determined what they did afterward.[18]

Many of these writers went on to take academic positions within the burgeoning institution of creative writing instruction. They taught literature and fiction at universities, ascended to higher leadership and management positions, and in some cases even founded new programs at other universities. World War II veterans who graduated from Iowa and Stanford would establish or direct creative writing programs at the University of Oregon (James Byron Hall, Iowa 1947), Miami University in Ohio (Milton White, Stegner Fellow 1948), the University of California–Santa Barbara (Edward Loomis, Stegner Fellow 1950), Southwest State and Murray State (Delbert Wylder, Iowa 1950), the University of California–Irvine (Oakley Hall, Iowa 1950), the University of Rhode Island (Leonard Casper, Stegner Fellow 1951), and Cornell University (James McConkey, Iowa 1953). Many others became professors of literature and creative writing at universities across the country.

In addition to positions within the university, several graduates influenced the field in other relevant ways. After writing his own novels and teaching at multiple universities, Ronald Cassill (Iowa 1947) founded the Association of Writers and Writing Programs in 1967, an organization that holds annual conferences to this day. He also become the editor of *The Norton Anthology of Short Fiction* for many years. Dean Doner (Iowa 1948) finished his professional career as the vice president of Boston University and was also one of the founders of the literary journal *Modern Fiction Studies*.

Veteran program graduates also found positions outside the academy, especially in publishing and journalism. Herbert Nipson (Iowa 1948) was the first Black student elected to the national journalism honor society (Sigma Delta Chi) at Penn State University. From 1949 through 1989, he was an editor at *Ebony* magazine, eventually rising to the position of executive editor in 1972. John Ferrone (Stegner Fellow 1951) spent more than thirty-five years in the publishing industry, working for Dell Publishing as well as Harcourt, Brace & World. Edward Blair (Iowa 1951) became the head of publications at Rocketdyne, a company that supplied rocket engines for the space program.

Bernard Taper, a naturalized citizen who was born in Scotland, spent two years in postwar Germany as one of the famed "Monuments Men" searching for art and cultural artifacts hidden away by the Nazis. He came to Stanford on a Stegner Fellowship in 1955, earning a master's in creative writing and later became a staff writer for the *New Yorker* and a journalism professor at UC-Berkeley.

While many veteran graduates of Iowa and Stanford went on to influence the literary field from within the academy or other adjacent institutions, others toiled away at their craft in relative obscurity, leaving their marks more locally by teaching at smaller community colleges and high schools. Robert Waring Hinwood, for example, had been drafted into the army in 1944 and, at only eighteen years old, found himself in combat in the Philippines. After earning his master's degree from Stanford on a Stegner Fellowship in 1952, he taught English at Monterey Peninsula College in California for nearly forty years until he retired in 1989. He died in 2007, leaving behind twelve poems and two unpublished novels, according to his obituary.[19] Bernard Hailperin served in Italy during the war and graduated from Iowa in 1948. He taught English literature, drama, and speech at Parsippany Hills High School in New Jersey. In 2009, he published a novel called *Children of Vesuvius*, which echoed his own wartime experiences. And Howard Winn (Stegner Fellow in 1952), a B-29 air crew veteran, taught English at Dutchess Community College in Poughkeepsie, New York, from 1958 until his retirement in 2005. In 2018, he published his first novel, *Acropolis*, about a small group of soldiers who attend Vassar College on the GI Bill—just as Winn had done.[20]

In postwar America, the GI Bill provided returning veterans with a much easier path into the literary field via the nascent institutions of creative writing programs. Veteran status conferred individuals with a new form of cultural authority that granted them a ticket from the periphery directly to the center of the literary field.[21] Whereas a writer like John Dos Passos struggled to find a publisher for his early work, World War II veterans, their pockets lined with financial support from the government, could attend universities like Stanford and Iowa and make connections with literary insiders such as Wallace Stegner, Paul Engle, and many others. The literary field itself became far more accommodating to veteran-authors immediately after the war than it had been to the veterans of the early 1920s.

CHAPTER TWO

That war veterans would become active participants in the institutions that helped bring them to the center of the field was perhaps an unintended consequence. The combination of the GI Bill and creative writing programs looking for students allowed war veterans to return home from Europe or the Pacific, spend a few years at a place like Iowa or Stanford—learning that they should "write what they know"—and come out the other end as teachers, program directors, magazine editors, and so on, shaping the postwar literary field well into the 1950s and 1960s in ways that, until now, have gone underappreciated.

We can't know for sure what lessons these veterans took with them as they spread across the country to teach the next generation of creative writing students or make editorial decisions at publishing houses, academic journals, and magazines. Tucked under their arms were likely copies of the notes they took as writing students with Stegner, Engle, and others, reminding them that personal experience was the primary source of textual authenticity. Viewed in this light, "the big X" that Elizabeth Tallent imagined and that Wallace Stegner sought was the personal experience of war and combat, and the instruction of a philosophy like "write what you know" was the first step toward the institutional curation of postwar memory. The veterans who took this advice, whether in the classroom or on their own, would find a readymade role model for their work in Ernest Hemingway.

Ernest Hemingway's War Writing Philosophy

No account of twentieth-century American war fiction can avoid a discussion of Ernest Hemingway. His celebrity in the wake of *A Farewell to Arms* (1929) and *For Whom the Bell Tolls* (1940) left him to wield his massive cultural authority around the literary field like a sledgehammer when it came to war writing. World War II veterans who became writers all wanted to emulate his style when they, too, returned home from overseas, often encouraged by Stegner, Hall, and other instructors who assigned Hemingway's story "Soldier's Home" as the canonical example of "understated self-reflection."[22] Later scholarship would consistently point to Hemingway as the primary influence on the war fiction genre after 1929. Alex Vernon notes that "every post-Hemingway American war veteran who has attempted to write serious

54

"Tell It Like It Was"

fiction about war and the military has had to contend with Hemingway's looming shadow."[23] Roy Scranton refers to Hemingway as the "high priest of combat gnosticism" in an article for the *Los Angeles Review of Books*.[24] "More than any other writer," Matthew Bruccoli writes, "Ernest Hemingway influenced what American writers were able to write about and the words they used."[25] Hemingway's views on war as fodder for the writer's mind are almost as canonical for the genre as his own literary works. War, for Hemingway,

> was one of the major subjects and certainly one of the hardest to write truly of and those writers who had not seen it were always very jealous and tried to make it seem unimportant, or a disease as a subject, while, really, it was just something quite irreplaceable that they had missed.[26]

Bruccoli observes that "the element Hemingway most admired in fiction was the accuracy that resulted from the writer's knowledge of the way it was, based on observation and experience, accurately reported. The word *truly* echoes throughout his nonfiction and fiction."[27] Hemingway says as much himself: "A writer's job is to tell the truth. His standard of fidelity to the truth should be so high that his invention, out of his experience, should produce a truer account than anything factual can be."[28] Though unspoken directly, one can feel the influence of both authority and authenticity behind Hemingway's words like the gravitational pull of a black hole.

Hemingway's views on war are strewn throughout his writings, both fiction and nonfiction. Leaning heavily on his experience as a volunteer ambulance driver in Italy during World War I, his early short stories such as "Soldier's Home" and "Big Two-Hearted River" intimated that the truth of war could hardly be communicated. *The Sun Also Rises*, his 1926 first novel, like "Big Two-Hearted River," is about the war without ever confronting it directly. In 1929, *A Farewell to Arms* followed the disillusioned path blazed by Dos Passos at the beginning of the decade. The novel's success would forever link Hemingway's name with the American fiction of the First World War. His reportage from the Spanish Civil War at the end of the 1930s led to *For Whom the Bell Tolls* (1940), another novel that, like his earlier works, would be read as autobiographical.

At the beginning of the World War II, Hemingway was one of the most popular writers in America, but his reputation among literary critics had fallen since his breakout in the 1920s.[29] Nonetheless, his work and his war experiences had afforded him a considerable amount of authority and credibility when it came to writing about conflict. In 1942, with the United States embroiled in global conflict, Hemingway edited an anthology titled *Men at War: The Best War Stories of All Time*. The book's intended audience was American service members en route to combat for the first time, and Hemingway's introduction to the volume speaks to his philosophy on what war literature can teach the uninitiated. "This book will not tell you how to die," he begins. "This book will tell you, though, how all men from the earliest times we know have fought and died. So when you have read it you will know that there are no worse things to be gone through than men have been through before."[30] The volume spans more than a thousand pages, and Hemingway's refrain throughout the introduction is that this collection can arm the fighting men with the knowledge that they are not the first to undergo the experience of war and battle:

> When you go to war as a boy you have a great illusion of immortality. Other people get killed; not you. It can happen to other people; but not to you. Then when you are badly wounded the first time you lose that illusion and you know it can happen to you. After being severely wounded two weeks before my nineteenth birthday I had a bad time until I figured it out that nothing could happen to me that had not happened to all men before me. Whatever I had to do men had always done. If they had done it then I could do it too and the best thing was not to worry about it.[31]

Hemingway also uses the occasion of the anthology's introduction to pronounce his judgment on several centuries of war literature, with particularly harsh words for the wartime writing of his own conflict. "In the last war there was no really good true war book during the entire four years of the war," he writes, arguing that the "only true writing that came through during the war was in poetry." He called the war years of 1914 through 1917 "the most colossal, murderous, mismanaged butchery that has taken place on earth. Any writer who said otherwise lied. So the writers either wrote propaganda, shut up, or fought."[32] It was only after the war had ended that

"Tell It Like It Was"

"the good and true books finally started to come out." These books, he continues

> were mostly all by writers who had never written or published anything before the war. The writers who were established before the war had nearly all sold out to write propaganda during it and most of them never recovered their honesty afterwards. All of their reputations steadily slumped because a writer should be of as great probity and honesty as a priest of God. He is either honest or not, as a woman is either chaste or not, and after one piece of dishonest writing he is never the same again.[33]

Only two World War I writers are mentioned by name as having produced anything worthy of inclusion in the collection: Frederic Manning (*Her Privates We*) of Australia and Henri Barbusse (*Under Fire*) of France. Hemingway calls Manning's 1929 novel "the finest and noblest book of men in war that I have ever read," and praises Barbusse's "courage" for writing and publishing such a realistic (that is, negative) account of the war while it was still underway, though he faults Barbusse for "screaming" too much. Hemingway's assessments — at least for World War I literature — were based less on the quality of a work's prose or other aesthetic values but rather the writers' stature as honest amateurs as well as his own standards of what should be considered "true" and "truth."

Hemingway also revises his take on *Three Soldiers*, now twenty years since its publication. He mentions that he would have liked to include an excerpt in the anthology because it was "the first attempt at a realistic book about the war written by an American," but that "on rereading it did not stand up." He argues that "the dialogue rings false and the actual combat is completely unconvincing. There are books like that, which are as exciting as a fine new play when they come out and, when you return to them after years, are as dead as the scenery of that play if you should happen on it in a storage house. . . . Its pall, and the lack of all clarity in the combat scenes, is what makes the Dos Passos book unreadable today."[34] It is worth recalling that Hemingway and Dos Passos, once friends, had a falling-out over political differences during the Spanish Civil War, something that may have influenced Hemingway's reappraisal of *Three Soldiers*.[35]

CHAPTER TWO

While many reviewers wrote highly of the anthology in general, Hemingway's introduction met with some criticism.[36] One reviewer remarked that Hemingway's tone suggested that "almost everybody else is wrong about war, and that only now has the great Interpreter collected the few immortal narratives, real and imaginary, that tell you what war is really like."[37] Indeed, that is exactly the sentiment that comes across in Hemingway's introduction, and not likely by accident. The capital he had accumulated as a writer since he began publishing stories about war in the early 1920s gave him the cultural authority to do this, and Hemingway was not about to pass up an opportunity to preach his views on war literature from such an influential literary pulpit—the soldiers for whom Hemingway had conceived the *Men at War* anthology were a captive audience, after all. Whatever the critical reception had been, the publisher wrote in the foreword to a 1955 new edition that the book was "so cherished by the G.I.'s of World War II." Regardless of what literary critics were saying, it was Hemingway's own words that were reaching the future writers of the war.

Hemingway and the Writing Workshop

The process that transformed Hemingway from a popular, best-selling author into a canonical figure of American letters began with the 1944 publication of an edited collection of his work called *The Portable Hemingway*. A year earlier, Viking Press had published the first in an envisioned series of "portable" books designed as cheap paperbacks to be sent to military personnel stationed overseas. Viking hired Malcolm Cowley, a writer and literary critic, to spearhead the Hemingway volume.

Cowley, like Hemingway and Dos Passos, had also served as a volunteer ambulance driver during the First World War and spent time with the famed Lost Generation of expatriate American writers living in Paris in the 1920s. He had accumulated a significant amount of authority and cultural capital as a literary critic in the 1930s and 1940s, despite some political setbacks—Cowley, an admitted Marxist, was forced to resign from a government job in the War Department in 1942 after coming under pressure from the House Committee on Un-American Activities.[38] After two years of essentially self-imposed exile, Cowley came to Viking determined to bring attention to what he believed were underappreciated writers, with Hemingway at the top of his list.[39]

Cowley used the opportunity as the book's editor to write an introduction that would reframe Hemingway as an artist of considerable symbolic depth. Benjamin Kirbach writes that "Cowley departed in his introductory essay from earlier critical assessments of Hemingway as emotionally sparse and overly masculine. Framed instead as essentially a tortured and submerged gothic writer, Cowley's re-evaluation is the dominant critical view today. And Hemingway's signature tip-of-the-iceberg style has perhaps become the most emulated in writing workshops."[40]

Reminiscing on his editing work of *Portable Hemingway* in an article published forty years later, Cowley noted that the book gave him a chance to "correct a general misestimation of Hemingway's work," arguing that he was "not merely an international celebrity but also an important figure in the history of American literature."[41] In the article, Cowley reprints the opening paragraph of his introduction to the Hemingway book as a way to defend his views on Hemingway's writing, which, in his view, were coming "under attack by the critical revisionists, a contentious sect." Most importantly within the introduction itself was Cowley's assessment that Hemingway's writing deserved a "kinship" with writers such as Edgar Allan Poe, Nathaniel Hawthorne, and Herman Melville —"the haunted and nocturnal writers, the men who dealt in images that were symbols of an inner world." Recalling that Cowley wrote this in 1944 and that *Portable Hemingway* became a bestseller, his inclusion of Hemingway on that list of the giants of American letters, obvious as it may seem now, elevated his name and his writing to a level of critical respect that was worthy of classroom instruction and study.

Cowley also discusses the scholarly gap in American literature for living writers to serve as models for the scores of new university programs after the war. He credits this gap as helping his *Portable Hemingway*, and later *The Portable Faulkner*, serve the interests of American literature and form the foundation of a new American canon. "I had portrayed both authors as representing an American tradition," Cowley writes, "as weaving American legends, as writing a prose that was rich in symbols, and as plunging into the human depths. By speaking in literary terms, I had helped to make them *teachable*."[42]

CHAPTER TWO

A teachable Hemingway became a powerful tool for the postwar American classroom. Aspiring writers were captivated by his writing style and his authorial persona, unable to resist the clarity of his sentences or the projected glamour of his lifestyle. Eric Bennett, whose *Workshops of Empire* examines how creative writing programs were employed as cultural weapons to counter Soviet ideology during the Cold War, argues that "Hemingway was *the* influence in writing workshops full of demobilized G.I.s. At the height of his fame in the mid-1950s, embodying the masculine individualism that the United States emphasized in its anti-Communist ferment, and offering a style easy to imitate, Hemingway stood center stage on college campuses."[43]

The intersection of Hemingway's writing and views on war with the rise of the workshop created a perfect storm of cultural authority that would overtake the institution. "In the years when the Iowa Writers' Workshop was first attracting talent," Bennett writes, "Hemingway provided—through a nexus of journalism, fiction, and celebrity—a paradigm for the postwar author. After the Second World War his legend would electrify creative writing programs directed by anti-communist liberals and filled with older students returning to school on the G. I. Bill."[44] These students, raised on a steady diet of "write what you know," saw in Hemingway a shining example of how personal experience could be converted into literary fiction. And veterans were not the only ones to fall under Hemingway's spell. Bennett points out that "even students not from a military background felt the influence,"[45] quoting from an essay that John Barth later wrote about his own time studying creative writing under a marine combat veteran at Johns Hopkins. Barth writes of his own workshop story that it was "largely derivative from Hemingway's 'Soldier's Home' without Hemingway's authentic knowledge of his material."[46]

The concept of narrative authenticity that comes from Hemingway's writing became an indispensable model for creative writing workshops searching for a balanced relationship between experience, imagination, and craft. Controlling the different legs of this authorial triangle—delicate restraint here, passionate expression there—was the workshop writer's challenge. Postwar writing aesthetics, at least at the highest levels, wanted more than a bucketful of unformed memories spilled onto the page. Hemingway, whose own wartime biographical details were well known (mostly due to Hemingway's marketing of himself), was the perfect example for the "right" way to transform combat experience into something artful.[47]

Greater than the Sum of Its Parts: World War II in American Fiction

What was the effect of the writing workshop and Hemingway on the fictional response to the Second World War? In 1954, Malcolm Cowley wrote an article titled "War Novels: After Two Wars" in which he reflected on four decades worth of American war fiction. He begins by observing that novels about World War II seem "to be little affected by the standards of the newer critics," and that "almost all of these are based on the experience of their authors." He continues:

> The experience calls urgently to be retold and, much more than civilian life, it takes the shape of stories with a beginning, a middle, and an end. The hero has adventures, and at last comes home; or he goes into action, suffers, and is killed; or again there may be a collective hero, a platoon or a ship's company that is brought together, becomes a living unity, and then is dissolved at the end of a campaign.[48]

Although Cowley gives the edge to the writers of the First World War for producing the greater individual works, he credits the writers of the Second World War for a better consistency than their predecessors as well as composing, as a group, a "sounder body of work." These writers "have been quick to master the tools of their craft," Cowley writes, noting that "on the average, their books are not only more smoothly and skillfully written than most war novels of the 1920s but are also better reporting of 'what really happened in action,' to borrow from Ernest Hemingway."[49] No doubt aware of how creative writing programs had adopted Hemingway for instructional purposes, Cowley writes that many of the more recent works employed what he dubbed "the Hemingway method" of depicting combat, something that he points out "can be learned from his books or studied in college courses," and which "most of the younger war novelists have followed . . . instinctively.

CHAPTER TWO

. . . Hemingway's battle scenes had a force and clarity that impressed the novelists who came after him. His method has become an accepted part of their technical equipment."[50]

Craft and technique, writing program buzzwords that had become two of the cornerstones of postwar literary aesthetics, had merged with a reportorial style to create a set of rules and expectations for war fiction. In addition to referring to Hemingway's influence on the war writer's "technical equipment," Cowley also considers the writers of World War II novels to be "good technicians, good reporters, and I should judge that they are also good historians."[51] Under this rubric, there is little room for imagination: the institutional curation of memory had reduced fiction writing to a straightforward form of experiential regurgitation restrained by the tools of the trade. Yet Cowley seems to fault this method for not leading to something greater, arguing that "the group of books is more impressive than the separate works of fiction. These are on a higher level of competence than almost all the first-war novels, but what they form is a tableland, not a chain of mountains."[52] On whether this is a defect or a virtue, Cowley hesitates. Once again blurring the distinction between fiction writers and historians, Cowley quips that "most of the young novelists might as well have been commissioned and trained in advance to write each his separate volume in a great collaborative history of World War II as seen by the fighting men. . . . Together the novels form a production of lasting value, one that may well be richer and more complete than the account we possess of any nation's part in any other recent war."[53] Viewing fiction this way echoes Hemingway's remark that a good writer of fiction "should produce a truer account than anything factual can be."[54]

By the 1960s, the veteran-author's cultural authority had become firmly embedded within the American literary institution. Postwar creative writing programs had adopted the basic tenets of combat gnosticism as part of their instruction, teaching students to "write what you know" and prioritizing the authority of experience as the foundational element of authenticity in the literary representation of war. At the same time, Ernest Hemingway's celebrity and views on war and war writing become the model for the post–World War II generation of writers, whether they had served or

"Tell It Like It Was"

not. Creative writing programs also used Hemingway's works as a major component of their curriculum, from a restrained style to the importance of a reportorial eye for detail. This combination pushed the genre into the waiting embrace of realism, an approach taken by the vast majority of the more than two thousand novels published about the war.[55] Most of those early works, though, have been forgotten, overshadowed by the war's small and arguably misrepresentative canon of novels that found new and innovative forms to elevate individual trauma into something more universal.[56]

At the end of all this, war writing is seen as a subject only for veterans; nonveteran-authored works about World War II are virtually nonexistent until decades later, when the war becomes a popular subject of historical fiction, something it remains today. Yet the belief that the truth of war is communicable through literature—from "telling it like it was" to Hemingway's introduction to *Men at War*—would distinguish the generation of World War I and II veterans from those who would serve in Vietnam, a war in which one of the defining phrases would signal a newfound attempt to defend the veteran-author's authority over the literary representation of war as never before: "You had to be there."

CHAPTER THREE

"You Had to Be There"

Vietnam and the Veteran's Consolidation of Authority

When Lieutenant Rufus Brooks is out to dinner with his wife at a fancy restaurant during his mid-tour trip home from Vietnam in John Del Vecchio's *The 13th Valley*, thoughts of his fellow soldiers constantly tug at his concentration. Irritated by "rich sons of bitches in here picking at their food," Rufus begins to tell his wife, Lila, about what his life has been like as a combat infantryman. Rufus quickly realizes, though, that "Lila doesn't want to talk about Vietnam."

> Rufus ran through explanations in his mind but he rejected each. He knew Lila was not interested in or capable of comprehending what his infantry unit was, what it meant to him. There was an *esprit de corps* among his men built on the deep concern each had for every other. They worked together, they fought together, they shared life and death. How can those words mean anything to someone who has not experienced it? Yet Rufus wanted to talk, wanted Lila to understand. But he could not talk.[1]

Rufus internalizes his conflict as the burden of his own experience. Desperate to connect with his wife on some level during his brief time home before heading back to Vietnam and more combat, Rufus finds only distance between them. He projects his feelings of sticking out as a military officer among civilians. He catches himself interpreting his wife's actions as designed to hide his service, for instance when she tells him not to wear his uniform ("'I'm not ashamed of it,' Rufus said simply, not defensively") or massages his hair ("Why are you doing that? Rufus asked himself. Does my short hair give me away? Does it offend you?"). Whatever he does, his thoughts remain with his men back in Vietnam, and in this moment he only wishes that his wife would listen to his war stories.

CHAPTER THREE

Yet in Rufus's mind, Lila isn't just uninterested in his war stories; she is *incapable* of "comprehending what his infantry unit was, what it meant to him." He mentions their camaraderie, the bond they share under the life-threatening conditions of combat, the way that a proximity to death created the revelatory conditions for an enhanced understanding of life. Rufus's conflicted emotions about the situation are punctuated first in the form of a rhetorical question—"How can those words mean anything to someone who has not experienced it?"—and then in another expression of his desire that Lila could understand him. He "wanted to talk, wanted Lila to understand," but in the end shackles himself with his own self-imposed silence.

At this point in the novel, there is little distance between Del Vecchio the author and his characters. Rufus's struggle to explain Vietnam to his wife reads as an expression of the burden of telling war stories, and as such comes across as an admission of the failure of representation to convey the essence of the experience. Whatever truth of the wartime experience that the author wishes to capture will, in this way, be lost on the civilian reader who either does not wish to hear the story in the first place or, even if the desire is present, is incapable of comprehending that truth. "You had to be there," as the saying goes.

Del Vecchio reaffirms this philosophical attitude in the novel's acknowledgments at the front of the book:

> Grateful acknowledgment is made to: A soldier on Firebase Rendezvous at the edge of the A Shau Valley during Lam Son 719, Spring 1971.
>
> He said to me, "You can do it, Man. You write about this place. You been here a long time. People gotta know what it was really like." And thus this book began.

The authority that this short passage establishes comes from a nearly unassailable position. Del Vecchio sets up the revelation in the first sentence, full of references to a place and time in Vietnam that would have little meaning to anyone who wasn't there: *Firebase Rendezvous, A Shau Valley, Lam Son 719*. Within the span of a single line Del Vecchio creates a division between those with knowledge and those without. Yet this knowledge is still based on facts that can be learned from history books or acquired through secondhand stories. The real punchline comes when the anonymous soldier, who urges Del Vecchio to "write about this place" and speaks in the grunt's vernacular, charges Del Vecchio personally with telling people "what it was really like." We are no longer in the realm of facts but something less tangible, something more personal, something perhaps—if we consider how Rufus feels at dinner with his wife—incommunicable no matter how authentic the story is written. Del Vecchio's decision to include this anecdote in 1982—eleven years after it happened—reads as a sly critique of the imaginative representations of the war that preceded him. None of this is to call the story out as apocryphal; whether a fellow soldier told John Del Vecchio that he must bear the burden of this story matters less than how Del Vecchio, as the novel's author, chose to use the encounter to frame his narrative.

The Vietnam War was a turning point in the veteran-author's place within the American literary field, and Del Vecchio's novel is but one example of how Vietnam veterans consolidated their authority over the literary representation of war by invoking a kind of rhetoric that valued personal experience over all other forms and sources of knowledge. Reacting against a counterculture movement that viewed soldiers as villains rather than akin to the heroes of the World War II generation, Vietnam veterans actively sought authority over the war's representation as a way to regain control of their image in society. They grabbed on to narratives that painted the war as a unique event in American history and combined them with the language of trauma to build a metaphorical fortress around their authority to interpret the war's meaning. Under these conditions, personal experience was no longer the primary source of narrative authority, it was the *only* source.

Vietnam's "Uniqueness" and the Rejection of Historical Truth

In May 1985, the Asia Society sponsored a conference that brought together a large group of writers, publishers, teachers, academics, and others to discuss "The Vietnam Experience in American Literature." The participants recognized that one of the dominant themes of the literature produced about the war to that point was the tension between fact and fiction. In a bibliographic commentary on the works discussed at the conference, John Clark Pratt—himself an author and veteran of the war—wrote that although one can read history to gain an understanding of what happened in

CHAPTER THREE

Vietnam, "it is from the fiction, though, that the real truth as well as the real progression of the war best can be seen."[2]

Pratt's assessment that fiction was the best form to get at the truth of the war recalls Hemingway's standards for fiction writers, whose understanding of the truth "should be so high that his invention, out of his experience, should produce a truer account than anything factual can be." The tension between history and fiction that Pratt and many other Vietnam veterans were grappling with was not a new debate; a related line of thought had come from the historian Hayden White a decade earlier. White's *Metahistory* (1973) approached historical writing from a narrative perspective, arguing that historians could not escape the biases—unconscious or otherwise—of their own linguistic and structural choices. Historical writing, in this view, could not be relied upon for a purely objective relationship to human events and experience. Postmodern thought would add yet another pillar of support to claims against the universality of historical truth. In *A Poetics of Postmodernism*, Linda Hutcheon noted that the postmodern "effects two simultaneous moves. It reinstalls historical contexts as significant and even determining, but in so doing, it problematizes the entire notion of historical knowledge."[3] The results of these intellectual developments were crucial for literary representations of war: if historical writing could be read as a kind of fiction, fiction could just as well be read as a reflection of history.

"In any war story, but especially a true one, it's difficult to separate what happened from what seemed to happen," Vietnam veteran Tim O'Brien writes in "How to Tell a True War Story" from his 1990 collection *The Things They Carried*, echoing the famous opening line from Kurt Vonnegut's *Slaughterhouse-Five*: "All this happened, more or less. The war parts, anyway, are pretty much true."[4] Although O'Brien's widely anthologized and analyzed story may be the most well-known example of this kind of writing, the inadequacy of historiography to describe the experience of Vietnam was a recurring theme from the very beginning. In a 1986 article on the historical consciousness of Vietnam War literature, for example, one scholar showed how a great number of Vietnam veterans who became writers dealt with the tension between fact and fiction by rejecting historical objectivity altogether: "It is precisely the belief that the *truth* of the Vietnam War

68

"You Had to Be There"

is accessible to the powers of rational historical analysis which many literary artists have found to be not only erroneous but contemptible."[5] Michael Herr's Dispatches (1977) became one of the best examples of this belief, a work of journalistic nonfiction that also rejects the capability of historical analysis to make sense of the war:

> Anyway, you couldn't use standard methods to date the doom; might as well say that Vietnam was where the Trail of Tears was headed all along, the turnaround point where it would touch and come back to form a containing perimeter; might just as well lay it on the proto-Gringos who found the New England woods too raw and empty for their peace and filled them up with their own imported devils.[6]

In this brief passage, Herr takes aim at what could be considered a fundamental task of historical analysis — identifying when the war began. The notion that "standard methods" were ill-suited to "date the doom" becomes embedded within an American historical consciousness that has known violence since its inception, with Herr creating a rhetorical link between Vietnam, the forced relocation of the indigenous Native Americans on the Trail of Tears, and even the Puritans (disparagingly referred to as "proto-Gringos"). Herr's book defies easy categorization; though technically a work of nonfiction, it routinely pops up in lists of novels about the war as well as in literary criticism and scholarship. The way Herr straddled the two genres (dubbed "New Journalism" by Tom Wolfe) put Dispatches in the position to become the perfect example for the debate between history and fiction as applied to the Vietnam War. Somehow, Dispatches came across as too real to be true.

Dispatches was one of the many works that functioned as "a genuine alternative to official documents, media reports, scholarly and popular histories," as John Carlos Rowe suggested. Other veteran-authored memoirs, novels, and personal testimony did the same, generating an "unusual competition" between official histories and subjective individual expressions, leading to what Rowe deemed a "confusion of personal account and historical knowledge" in the representations of Vietnam.[7] Through the proliferation of their works, Vietnam veterans were making the case that chronicles of their personal experiences should be considered as closer to the truth than anything a historical treatment could offer.

CHAPTER THREE

The veteran's authority to interpret the meaning of the war was even boosted by nonveterans who sought to amplify the veterans' voices as an alternative to historical accounts. "Vietnam was a brutal Neverneverland, outside time and space where little boys didn't have to grow up. They just grew old before their time," Mark Baker commented in *Nam: The Vietnam War in the Words of the Men and Women Who Fought There* (1981).[8] This oral history—Baker recorded and transcribed interviews with dozens of veterans—was deliberately framed as an antidote to a more traditional historical discourse, endowing a collective group of anonymous veterans with a rhetorical authority based on a structured presentation of their personal experience.[9] Baker's metaphor places that experience outside the bounds of a traditional reality and into a "Neverneverland" that marks it as something wholly different from everything that came beforehand. The fact that Baker was not a veteran himself only enhanced the authority of the veterans whose stories are transcribed as spoken but introduced with Baker's brief commentary; the reader is invited to identify with *Baker* as an outside listener of these veterans' stories through "a narrative perspective designed to bring us into a more personal relation with the veteran, but one that presumes the foreign quality of such an experience."[10] You might not have been there, the book suggests, but you can read these interviews and see for yourself what the history books can't teach you.

A corollary to the rejection of historiography that flows throughout the literary response to the war was the rhetoric of uniqueness that became part of the veteran's lexicon. It wasn't just that the experience of Vietnam was horrifying for those who served there, but that everything about it was described as unprecedented in American history. Authors and literary critics alike adopted this kind of rhetoric when writing or talking about Vietnam throughout the 1970s and into the early 1980s. In an early review essay published in 1978, one critic first says that Vietnam was "in countless hidden and obvious ways drastically different from every other war in our history" before remarking that "the weight of Vietnam's many sorry distinctions has exerted some curious effects on the literary attempts, in both memoirs and novels, to capture its singular quality."[11] Philip Beidler, a Vietnam veteran–turned–literary scholar, wrote in his early and influential

"You Had to Be There"

study *American Literature and the Experience of Vietnam* (1982) that "the experience of Vietnam, for those who underwent it, does seem in many ways to have been a thing genuinely peculiar unto itself, a self-contained world, a complete system."[12] Another literary scholar wrote in 1988 that for Americans, Vietnam "was qualitatively different from anything they had experienced in their history. . . . Vietnam was unique (and thus a unique literary response is called for) in a number of ways."[13] Scholars as recently as 2018 continue to refer to the Vietnam War as "an aberration of sorts, a long, unsatisfying conflict without the traditional narrative arc of crisis, struggle, redemption, and victory."[14]

The rhetorical characterization of the war as unique opened the door for criticism of conventional written history as less trustworthy than the veteran's personal experience, whether written as a straightforward memoir or thinly disguised as a novel; the difference between the two was often difficult to discern anyway. Michiko Kakutani, writing about the fictional response to Vietnam for the *New York Times Book Review* in 1984, argued that the traditional trope of the disillusioned returning soldier—born out of the literary memory of World War I—suffered "a dark revision" in the wake of Vietnam: "There are few opportunities for old-fashioned heroics—or any of the other conventional tests of manhood—in the cynical landscape of Vietnam. In Vietnam, simple physical and psychological survival is difficult enough." She continues, describing these novels as "urgent in tone, autobiographical in content," that "seem to have provided their authors with an emotional catharsis. . . . A flaw shared by many Vietnam novels, in fact, is that they do not become works of imagination; rather they retain the predictable shape and close-up, grainy texture of personal history."[15] For the vast majority of these novels, the attempt to replace the historical with the personal reduced their impact as works of art even as they contributed to a revision of the veteran's image in the American cultural imaginary.

The juxtaposition of real and imaginary, of fact and fiction, of truth and invention, had the effect of blurring the lines between the two and granting fiction a more authoritative form than, to some extent, historiography. The authors who wrote novels about Vietnam first and foremost wanted to capture the physical experience of the conflict, the transformation of the soldier who arrives as little more than a dressed up civilian on his first day and leaves a cold-blooded killer a year later. These are stories of initiation,

CHAPTER THREE

trials by fire and fury. For those who wrote about the war between 1965 and 1985—nearly all male combat veterans—the primary narrative focus of their works was the combat zone. Acclaimed novels like Tim O'Brien's *Going After Cacciato* (1978), Jim Webb's *Fields of Fire* (1978), Gustav Hasford's *The Short-Timers* (1979), John Del Vecchio's *The 13th Valley* (1982), and Stephen Wright's *Meditations in Green* (1983) all focused, in one way or another, on the experience of individual soldiers fighting, killing, and dying in the jungles of Vietnam. Even oral histories such as Baker's *Nam* emphasized how surreal the experience felt for many veterans. The argument that fiction was better suited to capture the truth of the war took hold precisely because of that surreality. One historian writing about the literary response to the war commented that "Fiction, it may be argued, is the literary mode which best expresses the history of the war in the minds of many soldiers who fought it and correspondents who reported it because they *experienced* it as fiction."[16] The uniqueness of the conflict in the minds of those who wrote about it thus gave way to a reversal of form whereby history became fiction and fiction became history. To fictionalize the experience of a combat tour in Vietnam was to preserve it in the amber of memory in a way that historiography never could.[17]

One aspect of the war that comes across as unique in its fictional response is the draft. As a theme, the draft makes its presence felt throughout many Vietnam War novels in a way that distinguishes it from the fiction written about the world wars, even though far more soldiers were conscripted for those conflicts than for Vietnam. Take Philip Dosier of Larry Heinemann's novel *Close Quarters*, or Paul Berlin in Tim O'Brien's *Going After Cacciato*, or James Chelini in John Del Vecchio's *The 13th Valley*. All three characters are drafted and sent to Vietnam, plucked from whatever lives they had been living and dropped into the middle of a hostile combat zone, forced to learn the ins and outs of tactical movements, patrol routes, standard operating procedures, and whatever other details they can absorb before they are either killed or learn enough to survive until the next firefight. "What in the world am I doing here?" Dosier wonders shortly after his first encounter with enemy fire:

> Why, oh why wasn't I born the Crown Prince or some Senator's brat, having myself a whipping boy. But I'm dumb. I'm just a fool. Always

"You Had to Be There"

wanting nothing more than to get along, just hoping to get by — a true son of the empire, trusting enough to buy that sorry myth of having to pay my dues — and so hauled off by the ears to sit on this cot and struggle around these woods, taking the cure. It was going to be a long year, too, or a short one.[18]

Del Vecchio's Chelini wonders the same thing:

What am I doing here, he thought. I'm just a kid, just a dumb kid. These are just kids, he said the words inside. The thought was a jumble of words and phrases, of pictures whirling and of names as ideograms. Kids from the suburbs, he thought. Rich kids. We're kids who've dreamed of far lands and exotic places, of the lands and wars of Hemingway and Mailer. Kids dreaming of seeing hobo jungles and shanties and of jumping a Steinbeck freight and of seeing America and the world.[19]

Both of these passages establish the characters as innocent of their circumstances before arriving in Vietnam. "But I'm dumb. I'm just a fool," Dosier says. "I'm just a kid, just a dumb kid," echoes Chelini. In each case, as well as in many other novels, the authors draft their characters into a place that they barely understand, a place that, when they compare it to the life they had before getting drafted, is unlike anything they had ever imagined.

Perhaps the most telling metaphor that testified to the view of the war as unique was the rhetorical division veterans made between Vietnam and "the World," often written with a capital W for even greater emphasis. In describing veterans' use of figurative language regarding everything from military operations to death, the enemy, and redeployment, Philip Beidler writes that those who were serving in Vietnam were forced to make their own "mental and metaphorical adjustments" as they set their watches on a 365-day countdown to return from a place "written off as too incomprehensible to exist."[20] Rather than reducing the idea of home to something more tangible, the Vietnam veteran enlarged a return home to something like returning to Earth itself. "People did not go home," Beidler writes, "they went 'back to the world.'"[21]

The rhetorical equivalence of home and "the World" is everywhere in

CHAPTER THREE

representations of Vietnam, from literature and film to, in Beidler's case, academic criticism. The language many veterans used to describe Vietnam —"unique," "surreal," "unfathomable"—created a deeper rhetorical division between those who were there and those who were not, separating the experience as something alien and otherworldly. Even a few examples from novels about the war capture the way that this particular metaphor burrowed into the minds of those who were there. The metafictional character "Tim O'Brien" in Tim O'Brien's *The Things They Carried* muses on his Vietnam experience two decades later: "Looking back after twenty years, I sometimes wonder if the events of that summer didn't happen in some other dimension, a place where your life exists before you've lived it, and where it goes afterward. None of it ever seemed real."[22] Sergeant Egan in Del Vecchio's *The 13th Valley* thinks, "It's all the Nam. . . . It don't fit onto the mind of the World so yer head shifts. It all makes sense." Or consider this exchange in Gustav Hasford's *The Short-Timers*:

> "It's crazy," Alice says. "It's just plain fucking crazy. I wish I was back in the World."
> I say, "No, back in the World is the crazy part. This, all this world of shit, this is real."[23]

In each of these novels, "the World" functions as a metaphor, a piece of language that takes the feelings of alienation and estrangement to the extreme. But Joe Haldeman, a physics major from Oklahoma who was drafted in 1967, makes the metaphor literal in his science fiction space opera *The Forever War* (1974). Though not strictly about Vietnam itself, *The Forever War* is a brilliant allegory about the war that leverages the science fiction genre to capture the complex feelings of returning home from war that goes beyond literary realism. Haldeman's protagonist, a thinly veiled autobiographical character drafted into Earth's unified military forces to fight against an alien race, returns to a planet that has aged hundreds of years while he has only aged two—the effects of time dilation and interstellar travel have, quite literally, transformed his home—the World—into something that he can no longer recognize.

The obsession with the "here" that was Vietnam, the need to understand that place with all its foreign contours, would drive so much of the early writing about the war, and the metaphorical confusion between the real and

"You Had to Be There"

the surreal is one of the great motifs of Vietnam War fiction. The importance of place, the location that divides Vietnam from "the World," set the conditions for the veteran's experience in the war as well as what it meant to come home. No wonder that the need to "come to literary terms with the experience of Vietnam," in Beidler's words, became one of the dominant themes of the war's fictional response.

The Vietnam veteran's claim to that war's uniqueness collapses under closer historical scrutiny, but it doesn't really matter—in the end, the rhetorical characterization of the war as unique found its way into American culture and stayed there.[24] For most people, believing that the war was unique allowed them to view it as an aberration, a stain to be washed away rather than evidence of a fundamental shift in American ideals. It would be another theme, though, that would come to define the Vietnam veteran's journey, building on the rejection of history, the rhetoric of uniqueness, and the incommunicability of the wartime experience. And it wouldn't stop there. In the years that followed, no other word would command more narrative authority within the cultural dynamic between veterans and American society: trauma.

The Cultural Authority of Trauma

In a 1984 article for Esquire magazine with the eyebrow-raising title "Why Men Love War," Vietnam veteran William Broyles Jr. wrote that the purpose of a war story "is not to enlighten but to exclude; its message is not its content but putting the listener in his place. I suffered, I was there. You were not. Only those facts matter. Everything else is beyond words to tell."[25]

Although this kind of attitude was not completely new—evident in the allusion to Walt Whitman's "Song of Myself" ("I am the man, I suffered, I was there.")—it nevertheless marked a rhetorical shift from veterans looking to "tell it like it was" to an ownership of narrative authority that actively excludes the nonveteran listener. This viewpoint appeared in the literary representations of the war almost immediately. There was little like it in the majority of novels written about World War I or II—by and large, communicating the experience of the war for those who weren't there was one of the major objectives of the fictional response to those conflicts. Previous generations of veterans may have argued that only those who have seen war

75

could effectively and authentically convey that experience through mediated representations, but there was still the implicit assumption that the truth of that experience *could* be conveyed. With Vietnam, the experience became something else entirely, something transcendental, sublime, and revelatory, a truth known only to those who were there, a truth beyond representation.

The political and social atmosphere following the war boosted veterans' claims to a greater degree of cultural authority than they had while the war was actively ongoing. In the wake of the war's conclusion and against the backdrop of the Watergate scandal, Americans' trust in government plummeted,[26] creating an opportunity for veterans to regain control of a narrative that had seen them "blamed by hawks for not winning and by doves for participating, [becoming] uncomfortable reminders of a conflict that caused unprecedented discord in this country."[27] During the late 1960s and into the early 1970s, veterans had been scapegoats, easier symbolic targets of scorn than the government that had sent them to war in the first place. But this changed as revelations of corruption took down Nixon and stained other public institutions as well. Vietnam veterans proved to be a useful foil to the impersonal bureaucracy of large institutions with shaky reputations, speaking with battle-earned conviction about the horrors they had seen—and committed—on behalf of their nation. They exposed the "moral hypocrisy of power," as Philip Melling puts it in *Vietnam in American Literature* (1990), speaking from "worm's-eye level" about the war as an antidote to the official government narratives that were becoming less and less trustworthy. "Just as the American public had been deceived at home, so the American veteran had been deceived by scandal on foreign soil. As a man who had witnessed the hypocrisy of power at first hand—and had suffered for it—the veteran was admirably placed to proclaim, in public, his knowledge of events and perception of the truth. Self-testimony was a duty."[28]

As Vietnam receded into American memory and the country sought to move on from years of protest and frustration, veteran-authors were more than willing to fill in the cultural gaps with their own narratives of personal experience. Indeed, there was a concerted effort in the 1980s toward the rehabilitation of the Vietnam veteran's image in American culture, an effort that coincided with the Reagan administration's defense-heavy, patriotic political rhetoric.[29] Paradoxically, the Vietnam veteran became a symbol of cultural unity going forward rather than a reminder of the bitter divisions

"You Had to Be There"

the war had engendered within American society. Thus, the decline of Americans' trust in the government in the mid-1970s was accompanied by an increased trust in Vietnam veterans. That increased trust in the veteran as a personal witness to government corruption afforded veteran-authors an enhanced authority over the narrative of the war, an authority that many of these veterans leveraged to fight back against the scapegoat image that had characterized them throughout the early 1970s.

It was the emphasis on personal suffering that became the source of the Vietnam veteran's newfound cultural authority, and the rhetorical shift from scapegoat to victim was the single most important development regarding the veteran's place in American society. Melling locates the origins of this shift in attitudes toward veterans alongside the emergence of a new conservative evangelical movement that believed the United States of the 1970s was in a "state of moral collapse." The role of the moral witness and personal testimony became a powerful source of authority in these circles, and the reframing of the Vietnam veteran's experience as a conversion narrative fit neatly into the movement. "To be struck down in conflict or singled out by God gave both the veteran and the evangelical the feeling that they were distinctive and had been marked out for a higher calling," Melling writes. "No longer the moral outcast of America the veteran could now become its moral tutor and, in some respects, its moral scourge; he could act the part of the visible saint who has had a conversion and undergone a sea change in the journey to Vietnam."[30] The veteran who had served and suffered in Vietnam returned home as though "born again"—he had witnessed the darkest chambers of humanity's capability and was now compelled to educate his fellow citizens about what he saw there.

A crucial element of this authority was a conformity to the proper antiwar narrative. The veteran-author's credibility came not only from personal experience overseas, but also from a more general stance against American involvement in Vietnam.[31] Recasting the Vietnam veteran's experience in terms of personal trauma fit into the proper antiwar, antigovernment attitudes of the mid-to-late 1970s, allowing veterans to regain control and authority over their own representation in the cultural imaginary. Historian Gregory Daddis writes that "both draftees who had served their yearlong tours in Vietnam and professionals remaining in uniform after war's end desperately needed an alternative, more positive, depiction of the returning warrior."[32] Thematic assessments of the first twenty years of Vietnam war fiction tend to come to similar conclusions. John Baky, who was the curator of LaSalle University's unrivaled collection of American imaginative representations of Vietnam, was perhaps best positioned to offer succinct appraisals of the first phase of Vietnam war novels through 1975 as characterized by a "propensity for vitriolic rage directed at the sources of political expedience that appear to keep good and decent citizen soldiers mired hopelessly in the tragically unwinnable combat of a foreign civil war," while the second phase through 1988 "continues the earlier trend of writing that employed thinly disguised autobiography as the narrative structure for the novel."[33] Ironically, narratives of trauma would prove to be the perfect solution, providing a kind of shield against criticism of the individual veteran's experience.

William Broyles's contention that war stories are only meant to put listeners in their place has roots in the evolution of war and memory culture over the last five hundred years. Historian Yuval Noah Harari has shown how the soldier's life and the experience of war carried little authority until the mid-eighteenth century and early nineteenth century.[34] Cultural changes brought about by the Enlightenment, the culture of sensibility, and Romanticism led to the idea of war as a "revelatory experience," and, as Harari observes, "Romanticism highlighted 'sublime' experiences as privileged sources for knowledge and authority, and war experience fitted perfectly to the Romantic definition of the sublime."[35] As war became linked to nationalism and patriotic glory rather than individual honor, nobility, or profiteering, the image of the common soldier improved within society and the experience of war became a newfound source of cultural authority.

Harari coins the term "flesh-witness" to describe this authority, emphasizing the physical component of its origins. As with the ideology of combat gnosticism discussed in chapter 1, the logic of flesh-witnessing can be summed up with the banner that "those who weren't there cannot understand," though flesh-witnessing goes beyond war experience as a kind of "secret knowledge" by linking personal experience with transcendental revelation.[36] Harari identifies this as "a potent new source of authority" that

"You Had to Be There"

began with Romantic conceptions of the sublime. The distinction between flesh-witness and eyewitness authority treads a careful line between experience and knowledge. Whereas eyewitnessing and testimony are confined to the realm of objective facts, flesh-witnessing is more closely related to feelings and bodily experience. This distinction imposes limitations on eyewitness authority, which Harari points out is "transmittable, and hence it is squandered by usage." This is the crucial point:

> Once a soldier tells the facts he knows, his audience knows them too. If the soldier wants to maintain a privileged authority to speak of war, he can base it only on other facts which he has yet to tell. Ultimately, the transmittable nature of factual knowledge leads to eyewitnesses losing their authority to experts such as historians. Whenever an expert takes the trouble to acquire the limited factual knowledge of several different eyewitnesses, he or she is bound to know more facts more confidently than any single eyewitness.[37]

In contrast to eyewitness accounts, which are limited to the recall and presentation of facts, Harari argues that flesh-witness narratives "convey authority" by emphasizing the division between the initiated and the ignorant; "the more flesh-witness accounts civilians hear, the less authority they have."[38] This inverse relationship between consuming the stories of war and one's understanding of it without having been there goes a long way to explain the sheer volume of literature written about Vietnam in the late 1970s through the 1980s.[39] It was a literary counterattack against the negative image of the Vietnam veteran in American society, intended not to educate its citizenry about the realities of the war but to grind into their minds their inability to understand — in other words, to put the listener in their place.[40]

The revelatory nature of war experience was initially seen as access to a special kind of knowledge, but that knowledge was not always related to trauma. In the years following the fall of Saigon, though, the authority of flesh-witnessing combined with the rhetoric of trauma to become a powerful source of cultural authority for Vietnam veterans. Trauma, in fact, came to be seen as the revelatory experience of war. This was especially true in the United States, where the vast majority of the population had no physical connection to foreign battlefields. Vietnam veterans thus recast their

CHAPTER THREE

experience as a form of traumatization, allowing them to regain a kind of moral authority as victims of the war rather than scapegoats for the war's conduct and failure.[41] This rhetorical shift granted them a source of authority to interpret the war that was practically incontestable—individual trauma cannot be questioned empirically while the owner of the experience controls its contours and chooses what information to reveal.[42]

Revisions to the Vietnam veteran's image through the merging of flesh-witnessing and trauma rhetoric culminated in what Roy Scranton has dubbed the "trauma hero," a trope so compelling and successful that it has been an American cultural stereotype ever since. "The trauma hero's revelation," Scranton writes, "is predicated on the idea that the subjective feeling of having undergone an experience offers a more robust claim to truth and a greater moral authority than do history, eyewitnessing, or other kinds of accounts that rely on observable evidence or reasoned argument."[43] With this formulation, the story of war became the story of trauma, and veterans became the bearers of that experiential burden on behalf of American society. They were to be pitied for what they went through, not scorned for what they did. It is no wonder that the overarching theme of so many works about Vietnam is how the individual American soldier, lied to and forsaken by his government, became traumatized by the very acts of violence he committed on behalf of his country.[44]

The negative image of the Vietnam veteran in American society immediately following the war quickly gave way to a more general distrust of government, a distrust exacerbated by the Watergate scandal and Richard Nixon's resignation as president in 1974. By the end of the 1970s and into the early 1980s, the perspective of the ground-level soldier—enhanced by the cultural authority of the trauma hero—started to seem more trustworthy. The veterans who wrote novels about Vietnam used their authority as flesh-witnesses to challenge the negative perception of the military in American society. Their novels overwhelmingly focus on the experience of war and Vietnam's combat zone, depicting soldiers as both agents and victims of their country while drawing sympathy for the plight of the common soldiers placed—often against their will—in a harrowing situation. The implicit valorization of the soldier's experience as the primary source of narrative authority gave the generation of Vietnam veterans the tools to control their own destiny in the war's collective memory.

"You Had to Be There"

There is something oddly compelling about trauma that is almost irresistible as a character trait.[45] War trauma in particular grants a certain aura to characters whose past is a magnetized mystery of unspoken experience. As such, the connection to the transcendental or the sublime endows war trauma with a kind of charismatic authority. The Israeli philosopher Avishai Margalit refers to this combination as a "moral witness" whose charisma "comes from having a special kind of experience which is elevated to some sort of high spirituality that makes the witness a moral force," an experience that differs from "calm, methodical observation" because of its revelatory nature.[46] Larry Heinemann seemed to recognize this in *Close Quarters* when he wrote about how Philip Dosier, upon coming home, would "buy a pair of dark glasses, the darkest lenses I could find, and save myself the trouble of people leaning close to me, whispering, 'Dosier. You know, you've got the oddest, strangest look in your eyes. Why is that, hey? What have you seen?'"[47]

It doesn't take much of a logical leap to see how the entire rhetoric of the Vietnam veteran's experience could lead to this point. Characterizing the war as a unique event in American history, dividing the jungles of Vietnam from the metaphorical "World" that represented American society, embracing the language of combat gnosticism and flesh-witnessing authority, and wrapping the experience of war within the veil of trauma all contributed to a new way of thinking about war fiction that consolidated the veteran-author's already privileged position within the literary field. What had begun after World War I with literary critics' aesthetic judgment that linked personal experience with narrative authenticity had ended with an authority to interpret war and conflict that superseded all other sources of truth and knowledge, from official government narratives to historical analyses. Armed with the authority of the flesh-witness and the rhetoric of trauma, veteran-authors spoke of war as a revelatory experience that cannot be communicated to those who were not there. That literary institutions implicitly endorsed this philosophy in creative writing programs only enhanced the veteran-author's status and identity within the field of production. Telling nonveterans that they had to be there or they wouldn't understand ensured that the experiential burden would remain theirs alone.

CHAPTER FOUR

"You Don't Have to Be a Veteran"

The All-Volunteer Force and the Dispersion of Authority

The evolution of the veteran-author's cultural authority during the first two-thirds of the twentieth century is the story of how one group of citizens began with no special knowledge or understanding of war to emerge as a class of writers who came to possess a dominance over the literary representation of war and conflict in American memory culture. Between the early 1920s and the end of the war in Vietnam, the American war fiction genre was built on the philosophy that personal experience, narrative authenticity, and literary authority were inexorably linked, making the genre the providence of veteran-authors and excluding most other voices until the immediacy of personal experience as a source of authority and authenticity faded into history.

Then something happened. In a policy change that would not immediately suggest an effect within the literary field, the United States abolished conscription in 1973 and transitioned to a professional, all-volunteer military. The days of compulsory military service were gone, and this decision would have consequences beyond the social relationship between the military and society, a relationship that in the nearly fifty years since has been characterized by a widening gap.

If only those who have experienced war can understand it, then, in an all-volunteer military, only those who choose to serve are condemned to bear the burden of that experience while the rest of the country carries on. This would be the logical conclusion of the combat gnosticism and flesh-witnessing ideologies that had characterized the genre of American war fiction since the 1920s. Extrapolating from this nearly century-long trend, one might expect that members of a professional military, asked to deploy on back-to-back rotations to the seemingly endless conflicts in Iraq and Afghanistan, would seek to own that experience and consolidate their authority over the literary representation of war in a way similar to what their predecessors did after Vietnam. And one might also expect that a population disconnected from these conflicts would gladly concede them that authority. After all, the shift to an all-volunteer force had only strengthened the veteran's interpretive sovereignty by walling off the rest of the population from the experience of war. The drifting of the civilian-military relationship and the social distance between those who fight and those who stay home would not, on the surface, suggest any structural changes to the genre's conventions.

As the civil-military gap unburdened most Americans from the consequences of foreign wars, though, a related shift took place within the literary field. Since the wars in Iraq and Afghanistan began, the veteran-author's near-monopoly on the literary representation of conflict has diminished significantly — as of 2020, veteran-authors account for less than half (twenty-three of fifty-nine) of the total number of authors who have published novels about the wars, a proportion unseen since before the early 1920s. The transition to an all-volunteer force has changed the war fiction genre in ways that, until now, have not been fully recognized or appreciated.

This chapter explores how the veteran-author's cultural authority over the literary representation of war has changed as a response to the social conditions created by American war culture after the end of conscription, leading to what I call a "dispersion" of contemporary war fiction authorship. This dispersion comes from two sources, both originating from the social distance between the military and American society that has emerged after the transition to an all-volunteer force. The first is the acceleration of the process in memory culture whereby current events become subsumed by the historical, transitioning from "happening" to "history" and shifting the source of narrative authenticity, as perceived within the field of reception, from extratextual to intratextual. Contemporary authors without the authority of personal experience in war are nonetheless writing what can be considered "historical" novels about them at a time that, viewed within the context of American literary history, is far earlier than would be expected.

Second, the social distance between the military and society has incentivized today's veteran-authors to reject the philosophy that only those who have experienced war can hope to understand it. Many veterans have actively

"You Don't Have to Be a Veteran"

written against that idea, because accepting it means that only those who volunteer are saddled with the burden of understanding. This has led to a pattern of veteran-authors ceding their authority by deemphasizing the need for personal experience as a source of narrative authenticity; it is a way for them to share the experiential burden of their memory with the rest of society.

From Happening to History:
War Fiction and American Memory Culture

When does happening end and history begin? Theories of historical fiction have yet to come to a consensus on this question, in part because the proximity to lived experience is a difficult concept to quantify.[1] But quibbling over the definition of historical fiction obscures the process by which the current event becomes history. Events may linger in collective memory long after the immediate ripples cease to affect culture and society. There is no magic number or formula to calculate how long ago in the past a novel must be set in order to qualify as historical fiction, though there is a logical point after which it becomes absurd to consider a writer's personal experience as an important component of a novel's authorship. In the beginning, experience, authority, and authenticity are linked, but they slowly decouple over time. As time passes and the event is no longer "contemporary," the event becomes open to interpretation and revision from newer sources without a direct connection to the experience, and the cultural authority of their literary representation becomes more pluralized.

As a subset of historical fiction, war novels fall along the blurry boundary between historiography and invention, often playing to the strengths of both to achieve a desired effect, what Tatiana Prorokova dubs "docu-fictions."[2] Authors seeking to represent the horrors of combat may simply dress their personal experiences in a thin cloak of invention and call it fiction. Others ignore history altogether in favor of making a larger point about the nature of war and humanity. In both cases, the amount of time that has elapsed between the events represented in the novel and when they actually occurred in history has an important effect on that literary work's critical reception. With the publication and reception of John Dos Passos's *Three Soldiers* in the early 1920s, personal experience became the dominant source of authenticity for twentieth-century American war fiction, and authenticity became the primary aesthetic criteria against which new war novels were judged.

There is a clear distinction between an immediate fictional response to an event and a novel written much later, though, especially for war novels. Early works leverage the immediacy of the events in order to convey a sense of experience, to depict what it was like to live through them. For the American wars of the twentieth century, there was a definitive end date after which direct experience of the war was no longer possible.[3] A timer begins, with each accumulated moment burying that experience under a heap of new days that weigh down its memory, potentially rendering it obscured or, in some cases, forgotten altogether. It is during these early times when veteran-authors since the 1920s have churned out war novels to preserve the experience of the war as a kind of literary fossil. Leveraging the authority of their experience, these veterans brought with them an instantly recognizable signal of authenticity that publishers could market to home front audiences.[4]

That novels of witnessing and experience are so salient during the initial years following a conflict should come as no surprise, especially in the American context where geographic distance from the battlefield has spared nearly all citizens from the war experience itself. The resulting hunger for stories that close the experiential gap is merely a reflection of how the lived experience of war remains at a distance, unlike for the civilian populations of nearly all other belligerents during the conflicts of the twentieth century. Memory culture incorporates veterans' novels into the historical record as individual stories that may or may not cohere into a distinct whole, often serving as a challenge to other mainstream narratives. After World War I, it was disillusionment over romanticism. After World War II, it was human tragedy over victory glow. After Vietnam, it was victimhood over scapegoating and blame.

As we have seen in the previous chapter, the overwhelming focus on "capturing the hell of the combat experience" that characterized the first twenty years of fiction about Vietnam, from 1965 through 1985, emphasized personal experience as its own kind of historical truth.[5] During the Asia Society's 1985 conference on the literature of the Vietnam War, William Pelfrey, a Vietnam War veteran–turned–novelist, restated the familiar line that "No one who has never been in combat can really understand the experience."

"You Don't Have to Be a Veteran"

Another combat veteran and fellow participant challenged Pelfrey's view, asking, "If that's true, why do you as writers about the combat experience bother to write about it? Who are you talking to? You're not telling me about combat. So if it cannot be explained to people who weren't there, who are you writing for, and why do you do it?" Timothy Lomperis summarizes Pelfrey's response:

> Bill Pelfrey admitted that war novelists do not write for other combat veterans but really more for the historical record. Like the World War I literature, the Vietnam War literature provides the veteran his distinctive perspective in the larger context of his generation. The literature gives a record of the veteran's emotions, a record, Bill feels, that can come only through fiction.[6]

In other words, one of the war novel's primary functions as a medium of collective memory is to capture and collect combatants' experiences for posterity. This implies that these authors want the best of both worlds for their novels, leveraging the emotional power of fiction while maintaining a semblance of historicity on par with, say, documentary. For the immediate fictional response to a war, this is effective. With time, though, the authority of experience fades, and memory cultures seek new ways to examine war and conflict through the lens of fiction.

As the temporal distance between the event and the fictional response increases, there is a shift in literary mode from novels of witness and testimony to novels infused with a greater historical consciousness. The former are rooted heavily in experience—either as the source of their authority or the goal of their representation—while the latter embed other stories within a historical landscape designed to question and challenge that consciousness. Memory culture scholar Astrid Erll refers to these works as "collective texts" that function as "vehicles for envisioning the past" and "create, circulate, and shape contents of cultural memory." Such texts "have to be able to resonate with a memory culture's horizons of meaning, its (narrative) schemata, and its existing images of the past. These are the grounds on which 'mnemonic authenticity' is generated."[7] The emphasis on memory and "mnemonic authenticity" thus implies a rhetorical shift away from witnessing and toward something greater. War novels function as media of collective memory—Erll uses the term "memory-making novels"

CHAPTER FOUR

(Gedächtnisromane)[8] — and when these novels move from the experiential mode to the broader realm of historical fiction their focus as an art form also shifts from a mere reflection of reality to an interrogation and interpretation of memory. Dalton Trumbo's 1938 novel *Johnny Got His Gun*, for example, reduced the suffering of the generation who lived through the First World War to a blind, limbless mute whose only wish is to die, while Thomas Pynchon's *Gravity's Rainbow* (1973) embedded the technological progress enabled by the Second World War within the Cold War discourse of perpetual terror and paranoia.

Much of this shift in literary mode comes down to how sources of narrative authenticity change over time. For an event that occurred outside living memory (that is, no one living was alive at the time of the event), it becomes irrelevant — aesthetically and otherwise — if an author has no personal experience with the subject of a historical novel. Readers and critics do not judge historical novels against standards of authenticity that privilege first-hand experience but rather against other markers of authenticity conveyed within the text itself. The farther one is in time from the historical events depicted in a novel, the more the ascription of authenticity is based on *intratextual* factors as they correspond with known historiography. In most cases, such factors include accuracy of historical detail, proper language use, avoidance of anachronisms, and so on.[9]

The converse of this is *extratextual* sources of authenticity. The closer one is to the historical events depicted in a novel, the more the novel's reception is framed in terms of the author's personal experience. It is only as the temporal distance between the event and the fiction based on that event increases that the markers of authenticity are more closely aligned with what is in the text itself. During the "happening" phase, writers without personal experience in a subject who wish to confront that subject in fiction may attempt to acquire authenticity based on research, interviews, site visits, and so on. This is precisely what Willa Cather did in her process writing *One of Ours*. Cather traveled to France to get a feel for the battlefields that claimed her cousin's life; today, a writer looking for research material can scroll through videos on YouTube or watch a Netflix documentary.

While these are admittedly different experiences and approaches to a writer's process, both involve the translation of extratextual elements into fictional prose. Cather's trips to France, for example, might have given her

"You Don't Have to Be a Veteran"

atmospheric insights into what a soldier would have seen and felt as he stood in a trench awaiting the signal to attack. Her authorial imagination would then convert her own physical observations of the terrain into a projection of her character's mental state. The intent is to enhance the realism of the writing by basing it on a real place and using her personal experience of that place as the foundation for her imaginative interpretation of past events. The same would be true of a writer today looking for similar imaginative insights through combat footage posted on the internet or other audiovisual sources. Contemporary writers have at their fingertips a seemingly endless stream of materials from which they can draw their descriptions. "In some ways," Ben Fountain writes, "the war has never been more accessible to those of us at home."[10] Or, as the narrator in Phil Klay's short story "Unless It's a Sucking Wound" puts it, "With the Internet you can do nothing but watch war all day if you want."[11] When it comes to extratextual research materials for fiction writing, this is certainly true; access to information and media has thinned the gap between firsthand experience and authorial imagination, even if the specific types of media have evolved.

The interaction of authority and authenticity during the formation of a conflict's collective memory changes over time. While the reimagination and revision of historical events through literary fiction is a well-known aspect of memory culture, it is the transition from current event to history that, for war fiction, begs for a deeper investigation. This ill-defined transition characterizes the interpretation of authenticity at different times, at first linking authenticity to the realm of facts and reality (and dominated by experiential authority) before broadening it to something less dependent on experience. As events recede in historical memory, the authority of experience declines, opening the events to reinterpretation, revision, and reimagining with the benefit of hindsight.

Even the very idea of authenticity itself depends on the historical moment in which a text is produced and received. Astrid Erll's concept of collective texts and their relationship to collective memory looks at how well a text's vision of an event fits within the existing meaning of the event as constructed by the development of its memory. "What is at stake when reading literature as collective texts," she writes, "is thus 'truth' according to memory."[12] This is not some objective historiographic truth, if such a thing exists, but rather a narrative's authenticity measured against the landscape of its memory. Underpinning this notion, however, is still the idea that authenticity comes from facts. Historian Hayden White approaches this question from a different angle, though. In writing about Toni Morrison and her process of using a historical figure as the starting point for her novel *Beloved* (1987), White describes his view of how history and fiction can interact and how imagination and invention can complement something like a historical record by providing "a subtext that was true in its *historical essence* but not strictly factual."[13] White is clearly moving beyond mere historiography in his conception of historical essence, taking things a step further by asking when the question "Is it true?" matters. Here, White distinguishes between "any account of the past presenting itself as a *historical* account thereof," in which questions of truth are relevant, and "discourses making reference to the real world (past or present) cast in a mode other than that of simple declaration" in which questions of truth are "of secondary importance." He highlights "artistic (verbal, aural, or visual) representations of reality (past or present)" as a prime example of these.[14]

The distinction between history and "historical essence," as White puts it, has implications for literary representations of war in which questions of authenticity and accuracy are often central to their criticism. If war novels are intended to preserve the experience of war—as witnessed by its combatants—for the historical record, then judging them against an absolute standard of authenticity and "truth" makes no sense; each individual experience possesses its own inherent authenticity and historical essence that may or may not match anyone else's. As an aesthetic value, the ascribed authenticity that comes with the authority of personal experience ignores the *fictional* element of literary representation, acting as a mere projection of an author's autobiographical details onto an otherwise historiographic plot line.

White's concern is what it means to "tell the truth about the past," and he refers to historical novels as "nondeclarative discourses" in which the accuracy of facts is less important than the emotions they convey: "Their truth may consist less in what they *assert* in the mode of factual truth telling than in what they *connote* in the other moods and voices identified in the study of grammar."[15] In formulating the narrative discourse this way, White suggests

"You Don't Have to Be a Veteran"

that the question answered by a literary representation of a historical event is not "Did it happen this way?" but rather "How did it feel to be part of it?"[16]

I n literary history there is a point when novels about war become less about capturing the experience of conflict and begin to use war as a historical setting. Dalton Trumbo was nine years old when World War I began, yet his novel *Johnny Got His Gun*, published in 1938, won the National Book Award and became a major piece of antiwar literature. Historical fiction about World War II has become almost a genre unto itself, with everything from middlebrow bestsellers (e.g., Kristin Hannah's *The Nightingale*) and prize-winning literary novels (e.g., Anthony Doerr's *All the Light We Cannot See*) to historical romances and action thrillers.

The temporal limits of experiential authority over an event's collective memory can be seen in the literary response to World War II. The veterans who returned home from battlefields in Europe and the Pacific did not, for the most part, buy in to the victory culture that took hold of the country after 1945. Most soldiers during the war did not know or care why they were fighting; they merely knew that they had to, and that winning the war—at great cost to human life—was the ticket home.[17] This was especially true of the soldiers in Europe, many of whom thought Hitler was bad but did not actually see him as an existential threat to the United States. The veteran-authored novels after the war sought to inject a dose of horrific reality into a population blinded by victory. In these novels, "the soldiers fight for no cause except to get home in one piece," as one literary historian wrote.[18] As the full extent of the Holocaust came to light throughout the following decades, though, the original motivation for fighting the war was revised as a fight for democracy and human rights. World War II became "the good war" in American memory culture because the moral links between fighting, dying, and justice were, in retrospect, crystal clear.[19]

Some veterans never came around to this view, struggling against the forces of memory culture that had grown to accept a certain version of the past as the correct one. "Throughout the twentieth century," Astrid Erll writes, "the task of remembering wars has proved a difficult issue in cultures of memory. Tensions arise usually within three or four decades after the end of a war, when its witnesses are still alive and claim—with all the authority

91

of the eye-witness — that their version of the past is the only proper one."[20] This tension applies even to those witnesses who had become canonical in their own right. Paul Fussell had served as an infantryman in Europe during the war, and his bitter views about it stayed with him his entire life. In 1989 he published *Wartime: Understanding and Behavior in the Second World War*, part memoir and part cultural study. Fussell's cultural authority when it came to war literature and culture was nearly unmatched in the years following the publication of *The Great War and Modern Memory* in 1975, but even he could not compete against the forces of collective memory that, in the more than forty years since V-J Day, had convinced Americans of the war's ultimate meaning and purpose. "Stupid and sadistic" were Fussell's words for it, saying that "some events, being inhuman, have no human meaning."[21] The book's critical reception was overwhelmingly negative; the memory of the war as a heroic struggle for democracy and human rights outweighed the authority of a single, albeit once influential, angry veteran.[22]

That doesn't mean that the authority of experience goes away completely, though. Vietnam War veteran Karl Marlantes published his novel *Matterhorn* in 2009, forty years after his combat tour, yet he still benefitted from experiential authority during the novel's critical reception.[23] But by that time the war had already opened up to other voices, and *Matterhorn* was surrounded by novels written by people who hadn't even been born when Marlantes was patrolling the jungles and valleys of Vietnam.

In fact, the Vietnam War provides a good example for the pluralization of authorship that comes with the transition to historical fiction. The fall of Saigon occurred nearly fifty years ago, but since the beginning of the Iraq War in 2003 contemporary novelists have returned to Vietnam with the benefit of historical hindsight, bringing with them the influences of their own time period and publishing a wave of new novels about the war. There have been at least a dozen, including several major prize winners, such as Denis Johnson's *Tree of Smoke* (2007) and Viet Thanh Nguyen's *The Sympathizer* (2016). There has also been a trend of women writing historical novels about Vietnam, a change in literary production that mirrors the increased role of women in the military. These novels include *Cementville* by Paulette Livers (2014) and *The Great Alone* by Kristin Hannah (2018), both of which follow in the footsteps of Bobbie Ann Mason's *In Country* (1985) by focusing on the home front either during or immediately after the war. And Tatjana Soli's *The*

Lotus Eaters (2010) reinterprets the course of the Vietnam War through the eyes of Helen Adams, a photojournalist from California who is drawn into the war's early days and spends ten years covering it through pictures. Helen acts as a reimagination of the original Homeric war stories—her name recalls Helen of Troy in *The Iliad* (some of her male colleagues in country even snidely refer to her as "Helen of Saigon"), and the ten years she spends in Vietnam parallel Odysseus's journey home in *The Odyssey*.

The publication of these novels, as well as the countless examples of historical novels about World War II or, for that matter, the Civil War, is empirical evidence that the authority of personal experience as a marker of narrative authenticity has a shelf life. The standards of what is valued as authentic war fiction shift based on the changing conditions within memory culture that link experiential authority with authenticity until that authority becomes overwhelmed by other sources. In 1985, the acclaimed author and Vietnam veteran Tim O'Brien spoke about the limits of facts and the importance of storytelling as a medium of memory: "I think that two hundred years, seven hundred years, a thousand years from now, when Vietnam is filled with condominiums and we're all going there to vacation on the beautiful beaches, the experience of Vietnam—all the facts—will be gone. Who knows, a thousand years from now the facts will disappear—bit by bit by bit—and all that we'll be left with are stories. To me, it doesn't really matter if they're true stories."[24] In 2009, Karl Marlantes can still publish his own experience-based novel about Vietnam, but he does so as the exception, no longer the rule. Today, Vietnam—like all of America's twentieth-century wars—is no longer happening; it's history.

Authority, Authenticity, and the Field of Production

The shift from extratextual to intratextual sources of authenticity does not happen in a vacuum. Book publishers, with an eye on market demands and commercial viability, are the ultimate gatekeepers of authorship whose own standards of authority and authenticity are what drive literary production. A writer hoping to enter the literary field and publish a novel has several steps to traverse before that novel goes out into the world, transitioning from the field of creation to the fields of production (e.g., agents and editors) and reception (e.g., critics and readers).

CHAPTER FOUR

Authenticity and authority play important roles during these field transitions from creation to production and production to reception, perhaps even more so for war fiction than for other genres less characterized by authenticity as an aesthetic value. Between the fields of creation and production are literary agents who present the first hurdle to publication. A previously unpublished writer who has written a novel must first gain representation from a literary agent, who then acts on behalf of the writer to sell the novel to a publisher.[25] Even catching the eye of a literary agent is often a herculean task; a 2012 article references one literary agency that receives around one hundred thousand queries per year and signs less than one new author for every ten thousand.[26]

Some of the evaluative criteria that agents use when deciding on which manuscripts to represent and which to reject are emotional connection with the work, judgment of the writer's artistic ability, and estimation of the work's market potential.[27] These are baseline criteria for any work of fiction hoping to get published. In my view, authenticity is a crucial metric that, for war fiction, underpins all three of these criteria, even if an understanding of what "authenticity" is can only be observed indirectly. An agent reading an unsolicited manuscript is unlikely to forge an emotional connection with a work that they do not see as authentic. The same applies to editors and book marketers at publishing houses who need to translate the logic of the novel into signals for readers (the field of reception). A war novel written by a veteran lends itself easily to this translation, as someone with the relevant experience is easier to market as authentic than someone with just a good story.

Authors without direct experience in war thus come to the table at an inherent disadvantage, at least from the logical position of actors such as agents and editors in the field of production. A veteran-author comes with a built-in set of marketing materials, desired or not, earned or unearned relative to the content of the story itself. A nonveteran author does not. Clayton Childress writes about the "name economy" and how successful authors (and publishers) are eventually able to signal readers simply by having their name on the cover of a book.[28] For war fiction, there is also what I call a "status economy" that operates within the logic of the genre — identifying a war novel as written by a veteran is a signal from the field of production to the field of reception that the reader can expect some murky notion of "authenticity" derived from the author's personal experiences. War novels

94

"You Don't Have to Be a Veteran"

written by nonveterans do not benefit from this status signal, so the field of production must find different ways to signal the field of reception that the work should be considered authentic.

These signals typically come from what Childress calls "secondary texts" or "writings *about* the thing rather than the thing itself."[29] Secondary texts help "translate novels into the logic of their new fields"—that is from an object of artistic creation to a commodity that must be marketed and sold to buyers—and "tend to recede from prominence once texts are safely embedded within fields."[30] Examples of secondary texts include book reviews, jacket synopses, and an agent's cover letter to an editor, but we can extend this to include blurbs from other authors as well as interviews and op-eds written by authors that directly or indirectly mention their works.[31] For veteran-authors of war novels, secondary texts may reinforce their status as veterans and emphasize the authority of their experience. For nonveteran authors, publishers may seek out blurbs from well-known authors of war novels in the hopes that their cultural authority will send a reliable signal to an uncommitted reader that the text is authentic. This may explain why, at least for many contemporary war novels written by nonveterans, the book release is accompanied by a well-placed interview or op-ed designed to attest to the author's "authority" to write about war.[32] The same logic applies to book reviews that perform a similar function, particularly if they compare the novel directly to another well-known work of war fiction.

Helen Benedict's 2011 novel *Sand Queen* is a good example of how a publisher may seek to strengthen the authority of an author without firsthand war experience. *Sand Queen* was one of the first novels published about the Iraq War, and Benedict was a journalism professor with no military background, though she had published a work of nonfiction about the war in 2009. One of the promotional blurbs for the novel came from Robert Olen Butler, a Vietnam War veteran and Pulitzer Prize–winning author of multiple works about the war: "Every war eventually yields works of art which transcend politics and history and illuminate our shared humanity. Helen Benedict's brilliant new novel has done just that with this century's American war in Iraq. *Sand Queen* is an important book by one our finest literary artists." Such a blurb has the effect of projecting some of Butler's authority onto Benedict, providing the potential reader with a positive signal through literary association. Similarly, the *Boston Globe*'s review of the novel called it

"*The Things They Carried* for women in Iraq," forging a link between Benedict and veteran Tim O'Brien, the most celebrated fiction writer to come out of the Vietnam War.[33]

In the end, agents and editors wield significant authority over which novels get published and which do not. For all we know, nonveterans have always been writing war novels at an even pace with veterans but publishing gatekeepers did not believe there was a market for them. The ability for authors today to bypass the traditional path through the field of production and self-publish their novels may provide some evidence for this, though as of 2020 most of the self-published works I have found about the wars in Iraq and Afghanistan have been written by veterans. This observation about the publishing industry's openness to nonveteran-authored war novels reveals an indirect approach to understanding the dynamics of authority within the field of production. Personal experience, while still one marker of narrative authenticity, is no longer its primary source.

The All-Volunteer Force and the Acceleration of History

For America's twentieth-century wars and their literary history, it was the norm for decades to elapse between the end of the war and the regular appearance of historical novels. For the conflicts in Iraq and Afghanistan, though, there has been no delay whatsoever. The temporal distance between happening and history for the war novel has collapsed into a social distance between the military and society; the wars in Iraq and Afghanistan are as far from the typical American's frame of daily reference as the war in Vietnam or, for that matter, the world wars.

The first part of this is a matter of empirical observation. As of 2020, there have been sixty-seven single-authored novels and short story collections published about the wars in Iraq and Afghanistan.[34] Accounting for authors who have published more than one novel, there have been fifty-nine authors.[35] Of these authors, twenty-three are veterans of the wars, thirty-one are nonveterans, and five have seen the wars personally but as something other than uniform-wearing service members (figure 3).[36] This last category is important, as these authors can credibly claim the authority of personal experience, but not as soldiers. More than one-third (twenty of fifty-nine) of these authors are women. American war fiction authorship has not looked

"You Don't Have to Be a Veteran"

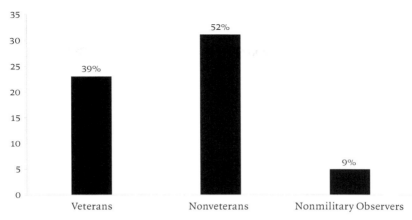

FIGURE 3. Contemporary war fiction authorship proportions according to the author's experiential background. "Veterans" include authors who served in the American military, "nonveterans" are those who did not, and "nonmilitary observers" are authors who spent time in Afghanistan or Iraq but not as a member of the armed forces (e.g., journalist, government civilian).

this way since before the publication of John Dos Passos's *Three Soldiers* in 1921, and the proportion of nonveteran and women authors upends the century-long trends of male, combat-veteran authorship within the genre.[37]

What these numbers represent is an acceleration of memory culture's previously slow process of converting a current event into a historical one and the dispersion of authority that came with it. Read together, these sixty-seven works represent a combination of the veteran-authored, experience-based novels — similar to the early fictional responses to previous wars — alongside an even greater number of novels written by nonveterans in search of some "historical essence," recalling Hayden White's words. While veteran-authors are still writing novels that engage with the wars in a personal way, the authority of experience and its equivalent narrative authenticity are no longer the genre's defining features. Armed with the tools of historical fiction, contemporary writers without personal experience in war are subjecting these wars to reimagination, reinterpretation, and interrogation of their meaning without waiting for any time to pass.

The catalyst for this acceleration has been the drifting relationship between the military and American society since the shift to an all-volunteer force, also known as the civil-military gap. Before the all-volunteer force, America's twentieth-century conflicts were shared cultural experiences. Although the domestic population was generally disconnected from the physical dangers of war, policies such as rationing, taxation, and other home front programs ensured a level of awareness, if not engagement, with the conflicts. Involuntary conscription also guaranteed that war would be a dinner table conversation topic for any American family with a man of military age. During Vietnam, for example, every household with a draft-age man was faced with a series of questions: What was his draft number? Should he volunteer for military service, potentially exercising some control of the type of assignment he would get, even as far as picking the military branch least likely to see combat (a side-effect known as "draft-motivated volunteers")? Should he gamble with his draft number, hoping that the tyranny of fate would miss him and land on someone less fortunate? Could he get a deferment? This was a practice that some found more successful than others, depending on factors such as marital status, education, financial wealth, and so on. Or, finally, out of options and devoid of hope, should he flee the country?

There was no way around this. During previous wars, in which a significant proportion of military personnel were conscripted into service from all over the country, there was a more even geographic distribution of experiential authority. The sheer percentage of people in uniform during the world wars and, later, Vietnam, combined with this geographic distribution of service, contributed to a broader dissemination of communicative memory and collective texts. Returning veterans upheld the oral tradition of the amateur storyteller, and whatever memories they shared became part of their family culture.

Since communicative memory is often conceived as the overlapping memories of three generations, family memory is of critical importance for understanding how historical events are communicated and interpreted within the small circle of close relationships.[38] But after nearly five decades of the all-volunteer force, direct family connections between service members and society have decreased, and families that do have military connections are more likely to perpetuate them, leading to what Amy Schafer calls a "warrior caste" within society, or a "trend in which a large proportion of those who do choose to serve come from military families."[39] The communicative memory of war that was once spread across the country is now mostly concentrated within the fraction of families whose sons and daughters have volunteered to serve. What's more, these families tend to be geographically isolated in small, rural areas near military bases, providing the average American citizen with far fewer opportunities to come into direct contact with war veterans.[40] Thus, the presence of the military in American society has declined—fewer people are directly in touch with the communicative memory of individual veterans, and the average American family has slowly become disconnected from even the idea of war.[41] If the war comes up during dinner conversation anymore, it is mostly at someone else's expense.

The end of conscription and the rise of the professional military has also led to an increased political appetite for using force as an instrument of foreign policy. With a professional force, the political price for supporting military interventions has declined because the overwhelming majority of Americans have no direct connection to those who would bear the burden of those use-of-force decisions. A Harvard Institute of Politics report in 2015 made this point crystal clear. When the research team surveyed younger Americans between the ages of eighteen and twenty-nine about the threat of the Islamic State in Iraq and Syria (ISIS), 60 percent supported sending ground troops to the region but only 13 percent said they would be willing to serve if more troops were needed.[42] This represents a "cognitive dissonance between military service and the use of force," in Amy Schafer's words.[43] David Kennedy, echoing the sentiment of many others in recent years, writes that the all-volunteer force "severed the link between citizenship and service. No American today is obligated to serve in the military."[44] The implicit threat of conscription that kept Americans glued to the nightly news broadcasts during Vietnam has today become an empty promise of ignorance.

While the civil-military gap has several dimensions, engagement is the one most critical to understanding the social distance between the military and society since the end of the draft.[45] In that sense, Americans' detachment from the military and war fits within a larger societal trend. Sebastian Junger writes that "the public is often accused of being disconnected from its military, but frankly it's disconnected from just about everything."[46] Robert Putnam made a similar case in his landmark study *Bowling Alone: The Collapse and Revival of American Community*, citing Americans' disengagement from civic participation since the 1960s.[47] Putnam's work focused on

American society more generally and predates the 2001 terrorist attacks that led to the wars in Afghanistan and Iraq, but others have advanced a similar thesis that examines disengagement specifically from the wars. Owen Gilman, for example, derides Americans' preference for "fantasyland" rather than confronting the costs and consequences of war, arguing that "instead of providing attention that would lead to depth of learning and understanding, citizens at home offer the most superficial of responses—a great vat of know-nothingness—and then turn quickly to something distracting, some facet of fantasyland, virtually anything that provides entertainment, distracts attention from reality, and demands no effort."[48] Author Ben Fountain refers to a "Fantasy Industrial Complex," observing that "our lives take place in the realm of fantasy, triviality, and materialism, and our senses and mental capacity become numbed as a result."[49]

The disengagement that Gilman and Fountain describe has the effect of removing the wars from Americans' sphere of political awareness and placing them into the same memory box as historical events. Where the draft during Vietnam made complete disengagement from what was happening all but impossible, this is not the case today. There is no draft. There are no war taxes. Indeed, the true costs of the war are obscured from public scrutiny, as more war fighting functions have been outsourced to private security contractors.[50] It has come to the point where the Pentagon's official count of deployed troops—when they provide the information at all—only captures a fraction of actual military activity on the ground and across the globe. Here's Ben Fountain again, in 2018: "Americans like the idea of breaking heads and drawing blood, but the burden of actual war? Not so much. And so the politicians pander, and we're more than willing to be pandered to. Throughout fifteen years of war there's been no appreciable rise in the tax rate, no mass mobilization, no call for sacrifice from the general population."[51] Rather than go to war in Iraq and Afghanistan as a nation, most of America was "at the mall," as Katey Schultz put it in the opening salvo of her 2013 short story collection, *Flashes of War*. The ease with which most modern Americans are able to disconnect from all but their most personally relevant matters has removed all kindling from whatever political spark may appear. With the all-volunteer force, modern American wars not only happen "over there," but they are fought by "someone else."

Untethered from the consequences of war, the American public has become less discriminating against different sources of narrative authenticity, effectively reducing the authority of experience in the same manner as temporal distance. On one hand, this feels like a bit of a paradox. The argument seems to be that when the relationship between the military and society was closer, the authority of experience mattered more as a marker of narrative authenticity when it came to cultural production. Today, with a yawning distance between the military and society, the veteran's experience still matters but converts into less cultural capital within the literary field because there is no longer a shared foundation for that experience. "Whether or not we actually served in Vietnam, those of us who were adults in the 1960s in America were involved in the Vietnam experience," Timothy Lomperis writes in "*Reading the Wind*," echoing the ending to Michael Herr's 1977 book *Dispatches*: "Vietnam, Vietnam, Vietnam, we've all been there." Before the all-volunteer force, it was American society that went to war, not just the military. The mobilization of troops came with a restructuring of civil priorities. These actions may have been small and had little impact on the daily lives of most citizens, but they were nonetheless impossible to ignore. And, of course, the realities of conscription meant that many families could be touched by the war whether they wished to be or not.

Under these conditions, which held broadly during World War I and World War II as well as the Korean War, the veteran's firsthand experience overseas meant a great deal within civil society, even though far more people were involved with the wars in some capacity than are today. Soldiers who returned home and chose to write novels about their experiences overseas were speaking to an audience with at least a passing familiarity with what that experience meant; despite their distance from American soil, the wars were shared cultural events with shared public memories, and the soldiers who had served returned home endowed with the authority to write about them.

If the value of personal experience has changed for the literary field, then so has the form of the cultural authority that, for the last hundred years, has rested on it. The veteran's cultural authority today is largely symbolic, stemming from a social environment that applauds the military from a safe distance while reducing the person wearing the uniform to stereotypes of heroes and victims.[52] The standards of authority and authenticity within the field of production (especially for literary agents and publishing house editors) have also changed to a point that more voices — many of whom cannot claim the authority of direct experience—nonetheless engage with the wars through literary fiction on the same level as the veterans who served in them. Even without defining what exactly an "authentic" war novel should look like, the greater proportion of contemporary war novels written by non-veterans provides indirect evidence that, in practice, actors within the field of the production have changed their conception of authenticity as it applies within the war fiction genre. The acceleration of history has primed readers to view alternate sources of authority over the literary representation of war without denigrating them as inauthentic, encouraging agents and editors (or at least not discouraging them) to publish novels written by nonveterans that, for previous wars, may not have appeared until years later. David Buchanan has written of the "cycle of war literature's production," arguing that

> Combat gnosticism determines (and hampers) how war literature is written and packaged and received. Meanwhile, experiential authority and personal wounding stand as the most important commodities to be debated and discussed while dissent and civilian perspectives on war are pushed to the critical background. . . . Yes, it takes time for war fiction to appear, but the temporal distance between war's event and its representation in fiction may only be necessary so that the dominant cloud of combat gnosticism can disperse.[53]

While this apparent requirement for authors without experiential authority to wait before they could publish war novels may have been true for the American conflicts of the twentieth century, it is demonstrably false today; the numbers simply do not support the contention that "the reader of contemporary war literature remains rooted in his or her desire for documentary verisimilitude."[54]

The Burden of Interpretation: Veteran-Authors Cede Their Authority

The dispersion of authority that came with American memory culture's conversion of temporal distance into social distance has been accompanied by a pattern of veterans rejecting the ideologies of combat gnosticism and flesh-witnessing, ceding the cultural authority over the literary representation of conflict that they had come to possess throughout the twentieth century.

"You Don't Have to Be a Veteran"

Taken to its extreme, combat gnosticism not only contends that only those with personal experience in war and combat could possibly understand it, but also that these veterans are the only ones who can write authentically about war in general. Accepting this premise means trapping veterans in an echo chamber of memory that merely reflects their own voices back at a diminished volume. Thus, in response to the social conditions created by the shift to an all-volunteer force and the unburdening of the civilian population from the consequences of foreign wars, contemporary veteran-authors have rebelled against the attitude that places personal experience on a philosophical pedestal over all other sources of knowledge, publishing articles and reviews that seek a more pluralized understanding of authority in the hopes of sharing the burden of memory with the rest of the American population.

Contrasting the publication of Kevin Powers's *The Yellow Birds* and Ben Fountain's *Billy Lynn's Long Halftime Walk* in 2012 provides an instructive case study to see how veteran-authors began to revise their conception of narrative authority. Powers was one of the first veterans of the Iraq War to write a novel about it, and *The Yellow Birds* conformed to many of the genre's traditions and conventions by focusing on the traumatic experience of its narrator, Private John Bartle, as well as the lingering psychological effects of that experience once Bartle returns home. Structured partly as a mystery—the reader knows that Bartle's fellow soldier Murphy is dead and that his death occurred under strange circumstances—*The Yellow Birds* is concerned with Bartle's emotional stress and difficulty coping with whatever it was that happened in Iraq.

As a veteran-authored novel that dealt thematically with traumatic experience, *The Yellow Birds* seemed poised to continue the tradition of American war fiction where the fictional response to the Vietnam War had left off. "The *All Quiet on the Western Front* of America's Arab wars," blurbed Tom Wolfe on the front cover. On the back, comparisons are made to Hemingway, Tim O'Brien (twice), Norman Mailer, and even Herman Melville. Readers were given no reason to doubt that this was the novel that belonged in the hitherto empty space on the shelf of canonized literature reserved for America's war in Iraq.

A running theme in book reviews and interviews with Powers was an obsession with autobiographical details. Powers had enlisted in the army at seventeen, a fact that not a single interviewer or reviewer failed to mention.

He served in Iraq from February 2004 to March 2005, and he sets *The Yellow Birds* in the same time and place (though he rearranges the letters of the actual Iraqi city of Tal Afar to become "Al Tafar"). "I guess the inevitable question," Jeffrey Brown begins in an interview for *PBS NewsHour*, "I'll get it out of the way quickly, is how much of the book, the novel, is based on your experience?"[55] In this interview, as with others that ask the same question, Powers refuses to take the bait that would link the novel's content with his service in Iraq, stating directly that "the actual events that take place in the novel are not events that I experienced myself, but I think the kind of emotional core of the book was something that I identified with very strongly. This sort of interior life of the narrator, especially as something that I felt, those emotions are things that I felt myself."

Four months before *The Yellow Birds*, Ecco Press published Ben Fountain's *Billy Lynn's Long Halftime Walk*, a darkly sardonic depiction of how far apart the military and American society had drifted. Taking place at a Dallas Cowboys football game on Thanksgiving Day, *Billy Lynn* sets a mirror to American war culture after 9/11 and is deeply disturbed by its reflection. The novel is focalized through Specialist Billy Lynn, a nineteen-year-old soldier from Texas whose squad was filmed by an embedded news crew while fighting off an enemy ambush. Billy is hailed as a hero for his actions during the battle and his squad has been sent around the United States on a two week "Victory Tour" to boost morale back home, but Fountain is less interested in Billy's psyche than in exploring the gap between his experiences in Iraq and the home front mindlessness of his fellow citizens. Unlike *The Yellow Birds*, which is split evenly between the combat zone and the home front, *Billy Lynn* takes place entirely in the United States, with the exception of a few brief glimpses of Billy's memories from Iraq.

The Yellow Birds and *Billy Lynn's Long Halftime Walk* thus make for an interesting pair for comparison. Other than dealing with the Iraq War, they could not be more different in style, content, theme, or author—one is a lyrical meditation on combat and trauma by a young author who had personally been to the war, and the other is a biting satire of American society's relationship to soldiers (including veterans like Kevin Powers) by an author with no personal experience in the military or the wars. Both novels fit well into the genre's tradition of trauma heroes, even though in my view Fountain's protagonist can be read as a critique of the trauma hero myth.[56] But where *The Yellow Birds* represents the more traditional experiential-based novel typical of the early fictional response to wars in American literary history, *Billy Lynn* reads as an example of a contemporary historical novel about the war. Fountain embeds the narrative within the historical landscape, anchoring it to reality through a mixture of real historical figures (e.g., references to President George W. Bush, John Kerry, as well as various Hollywood actors) and phrases of the time; one character says "there are no cut-and-runners here," echoing the way Republicans used the phrase as a pejorative to attack Democrats for their call to withdraw troops from Iraq in 2006.[57]

Both novels were nominated for the National Book Award that year, and the subject of narrative authority came up in an interview with Powers and Fountain in the *New York Times* that took place just days before the awards ceremony. The interviewer asked Fountain, "Ben, as far as I know, you were never in the military. What spurred your decision to write about the soldiers in your novel, and what kind of research did you do about the characters?" Fountain, then as he has ever since, downplays his own authority with his response: "It wasn't an idle or trivial thing for me, undertaking a book like this. Since I've never served in the military, never been in a shooting war, I felt like I had to earn the right to write a book like this. I'm still not satisfied that I had the right to do it." Powers is having none of this, though:

> I think Ben's obvious conscientiousness with regard to the seriousness of the subject matter is probably a not insignificant reason why "Billy Lynn" is so good. There seems to be a correlation between this attitude and good, true art that is far more useful as a metric than whether or not experience equals any kind of authority in artistic expression, which for the record I'm pretty sure it doesn't.[58]

In this interview, Powers and Fountain are placed on even ground — both are debut novelists nominated for the same award (though they both lost) who wrote very different novels about the Iraq War. Instead of reasserting his experiential authority, Powers instead reframes the aesthetic criteria for artistic expression in terms of the author's attitude toward the subject of war. Further, Powers's consistent emphasis on identifying with the "emotional core" of his novel has shades of Hayden White's "historical

CHAPTER FOUR

essence." The effect of this is to grant Fountain the same narrative authority as Powers by encouraging the experience-based novel and the contemporary historical novel about the war to coexist and be judged against the same aesthetic criteria.

Powers would not be the last veteran-author to argue against the authority of experience as the basis for narrative authenticity. In a 2014 article for the *New York Times*, Iraq War veteran Phil Klay—whose collection of short stories, *Redeployment*, would win the National Book Award that Powers and Fountain had narrowly missed—calls the insistence that only veterans understand the trauma of war a "failure of the imagination."[59] He argues that "the notion that the veteran is an unassailable authority on the experience of war shuts down conversation." Read along the continuum of modern war writing that stretches back to the First World War, Klay's words have the effect of a direct rebuttal to the Vietnam-era refrain "You had to be there."

Two years later, Iraq War veteran and novelist Matt Gallagher wrote an article for the online magazine *Literary Hub* with the title "You Don't Have to Be a Veteran to Write about War." "Authority is writing's lifeblood," Gallagher opened his essay, before arguing that "it's high-time that writers and readers of contemporary war literature alike recognize that experience is not the same thing as authority."[60] To bolster his argument, Gallagher invokes a tradition of literature that stretches from Homer, Shakespeare, and Stephen Crane to Bobbie Ann Mason and even Ben Fountain. "Experience is not the same thing as authority," Gallagher says, adding his voice to that of Powers and Klay. These writers would be followed by others, including army veteran Brian Van Reet, who, in a January 2019 speech at the American Library in Paris, argued that "we should refine and complicate our ideas of what a war book is and who war writers are. . . . [W]e should broaden our idea of what war literature is and who produces it. It's certainly not a genre limited to writers who are also war veterans. Many of the best books I've read on war were written by civilians."[61] A few months later, Matthew Komatsu, an air force veteran, wrote in his review of Jon Chopan's *Veterans Crisis Hotline* that "war literature is no longer the sole dominion of those who've participated directly in combat."[62]

It has not just been veteran-authors taking this stance; veteran-scholars have done the same. In contrast to Paul Fussell and other scholars, such as Philip Beidler and Samuel Hynes, who embraced the authority of experience, veterans of Iraq and Afghanistan who have themselves become scholars have consistently written *against* combat gnosticism. David Buchanan (an air force veteran) has a long screed against combat gnosticism and "the anxiety of authenticity" in his book, *Going Scapegoat: Post-9/11 War Literature, Language and Culture* (2016). In *War Narratives* (2019), Caleb Cage (an army veteran) rejects the superiority of the individual soldier's perspective and argues that "the most trustworthy perspectives from these wars have come from fiction written by both veterans of these wars and civilians."[63] Behind the word "trustworthy" is the shadow of authenticity that has so often been associated with veterans, but Cage's inclusion of civilians here suggests that the most trustworthy narratives are not necessarily those offered by veterans but rather whoever chooses to express themselves in fiction, echoing an argument also made by many Vietnam veterans but without excluding those who weren't there. Roy Scranton (army veteran) embeds his dismissal of combat gnosticism within a larger critique of the trauma hero narrative, writing first that "in contrast to eyewitnessing and historical accounts, the authority of experiential truth requires no corroboration" before noting that "the trauma hero narrative, the story of the martyr who bears the psychological wound that both is and is caused by a revelatory encounter with truth, testifies to our persistent cultural sanctification of war. The trauma hero's claim to revelatory truth supersedes the juridical, legislative, journalistic, scientific, and scholarly contests that establish consensus in secular liberalism, invoking instead a transcendental, mystic, subjective authority."[64]

I would be remiss if I did not add myself to this list; one of the main arguments of this book is an agreement with those veterans of Iraq and Afghanistan who believe that the literary representation of war is too important to be left only to veterans. Yielding the authority and responsibility to create imaginative interpretations of the nation's conflicts to veterans alone absolves the rest of the population from a certain degree of emotional investment. There are many forces at work, though, and the influence of Paul Fussell's *The Great War and Modern Memory* on literary scholarship continues to reverberate even today. Despite the steady campaign of veteran writers and scholars downplaying the authority of experience, it remains the genre's most widely assumed characteristic.

CHAPTER FOUR

Recalling Harari's terms from the previous chapter, contemporary veteran-authors and veteran-scholars are rhetorically favoring the authority of the eyewitness while downplaying the authority of the flesh-witness. The transferability of eyewitness authority from storyteller to listener then becomes a crucial building block to repair the civil-military gap, as the veterans' stories are no longer designed to exclude civilians from participation and understanding but rather to welcome them through narrative engagement. In the end, veterans *want* to unburden themselves from the sole responsibility to experience and understand these wars; encouraging nonveterans to write novels about them is one of many ways to do so.

The dispersion of authority over the literary representation of war in American memory culture represents the bookend of a process that began in 1921 and lasted nearly one hundred years. The veteran-author's accumulation of authority between World War I and Vietnam faced a disruption after the shift to a professional military, and the social gap that has characterized the civil-military relationship has helped reshape the war fiction genre to reflect the changes in American society since the 1970s. Today, as writers continue to subject the wars in Iraq and Afghanistan to fictional treatment, the veterans who have volunteered to serve and then returned to write their own novels are doing so mindful of what came before them but unafraid to reject conventional wisdom about who should write about war and what should be considered authentic.

The chapters that follow show how the changing relationship between the military and society since the end of the Vietnam War has done more than lead to a dispersion of war fiction authorship (*who* is writing about war); it has also influenced how contemporary war novels function as media of collective memory by shifting the narrative emphasis from the combat zone to the home front, and affected who gets remembered in these stories by broadening the protagonists to include more than just male American soldiers.

CHAPTER FIVE

"The New Battle"

The Civil-Military Gap and the Shock of Coming Home

The dispersion of war fiction authorship described in the previous chapter has been accompanied by a shift in narrative content in which contemporary war novels place far more emphasis on the home front compared with the novels written about the Vietnam War. What took the post-Vietnam generation of writers more than a decade after the conflict's end to see as an important element of the war experience has been at the forefront of the contemporary novels of Iraq and Afghanistan. These works have depicted the process of coming home far more extensively and with a greater depth than those written about Vietnam. Foregrounded are the jarring experiences of redeployment, the psychological challenges of reintegration, and the emotional toll of moral injury. Imaginative re-creations of these experiences seek to contrast images of the self at war and at home, using the disconnect between the veteran's experience and the unaffected American society as a driver of narrative tension. These novels reflect not only the changing nature of contemporary warfare but also the drifting relationship between the military and American society.

The influence of the civil-military gap on the content of contemporary war fiction has been to challenge the primacy of combat experience as a source of narrative authority. Veterans of Iraq and Afghanistan have fought in conflicts where direct combat with an enemy force has been far less common than the psychological stress of the unknown — from roadside bombs and incoming rockets to insider attacks by host nation allies. These veterans have been deployed to morally complex environments within and among fractured populations beset by insurgency, and their institutional training has deemphasized battlefield violence as an element of operational and strategic success. When they come home, veterans return to a nation almost completely disconnected from their overseas experience. The dissonance between that experience and the positive but superficial welcome veterans receive upon redeployment has contributed to a kind of "reverse culture shock" that includes difficulties adjusting to life at home after war. Post-traumatic stress and moral injury have replaced physical scars as the wars' "signature wounds,"[1] worsened by a return to a society that thanks veterans for their service but does not know much about them or what they have been through.[2] Consequently, the domestic social conditions of the civil-military gap as well as the nature and training of counterinsurgency warfare have transformed the defining experience of an overseas deployment from combat to coming home, and the literary effects of this transformation have manifested themselves in the narrative content of the wars' fictional response compared to the war fiction to emerge after Vietnam.

War, Combat, and the Defining Experience of Conflict

In March 2009, the United States House of Representatives Committee on Veterans' Affairs held a hearing titled "The Nexus between Engaged in Combat with the Enemy and Post-Traumatic Stress Disorder in an Era of Changing Warfare Tactics."[3] The intent was to determine if the government's official definition of "engaged in combat with the enemy" was too narrow to encompass the reality of military service in Iraq and Afghanistan. The chairman, Representative John J. Hall (D-NY), opened the hearing by noting that since the Civil War, Congress had recognized that soldiers who were wounded in battle should be entitled to some form of disability compensation. In the years that followed, the statutory requirements for compensation consistently specified combat engagements with enemy forces as the necessary source of a soldier's injuries. By the end of World War II, disability ratings began to include provisions for "War Psychosis," a term similar to "Shell Shock" or "Battle Fatigue" that accounted for nonphysical injuries but was still linked to prolonged exposure to combat and danger. These terms would be replaced by post-traumatic stress disorder (PTSD) in 1980. As a way to broaden the definition of combat to allow PTSD diagnoses for soldiers who were not actually in direct contact with the enemy, Hall notes that "the nature of wartime services changed, as many can agree. Warfare encompasses acts of terrorism, insurgency, and guerilla tactics. No place is safe and the enemy may not be readily identifiable."[4]

Hall's more expansive definition of combat comes at a time when direct

"The New Battle"

clashes with enemy forces for territorial control have been far less frequent compared to the Vietnam War and other twentieth-century conflicts, challenging the primacy of combat experience as a source of narrative authority within the war fiction genre. Most soldiers no longer experience combat in the more conventional sense of frequent, direct engagements with enemy soldiers, and the military's approach to the counterinsurgency even downplays the importance of violence and killing as elements of victory. The psychological and moral aspects of counterinsurgency have replaced the physical threat of battlefield violence as the defining characteristics of the wars in Iraq and Afghanistan, and combat no longer functions as an experiential dividing line that endows veteran-authors with the sole authority over the literary representation of the wars.

With the exception of the opening phase of the US-led invasion of Iraq in March 2003, the vast majority of soldiers deployed to Iraq and Afghanistan never engaged the enemy in pitched battles, nor even had occasion to fire their rifles. Further, once the invasion ended and transitioned into an extended occupation,[5] the nature of the conflict changed from maneuver warfare against an organized and uniformed enemy force to a counterinsurgency, a type of conflict in which combat is often seen as antithetical to a mission whose goal is to build security and stability among a population. According to a definition from the US State Department, counterinsurgency is "the blend of comprehensive civilian and military efforts designed to simultaneously contain insurgency and address its root causes. Unlike conventional warfare, non-military means are often the most effective elements, with military forces playing an enabling role."[6] The Department of Defense guidance on fighting a counterinsurgency also deemphasized the role of combat as an element of operational and strategic success. In Iraq and Afghanistan, for example, the rules of engagement provided soldiers with strict guidelines that told them when they were allowed to fire their weapons. Killing the enemy took a back seat to protecting the population. David Kilcullen, a military strategist who advised senior US military and civilian officials in Iraq between 2005 and 2008, writes that one of the fundamental considerations in a counterinsurgency is "to act with respect for local people, putting the well-being of noncombatant civilians ahead of any other consideration, even—in fact, especially—ahead of killing the enemy."[7] Rather than entrenching themselves in foxholes waiting for an enemy attack, soldiers were routinely tasked with building relationships with local civil and religious leaders. Measurements of success came not in the form of territory gained and held or dubious metrics like Vietnam's infamous "body count" but in terms of training local security forces, supporting good governance, encouraging economic development, and so on.[8]

The way of fighting and measuring success in the Afghanistan and Iraq counterinsurgency campaigns meant that these conflicts were not defined by combat but by cultural sensitivity, moral judgment, and an ever-present simmer of danger in the form of small bands of insurgents employing low-tech weapons to attack technologically superior American forces. Ambushes and skirmishes became less frequent as insurgents began to favor indiscriminate mortar and rocket attacks that rained down on forward operating bases. Insurgents also infiltrated allied police and military forces, turning their weapons on Coalition troops from inside the protective confines of their secure perimeter in so-called "Green on Blue" incidents. Driving on any road brought the dread of encountering the wars' biggest battlefield killer, the improvised explosive device (IED), or roadside bomb.[9] The sum of all these factors meant, as Hall argued, that no place was safe from all danger—something that made the psychological stress even worse.[10]

One could argue that the war in Vietnam was also characterized by psychological factors rather than territorial gains and losses, but this misses the actual frequency of combat engagements and comparative threat of violent death. A back-of-the-envelope calculation for combat exposure from Vietnam to Iraq and Afghanistan gives a good idea of the scale involved. To do this, I aggregated the total number of troops killed or wounded in action as a percentage of the total who served in country. For Vietnam, there were 351,078 casualties (303,644 wounded and 47,434 killed in action as a result of hostile fire). The number of troops who served in Vietnam between 1964 and 1975 was approximately 2,594,000, giving a total casualty percentage of 13.5 percent. For Iraq and Afghanistan, there were 58,422 casualties between 2001 and 2019 (52,981 wounded and 5,441 killed as a result of hostile fire). The number of troops who served in these conflicts as of 2018 was approximately 2,770,000, for a total casualty percentage of 2.1 percent. Note that this is a rough estimate; a soldier can experience combat without becoming a casualty and thus would not be included in these statistics. They also provide only a static picture and do not account for differences depending on when an individual was deployed (e.g., during the invasion of Iraq in 2003 or after the Sunni Awakening in 2007). Nonetheless, these numbers provide a reasonable lower bound for comparison, and they suggest that, on average, more soldiers deployed to Vietnam experienced combat action than those who served in Iraq and Afghanistan.[11] As it was, I believe that the American soldier's experience in Vietnam was still characterized by combat and engagement with the enemy in a way that differs from the experience in Iraq and Afghanistan, even if that enemy was elusive and fought using guerrilla tactics. Postwar criticism even pointed to the army's unwillingness to move past a tactical mindset focused on overwhelming firepower and recognize Vietnam as a counterinsurgency as a reason for the war's ultimate failure.[12]

Within the literary field, though, the more conventional image of combat has been at the heart of the war fiction genre's most prominent characteristics. War has always been a far broader subject and set of experiences than battle or combat, but academic treatment of the subject, and particularly in literature, tends to blur the distinction between the two.[13] In fact, in Wallis Sanborn's *The American Novel of War: A Critical Analysis and Classification System* (2012) — the only contemporary study that seeks to establish a set of characteristics that define a war novel and its content — Sanborn limits his text selection exclusively to works that are "by and of combat — in theme, in topic, in element. . . . All the novels of war in this study have extended scenes of battlefield violence, and all of the texts deal with the physical, psychological, emotional, and intellectual traumas that the combatants undergo before, during, and after battle."[14] He explicitly excludes novels that "take place primarily out of the war zone or have primary non-war thematic elements like 'love in a time of war' or 'issues at home during a time of war' or farcical non-war premises." If there's no combat, it doesn't count.[15]

Despite Sanborn's approach to classifying works within the genre as well as other similar war fiction scholarship, I contend that there is a fundamental difference between the literary representation of combat and the holistic representation of war. Critical obsession with combat as the focal point of war fiction seems to come from the question of how literature can address the aesthetic representation of violence and suffering on a massive scale. It's less about how writers of all backgrounds interrogate the origins, causes, effects, and meaning of war as a lamentable element of humanity, but rather how the brutality of the battlefield is rendered using written language. Yet war is more than those bursts of violence, brief or sustained, and for many contemporary writers the far more interesting question is what happens afterward.

In fact, the experience of homecoming has taken over from combat as the defining narrative element of contemporary war fiction.[16] The disruptive effect of an overseas tour in Iraq or Afghanistan serves to contrast American society with wartime experience, even if that experience is no longer primarily characterized by combat in the same sense as during previous wars. Rather than afterthoughts to a story of action and survival, the psychological and moral dimensions of life after combat have *become* the story.

In that sense, veterans and nonveterans find themselves in similar positions as fiction writers. Mimetic realism and portrayals of combat have given way to social, psychological, and moral struggles. None of these themes suggest that having served in the military or spent time in a combat zone gives a writer access to special knowledge or understanding for telling a war story. The authority of the "flesh-witness" described in chapter 3 collapses under the weight of competing psychological conditions that rival the "extreme bodily conditions of war: hunger, cold, exhaustion, injury, the presence of death — and occasionally the thrill of killing and the exhilarating adrenaline rush of combat" that had previously served as the veteran's source of experiential authority.[17] Flesh-witness authority is confined to the experience of battle and combat, but the argument that only those who have experienced combat can understand war requires a metonymic reduction of war to the tactical realm of bombs, bullets, and bayonets — a metonym that breaks down under the battlefield conditions of Iraq and Afghanistan.

The Social Conditions of Homecoming during Vietnam

The veterans who returned from Vietnam did so alone and reentered a society that was bitterly divided about the war from which they had just come home. Unlike the veterans of the world wars and the Korean War, who redeployed with their fellow soldiers via maritime transport ships after the duration of the conflict, soldiers deployed to Vietnam for one-year tours, counting down the days until they boarded an airplane bound for the United States. They returned "lonely and alone," according to historian James Wright. "They flew on charter flights and entered a terminal and went back into civilian life. . . . [T]he logistics of arrival alone deprived them of any sense of accomplishment or service."[18] The homecoming experience became a process of alienation: first, alienation from any kind of group cohesion that might have existed had they redeployed as units rather than individuals, and second, alienation from the society to which they returned. From green recruit—whether drafted or volunteered—to combat-hardened veteran merely counting days until his DEROS (Date of Expected/Eligible Return from Overseas), the individual nature of the Vietnam veteran's experience became one of the conflict's defining features.

They were lonely, alone, and above all feeling abandoned by the country that sent them to fight. "There is little doubt," Wright observes, "that many veterans came home from Vietnam feeling frustrated if not angry and generally feeling unappreciated by a nation that had turned its back on their war."[19] They compared themselves, fairly or not, to the victorious and celebrated veterans who returned home after World War II. For veterans of Vietnam, feelings of dejection accompanied the absence of operational closure. Branded as scapegoats for the first military failure in American history, veterans returned home with the sense that they had done their duty as their country had demanded under morally ambiguous and strategically questionable circumstances only to find their image and reputation in tatters.[20] They were bitter about how their country treated them, and that bitterness found its way into a great deal of the veteran-authored fiction published in the 1970s. Take it from Private First Class Henry Winsted, drafted just out of college, in William Pelfrey's 1972 novel The Big V: "What are we gonna do when we get back? Fuckin hippies, fuckin protestors. Fuckin VFW. Who's gonna understand? Who's gonna give a fuck?" Or Corporal Joker in Gustav Hasford's The Short-Timers, who knows that "those of us who survive to be short-timers will fly the great speckled bird back to hometown America. But home won't be there anymore and we won't be there either. Upon each of us the war has lodged itself, a black crab feeding."[21]

The social conditions of redeployment for Vietnam veterans trace their origins to the preceding decade. While Cold War tensions led to an expansion of the active-duty force in the 1950s and 1960s, the domestic social and political climate began to change. The escalation of American military involvement in Vietnam paralleled the "hawk versus dove" debate back home, and media coverage gave the impression of increased polarization across

CHAPTER FIVE

the country. Conscription and the draft became highly charged and controversial topics, even though only one-quarter of the American forces in Vietnam were draftees (compared with nearly two-thirds during World War II).[22] Nevertheless, the notion that citizens could be forced to serve, and possibly die, in a war they did not support became fodder for antiwar activists, and by 1972 the proportion of Americans who identified as against the war was more than two out of three.[23] "The difference during the Vietnam War," according to Loren Baritz, "was not the number of Americans who disagreed with government policy, but the number who took to the streets."[24]

With public opinion increasingly against American involvement in the war, veterans coming home were forced into the awkward position of defending their wearing of the uniform at all. There was a sense that those who had served in an unpopular war were themselves somehow culpable for its outcomes, in some ways as guilty as those who had sent them there in the first place.[25] The massacre of Vietnamese civilians at My Lai in March 1968 and television reports of widespread drug use among deployed soldiers led to the stereotyping of veterans as murderers and junkies. A vocal antiwar movement fought a discursive battle with the government, catching veterans in the crossfire. The image of the returning veteran, psychologically scarred and facing the rejection of society, found its way into works of fiction and other imaginative representations of the war. Throughout the 1970s and 1980s, the prototypical representation of a Vietnam veteran in television, film, and literature was of a psychopath, a social outcast who might snap at any moment, willing and able to kill as he had done during the war. Rather than a celebrated hero of democracy, the stereotypical Vietnam veteran in cultural productions of those years was a traumatized killer who posed a danger to society.[26]

These social conditions became one of the defining features of the fictional response to the war. Novels about Vietnam tended to characterize the home front as an antagonist, another obstacle for the returning veteran to deal with. Maureen Ryan observes that common homecoming themes in the early narratives of the Vietnam War were set up as a contrast with the reality of how World War II veterans returned: "Over and over again, in early popular texts arising from the war, the veteran returns from Vietnam not as a welcomed hero, feted with the parades and celebrations that greeted his father

"The New Battle"

after his war—the 'good' war—but as a scorned 'baby killer,' harassed by antiwar activists, misunderstood by embarrassed families, neglected by a government and a military distracted by the unpopular and increasingly disastrous war, and by a home front driven by internal conflict."[27] Drawing on a range of texts, Ryan observes a common theme that the true enemy of the American soldiers was neither the Viet Cong nor the North Vietnamese but the people back home who didn't support them: "Once again, if you weren't there, not only don't you care, you are actively hostile to the defeated warriors."[28] In the handful of novels about the Vietnam War that explicitly depict the experience of coming home, Ryan writes that "there is really only one story—the country's ongoing betrayal of its soldiers who returned to an alien home."[29]

Despite the widespread cultural view that American society uniformly spat—literally as well as figuratively—on those who had served in Vietnam, there is some evidence to the contrary. A 1971 poll showed that the vast majority of Americans believed that Vietnam veterans "deserved the same 'warm reception' as those who fought in previous wars, even as 61 percent thought they were sent to a war 'we could never win.'"[30] Sociologists and historians have combed through the media archives of the 1960s and early 1970s to find the origins of the collective belief that protest movements antagonized troops more than they did policymakers, but most have failed to find much supporting evidence.[31]

For many Vietnam veterans, though, actions told another story. Karl Marlantes wrote of his own homecoming in his book *What It Is Like to Go to War*.[32] He had been back "perhaps a month" and was walking around town in uniform when a group of "young people, my age, began to follow me down the street on the opposite side, jeering, calling me names, chanting in unison. They were flying the flags of North Vietnam and the Viet Cong." He saw signs at restaurants and bars that said "No Military!" and two of his fellow young officers were "murdered, gunned down from a passing car in their dress whites outside a hamburger joint on M Street."[33]

Marlantes recounted his experience in 2011, more than forty years after his tour in Vietnam. Individual memories have clashed with the war's collective memory ever since; the contentious nature of the Vietnam veteran's homecoming experience continues even as the immediacy of the experience

CHAPTER FIVE

is all but lost to living memory. In that time, fictional works have shaped the memory of what it was like to come home from Vietnam, a collective vision that has been used as a benchmark to gauge the homecoming experience for veterans of Afghanistan and Iraq.

The Reverse Culture Shock of Coming Home from Iraq and Afghanistan

Somewhere between the end of the US withdrawal in Vietnam and the darkest days of the insurgency in Iraq, American society learned to separate its feelings about war from its opinions of those who fought it. Rather than confronting an angry, antagonist populace, the uniform-wearing Iraq or Afghanistan war veteran confronts apathy cloaked in patriotic appreciation. Lamenting the lack of American civic engagement with the wars, Owen Gilman writes that coming home from war for contemporary veterans is as much of a challenge as going to war in the first place. He argues that "going to war and then representing the experience of war constitute only two elements of a three-part sequence. The final consideration explores the way circumstances in American culture currently bedevil veterans, making their home a kind of hell. As long as average Americans are preoccupied with superficial nonsense, veterans will feel marginalized to the point of nonexistence."[34]

The unburdening of American society from the consequences of war has been expressed repeatedly in the homecoming stories of contemporary war fiction. Characters who served in Iraq or Afghanistan experience a "reverse culture shock" as they return to a nation that has carried on in their absence as though nothing had changed.[35] "We took my combat pay and did a lot of shopping. Which is how America fights back against the terrorists" the narrator of Phil Klay's story "Redeployment" quips shortly after his own homecoming, satirizing the disconnect between his time in a combat zone and the consumerist mentality that grips American society.[36] Or consider the sentiments of Billy Lynn, the protagonist of Ben Fountain's *Billy Lynn's Long Halftime Walk*: "He wishes just once that somebody would call him baby-killer."[37] Billy is so uncomfortable with how he and his fellow squadmates have been transformed into heroic symbols for the Thanksgiving Day halftime show at the Dallas Cowboys stadium that he actively hopes to be

"The New Battle"

verbally abused for his service with the same epithet hurled at his Vietnam-era predecessors.

Because only those Americans who choose to serve become preoccupied with the wars, the rest of the country is free to deal with "superficial nonsense," as Gilman puts it. The violence in Iraq and Afghanistan hardly registered in the average American's daily life, and the infrequent social contact between members of the military and most American citizens has led to a lack of understanding between those who serve and the rest of the nation. A 2016 study revealed that a large number of nonveterans were prone to answer "don't know" or "no opinion" to questions posed about the military, a response that contradicts most Americans' willingness to answer questions about topics they know little about.[38] The study's authors believed that this hesitance comes from a lack of social contact between the military and most Americans, and that most Americans are, in fact, aware of their own ignorance when it comes to military service. "Americans have less direct contact with service members," the authors write, "but portrayals of the military in movies or on television are common. It might be that these depictions of the military do little to bridge the gap and that they instead only highlight the fact that military service has little to do with the lives of average Americans."[39]

Nowhere is this gap more prominent than during a veteran's redeployment. The contrast between the war zone and the home front often becomes overwhelming for returning veterans, and contemporary fiction writers—veterans and nonveterans alike—have homed in on this disconnect to put the relationship between the military and American society in the starkest possible relief. The soldiers in contemporary war novels who return home, whether for good or simply on mid-tour leave,[40] often react viscerally to what they see as the frivolity of an American society unconcerned with the wars. In some cases, authors depict homecomings that are deliberately short-lived, as the soldiers are only back in the United States for a few weeks before they return overseas. The narrative structure of these scenes, which interrupt the "war story" for a brief return to civilian life before abruptly returning, mirrors the emotional effects on the soldiers. They leave the combat zone, but, as with redeploying soldiers from Vietnam, they do so as individuals without the social benefits of having their friends and fellow soldiers nearby. In Siobhan Fallon's *You Know When the Men Are Gone* (2011), for example, David

CHAPTER FIVE

"Moge" Mogeson goes home to Westchester County, just north of Manhattan. Overwhelmed by the sheer excess of an American grocery store, he gets the urge to punch a woman who is complaining to one of the employees that they don't have the specific brand of cereal that her daughter likes (a direct contrast to the young Iraqi schoolchildren Moge has seen who have few supplies and barely anything to eat). "Everything at home annoyed him and he knew it was irrational and misplaced." He also decries the lack of media coverage about the wars:

> Did one missing woman in Missouri — sure, she was pretty, a wife
> and the mother of three — really need to be the headlining story
> on every single news program when there were American soldiers,
> mothers and fathers, wives and husbands, dying in Iraq and Afghanistan? Why weren't Larry King and Barbara Walters interviewing their
> grieving families or telling their intricate life stories?[41]

Moge rejects the banalities of home — unable to care "when [his girlfriend] Marissa told him about her second-graders with their video games and peanut allergies, or when his mother complained about gas prices, or when his father had a lousy day of golf." Instead, he thinks that "something was wrong with him, some part of him was still keyed into Baghdad" and that "everything that he thought would make him happy here at home suddenly seemed so inconsequential."[42]

Moge may find the physical presence at home disorienting, but other characters discover that their very idea of home has become conflated with war. In Stephen Markley's Ohio (2018), army veteran Dan Eaton feels "relieved" as he flies back to Baghdad after his R&R leave. After he is shot in the chest on his second patrol — saved by his protective body armor — he realizes that, in Iraq, "he felt more at home than he had the previous eighteen days in his mother's gaze, in his father's humor, in [his girlfriend] Hailey's arms." Whatever comforts he might have expected from home fall flat, and Eaton's conception of home as a place becomes unmoored: "Home is a roving sensation, not a place, and for a large chunk of his life, the feel of that bullet to the chest, that was home."[43]

In army veteran Roy Scranton's War Porn (2016), one of the protagonists — a junior enlisted soldier named Wilson — brings with him the feelings of discontinuity between home and the combat zone when he flies to Oregon

120

"The New Battle"

for R&R. Scranton mirrors this discontinuity with a nonlinear narrative structure; Wilson's two sections of the novel are embedded within three other plot lines and separated by more than one hundred pages. The second half of his storyline begins with his return to Iraq from R&R. Internally, he expresses excitement. Thinking about his fellow soldiers, Wilson "wanted to see their faces. They understood. They knew this shit world we lived in, knew it all better than anyone I could talk to back in Oregon."[44] When he tells his sergeant about what it was like back home, he focuses on the airport as the symbolic divider between war and home:

> It's weird man, coming back. At the Dallas airport, there was this line of flag wavers, and anytime anyone found out I was in Iraq, they got all serious and shit, started thanking me and telling me what a great thing I was doing. I didn't know what to say. Like, hell yeah, fuck hadji! I mean, what the fuck?[45]

Other characters react negatively to what they perceive as the "fantasy-land" of American society that Owen Gilman describes. Lauren Clay in Cara Hoffman's *Be Safe I Love You* looks around and thinks that "she'd come home to a world of fragile baby animals."[46] In Roxana Robinson's *Sparta*, returned veteran Conrad Farrell twice loses his temper while in a restaurant at what he perceives as the ignorance and indifference of his fellow citizens. The first time he is with his girlfriend and nearly flies into a rage at a woman whose purse hit him:

> What made him so wild, what made him swell with rage, was the fact that no one here knew anything, no one here understood about the real world. No one understood what you looked for on the street (risk assessment), how you cleared a room (always moving as a team, though you had to slip through the fatal funnel one by one), how many shots you fired to kill someone (three), how you identified yourself on the radio (company, platoon, individual), how to establish a perimeter, or what the risks were in a room like this, filled with moving people and noise. They knew fuck-all here, everyone.[47]

Conrad's identity has become so consumed by his military experience that he associates the tactical elements of combat with the "real world" and criticizes the other patrons at the restaurant for not knowing anything.

CHAPTER FIVE

Conrad's internal seething at the people's lack of what he deems important knowledge leads him to compare his service to the veterans of World War II:

> He wondered if this was what it had been like after World War II, soldiers arriving home from the battlefield to all those beaming civilians. But back then the soldiers had had a critical mass, and the war had been a national effort. Not like this, where no one could even find Iraq on the map. No one knew why we were there, no one could remember if we'd found WMDs or not.[48]

Later, having lunch with his father, he appraises the crowd as "mostly men in suits. . . . Dark suits and white shirts and dark silk ties, an unmistakable sense of self-satisfaction. They were a few years older than him, not much. They seemed completely at ease, talking and laughing. What had they ever done in the world? But here they were, in suits, unfolding their napkins, ready to order sushi-grade tuna steaks, and headed for long and rewarding careers." He then refers to the restaurant as a "parallel universe, where he was absent."[49] Conrad's irritation isn't just at what he assumes is their apathy — he never actually interacts with any of these characters — but also the comfortable lifestyle they enjoy while two wars are going on overseas.

Even characters who do speak with civilians often find the interactions to be superficial and unsatisfying. In veteran-author Michael Pitre's *Fives and Twenty-Fives* (2014), Donovan, one of the novel's protagonists, finds himself talking with a Korean War veteran at the airport USO after his flight is canceled. They bond, even if Donovan is reluctant to do so, in a way that suggests that his service will never leave him (something he confirms later while attending graduate school). Tippet, the Korean War vet, brings over two girls to talk to him, as though that's the only way to cheer up a brooding war veteran. He tells the girls that Donovan just came home from Iraq, and they respond with the standard reactions: "Oh, wow"; "That is really just so amazing"; "Thank you for your service."[50] Like Conrad Farrell, Donovan projects his own version of these girls' futures and the sad role he believes he is destined to play in them:

> The brunettes introduced themselves, but I couldn't process their names. They reminded me of girls I'd known in college. Perfect and put together. They'd both be married any minute, and the conversa-

"The New Battle"

tion we were about to have would become a story at cocktail parties. They'd stand next to their husbands and tell the story of the Iraq vet they once met. How he was drunk beyond belief in the airport.[51]

The most extended take on the reverse culture shock of homecoming is Ben Fountain's 2012 satirical novel *Billy Lynn's Long Halftime Walk*. Specialist Billy Lynn and his squad are spending two weeks traveling the United States on a "Victory Tour" after an embedded news crew caught them on camera fighting off an enemy ambush in Iraq. Billy in particular is hailed as a hero after he rushed to the aid of his wounded sergeant as two enemy fighters were attempting to abduct him. Although the novel takes place entirely in the United States, the few moments of reflection about combat that flow through Billy's thoughts provide an important counterbalance to the extravagance that awaits the Bravo Squad at the Dallas Cowboys stadium on Thanksgiving Day—the last day before their return to Iraq—where the soldiers have been enrolled to participate in the game's halftime show.

The heart of the novel is Billy's assessment of, and interaction with, his fellow citizens. Mobs of civilians thank Billy for his service and praise him for his bravery based on a few minutes of combat footage they've seen of him on the news. They project their own thoughts, emotions, and opinions about the war onto him. They look to him for reassurance and to assuage their guilt for not facing the consequences of war themselves. In the end, the reader hears Billy's thoughts and finds him to be more complicated than the people he meets likely think he is. He takes a deep interest in the stadium crowd and its constituents, likening "all the varieties on display" to "a migration scene from a nature documentary, all shapes, ages, sizes, colors, and income indicators, although well-fed Anglo is the dominant demographic." His thoughts continue:

> Having served on their behalf as a frontline soldier, Billy finds himself constantly wondering about them. What are they thinking? What do they want? Do they know they're alive? As if prolonged and intimate exposure to death is what's required to fully inhabit one's present life.[52]

Billy's erudite and philosophical introspection is more than one might expect from a nineteen-year-old army specialist, but perhaps that is precisely

CHAPTER FIVE

Fountain's point. Age is not a prerequisite for knowledge, Billy realizes, twice musing that "Iraq ages you in dog years."[53] Comparing his own knowledge—gained through his experience in Iraq—to the people he encounters at the stadium, Billy infantilizes them:

> No matter their age or station in life, Billy can't help but regard his fellow Americans as children. They are bold and proud and certain in the way of clever children blessed with too much self-esteem, and no amount of lecturing will enlighten them as to the state of pure sin toward which war inclines. He pities them, scorns them, loves them, hates them, these children. These boys and girls. These toddlers, these infants. Americans are children who must go somewhere else to grow up, and sometimes die.[54]

Billy equates childhood with innocence and thinks of Americans as innocent and ignorant of the ways of the world that would force them to "go somewhere else to grow up." He also upends the civilians' expectations of him, even if he only does so in his private consciousness while putting on a performance for the audience around him—"Bravo," Fountain's chosen letter of the military alphabet to refer to the squad, even suggests a kind of post-performance applause.[55] The tension between his fellow citizens' praise one moment and their indifference the next confuses him. "Being a Bravo means inhabiting a state of semi-celebrity that occasionally flattens you with praise and adulation. At staged rallies, for instance, or appearances at malls, or whenever TV or radio is present, you are apt at some point to be lovingly mobbed by everyday Americans eager to show their gratitude, then other times it's like you're invisible, people just see right through you, nothing registers."[56]

This dichotomy of praise and indifference comes from a place of guilt, Billy thinks. He again marvels that "no one spits, no one calls him baby-killer. On the contrary, people could not be more supportive or kindlier disposed, yet Billy finds these encounters weird and frightening all the same." Billy detects a hidden truth beneath their praise: "There's something harsh in his fellow Americans, avid, ecstatic, a burning that comes of the deepest need. That's his sense of it, they all need something from him. . . . They say thank you over and over and with growing fervor, they know they're being good when they thank the troops and their eyes shimmer with love for them-selves and this tangible proof of their goodness."[57] Fountain employs Billy as a mirror to reveal Americans' superficial gratitude to those in uniform as a form of affirming their own sense of righteousness. The civilians who thank Billy seek his approval, an acknowledgment that they are doing their part by not repeating the treatment of veterans during and after Vietnam. That they "shimmer with love for themselves" and see their praise of Billy and the troops as "tangible proof of their goodness" suggests a need for absolution that can only come from veterans. Yet the shockingly positive reception that Billy and the Bravos receive — blown to over-the-top proportions throughout the novel — is merely a glossy mask that covers the inherent ugliness of the unbalanced civil-military relationship.

The New Battle:
Post-Traumatic Stress and Reintegration

The psychological challenges of homecoming for contemporary wars can have consequences just as lethal as an enemy bullet; between 2013 and 2019, more than 45,000 veterans and active-duty military members took their own lives, a number that dwarfs the 5,437 troops killed by hostile fire.[58] An open acknowledgement that veterans may confront a range of behavioral and mental health issues has spawned a trove of scientific research as well as popular writing on the subject.[59] In his book *Tribe: On Homecoming and Belonging*, journalist and veteran war correspondent Sebastian Junger observes that "today's veterans often come home to find although they're willing to die for their country, they're not sure how to live for it."[60] As many of the characters in contemporary war fiction learn, redeployment from the combat zone is merely the first step in the reintegration process, and it is here where the bulk of the fictional response to Iraq and Afghanistan spends its narrative energy.

And with good reason. Today's American military has the highest re-ported rates of post-traumatic stress in its history.[61] The source of this trauma is not always related to combat exposure, though. Veterans of Iraq and Afghanistan "return from wars that are safer than those their fathers and grandfathers fought," Junger writes, "and yet far greater numbers of

CHAPTER FIVE

them wind up alienated and depressed. This is true *even for people who didn't experience combat*. In other words, the problem doesn't seem to be trauma on battlefield so much as reentry into society."[62]

This is the society that has become disconnected from its nation's wars, and the fictional veterans who return home from overseas must confront the apathy of their fellow citizens head on. Although fiction that dealt with the Vietnam War's domestic aftermath and issues of reintegration started to appear in the early 1970s, these novels were still far outweighed by combat zone narratives.[63] Later novels took up the theme more frequently; Bobbie Ann Mason's *In Country* (1985) and Larry Heinemann's *Paco's Story* (1987), for example, cover the home front territory in great depth, providing at least a rough sketch for the kinds of works that would be written about Iraq and Afghanistan.

Mental health challenges and substance abuse loom large as themes in many contemporary war novels. Alcohol and drugs in particular play a crucial part in many of these works, including the reintegration of a combat-wounded helicopter pilot in Kristin Hannah's *Home Front* (2012), a troubled veteran's brief but powerful appearance in Mark Doten's *The Infernal* (2015), nearly all of the characters in Jon Chopan's story collection *Veterans Crisis Hotline* (2018), and the lurking presence of heroin and opiates in Stephen Markley's *Ohio* (2018) as well as veteran-authored works including Michael Pitre's *Fives and Twenty-Fives* (2014), Jesse Goolsby's *I'd Walk with My Friends If I Could Find Them*, Brandon Caro's *Old Silk Road* (2015), and Nico Walker's *Cherry* (2018).

Veteran suicide is another theme for novels interested in following the psychological journey of a returned veteran down its darkest possible path. Air force veteran Matthew Hefti's *A Hard and Heavy Thing* (2015) is constructed as a novel-length suicide note from war veteran Levi to his best friend Nick. The novel begins with an "Adumbration," a word that means both "sketch" but also — more literally translated from the Latin —"foreshadowing," and Hefti employs an intricate narrative structure in which Levi writes of himself in third person, occasionally breaking into the main narrative with parenthetical first-person comments:

He could not make sense of all that had happened, but he had to explain it somehow. He owed his friend that much. So he left the river

126

"The New Battle"

for home, where he wrote and remembered. He wrote in such a way as to ignore his ego, a task that still remained difficult despite his narrative tricks.

[I did exactly what you told me to do, Nick. Didn't you tell me to just write the stupid book already? And that even doing the worst thing on the planet had to count for something? Well I can't think of anything worse than what I'm about to do, which is why I think you deserve an explanation. And maybe after you read it you'll realize why I don't have the hope that you have. The truth is this: We begin and end alone.][64]

Characters who begin to think about suicide feature in other works by veterans as well, including Phil Klay's *Redeployment*, Jesse Goolsby's *I'd Walk with My Friends If I Could Find Them*, Odie Lindsey's *We Come to Our Senses*, Elliot Ackerman's *Waiting for Eden*, and Nico Walker's *Cherry*. In *Cherry*, the nameless narrator goes to the VA hospital when he is thinking about killing himself. Later he has an appointment with another doctor named Kaufmann whom he could see "for free because the government was giving him money to study on people like me."[65] Dr. Kaufmann sends him to a drug counselor at the local hospital who rubs him the wrong way and thinks that he is a liar:

He asked me what I was seeing Dr. Kaufmann for. I said I thought I was seeing Dr. Kaufmann for PTSD and he asked what could I have PTSD from and I said I'd been in Iraq. He asked me when. I said I'd got there in '05 and left in '06. He said the war had been over by then. So I left because I couldn't stay there.[66]

The simple staccato of Walker's sentences here highlights the gravity of the interaction. The narrator, who earlier admits, "I was pretty fucked in the head, and I was being a sad crazy fuck about some horrors I'd been through," confronts a civilian doctor who immediately belittles his trauma.[67] The doctor's ignorance about the war clashes with the narrator's experience to the point that he simply leaves rather than seek treatment. His mental health remains questionable for the rest of the novel, becoming overshadowed by his drug addiction in such a way that the link between his Iraq deployment and subsequent substance abuse is always present.

Although themes of mental health, post-traumatic stress, and reintegration do feature in many veteran-authored novels, they are never the work's

CHAPTER FIVE

sole focus. In contrast, two novels by nonveterans — Roxana Robinson's *Sparta* and Cara Hoffman's *Be Safe I Love You* — depict the psychological struggles of returned veterans as they fight a losing battle against post-traumatic stress on their descent toward attempted suicide. *Sparta* opens while Conrad Farrell, a Marine Corps officer returning from Iraq, is still in the airplane en route home. Conrad's thoughts drift back and forth between where he was and where he is going: "What came into his mind was the place he had left, which was still there. He was here, descending over this place, cool, verdant, silent. The place he had left, which was still there, was arid, brown, deafening. Suffocatingly hot, heat pressed over it like a mattress. At this moment, while he was here, that place was there. But he could not hold both places in his mind at once. Trying to do so felt risky."[68] The contradiction between space and place, emphasized further by the airplane that exists somewhere in between, sets up the struggle throughout the novel between the person Conrad feels he once was and the person he feels he is now. The sudden change of landscape and place is a jarring transition, something that veterans have spoken about since Vietnam. Trapped in the flying machine that carries him between points, Conrad "couldn't imagine what lay ahead: civilian life seemed unthinkable. He couldn't remember what it was like" while at the same time "he didn't want to remember what lay behind him in Iraq. He couldn't bear the images that rose up as soon as he closed his eyes."[69] Conrad's emotional and psychological transformations begin here and remain the focal point of the rest of the novel as he struggles with what appear to be the symptoms of post-traumatic stress. No matter how hard he tries, he cannot escape the gravity of those images, whatever they may be.

Be Safe I Love You also begins in an airport. Lauren Clay, a classically trained singer who enlists in the army to support her family, returns home after a tour in Iraq burdened by a memory that she cannot shake, one of the "invisible wounds of war."[70] Like Conrad, Lauren "was back but didn't feel so far away from Iraq."[71] And, again like Conrad, she experiences the dissociate feeling of self while reflecting upon her decision to join the military in the first place: "Now it seemed like that had all happened to another girl. That mind, that decision, belonged to another girl."[72] All this before she has cleared the baggage claim.

Lauren returns home from Iraq with "no red flags" on her mandatory post-deployment health assessment; according to an army psychologist's initial

"The New Battle"

evaluation, Lauren was "a model soldier," and "had not been concussed or injured or suffered an amputation. She had not been sexually assaulted or gotten pregnant on her tour, and she had no medically unexplained symptoms."[73] In keeping with military policy at the time, Lauren had filled out a form designed to evaluate her mental health as she prepares to leave the army and transition back into the civilian world. "Based on Clay's answers on the form, Dr. Klein felt she was not at risk for major depressive disorder. She did not appear to have signs of PTSD or markers for addiction, suicide, or committing acts of domestic violence. Klein scheduled an in-office meeting to discuss factors related to combat and operational stress: normal stuff, expected issues for returning service members."[74] Hoffman uses this scene to contrast Lauren's lack of physical injuries with the moral injury she has sustained for having killed civilians, a plot point withheld until much later in the novel. As Dr. Klein realizes that she made a mistake releasing Lauren so quickly, she thinks that "contrary to the folk wisdom of families and spouses and others who never make it down range, home is not always the safest place for a returning warrior."[75]

Robinson and Hoffman each find ways to have their characters reflect on their own transformation, ways in which they no longer feel like the people they once were. Neither Lauren nor Conrad recognize themselves, either in the mirror or in pictures taken before their combat deployments. In both novels, the narrative structure reveals bits and pieces of their experiences in Iraq and does so only after beginning their stories immediately upon arriving home. What one might assume should be a moment of joyous celebration and relief upon returning from war is, for both characters, only disorienting.

In Sparta, Conrad's inability to separate himself from his military identity contributes to his reintegration challenges. He keeps in touch with his former marines and fellow officers via email, unable to move on or disconnect completely from his former life. Corporal Anderson, one of the squad leaders who had been under Conrad's command, jokes about reenlisting because "in a weird way I miss the big sandbox."[76] Conrad then thinks "he didn't like the thought that this war had changed men inside, twisted them somehow so they couldn't fit back home. The joke wasn't a good sign."[77] Not only does Conrad correspond with the men he served with via email, he "check[s] the military blogs" every day, which were "news from his tribe, living filaments

CHAPTER FIVE

connecting him to the life he had known."[78] This practice is echoed in Phil Klay's story "Unless It's a Sucking Chest Wound," where the protagonist frequently checks the internet for updated lists of soldiers killed in action. As the novel progresses, Conrad's mental state deteriorates further; he begins taking sleeping pills and, like so many veterans in contemporary war fiction, drinks alcohol to numb himself at night and keep the memories of war at bay. He becomes suicidal, and he learns that Anderson, his former soldier, actually does commit suicide after a long foreshadowing process.

In *Be Safe I Love You*, Lauren is unable to cope with the guilt that comes from having killed three innocent Iraqi civilians and losing one of her own soldiers in the same incident. Like Conrad, Lauren feels herself as apart from the society to which she has returned, though her voice comes across more cynically about the war:

> She was not living side by side with the rest of them anymore. . . . She could see what people were thinking and what they were going to say before they said it. She'd been like this before she left for Iraq, but now it was excruciating the way she knew every little thing that would happen. The way she could see people thinking things about her they wouldn't say. *The filthiest secret of all is hiding in plain sight all over the world; they put up monuments to it and have parades.* But when it's just you, just one person alone in the same room with them, they stare, watch you like you'll do something wrong now. Because deep down they knew you were doing something wrong in the first place. All that training was not for rescuing kittens from trees.[79] [emphasis added]

That "filthy secret" may be about the divide between those who sign up to kill and those who stay behind, that war is inherently about killing other human beings and no amount of glorification will remove that stain from the memories of those who wore the uniform. The tone here is far angrier and sharper than, for example, Kristin Hannah's *Home Front*, which acknowledges the psychological toll of coming home from war while brushing aside the morality of participation. Even Conrad Farrell's father tells his son, "It looks as though you feel bad about something . . . but everything you've done you should feel proud of."[80] There is no pride for Lauren, though, who looks at her fellow citizens and imagines that "deep down they knew you were doing something wrong in the first place," recognizing that military

"The New Battle"

training is for war and killing other human beings, "not for rescuing kittens from trees."

Without anything positive to take from her experience and ground her in her new reality, Lauren turns toward the darkness. She hallucinates images of the family dog who died shortly before she came home from Iraq. Daryl, a fellow soldier whose existence provides her with a driving force and mission to go see him, is revealed to have been killed in action. Lauren only comes to grips with that reality after driving up to Daryl's house and meeting his wife. This takes her to the breaking point, leading her to the conclusion that she never really returned home at all:

> She looked away from him [Danny], watched to see if Sebastian [the dog] was still in the car. She knew why only she could see him. She knew why she had believed Daryl was home too. She knew what she was. A ghost and her dog, but somehow she'd forgotten that she had not returned at all. The woman she was supposed to be, was meant to be, would have been, could never exist at all now, and she was stuck dragging around this ruined version of herself. She owed it to the memory of her real self to get rid of this doppelgänger that she was trapped inside, some false and foreign shadow that was no more alive than the dog.[81]

She remembers that "the plan had always been to join Daryl and she had managed to forget what that really meant. But she would not forget again."[82] In seeking to "get rid of this doppelgänger that she was trapped inside," she comes up with a plan to end her own life.

In the end, though, the suicide attempts in both novels are thwarted by the protagonists' younger brothers. In Lauren's case, her brother Danny literally saves her life from hypothermia in the cold Canadian snow, a symbolic reversal of Lauren's own protective instincts. For Conrad, a confrontation with his younger brother Ollie reveals his intent to commit suicide, and although the resolution does not feel satisfying given how much difficulty Conrad has experienced throughout the novel, he nonetheless fights away his demons and appears to be making progress at the end. The same goes for Lauren, who is given a second chance to attend a prestigious music school. In both novels we are given a picture of traumatized veterans who struggle to deal with their experiences in the war. Guilt and memory drive them close to taking their own lives, yet they are both pulled back from the brink at the last minute and given a second chance at redemption.

What does it mean that both *Sparta* and *Be Safe I Love You* end with positive, if somewhat hesitant endings? Both portray protagonists who joined the military out of a sense of obligation only to return with emotional damage that drives them to suicide. Conrad Farrell and Lauren Clay each come home feeling as though they are no longer the same people as when they left. They both are dealing with some form of post-traumatic stress, an inability to separate themselves from their lives in uniform, and are initially unable to reintegrate and resume their former lives. Both suffer from moral injury after having seen or caused the deaths of innocent civilians. Both slowly tumble toward attempted suicide, though from a chronological perspective Lauren's downward spiral occurs much sooner than Conrad's.

The sad truth is that veterans who have taken their own lives cannot tell their stories, and it is within this space that many contemporary fiction writers attempt to extract meaning and understanding by creating characters who survive their post-deployment battles. The psychological stress of reintegration presents a perfect storm of conflict that many nonveteran authors of contemporary war fiction have found irresistible. Conrad Farrell and Lauren Clay are just two examples of veterans struggling with post-traumatic stress, and, at least in Clay's case, there are heavy undertones of the other recurring theme in fiction about the home front: moral injury.

Moral Injury as a Reaction to Lack of Consequences

There is a distinction between post-traumatic stress disorder—a physiological response to intense fear and relived traumatic experience—and moral injury, which is more like an array of complex feelings in search of a simple remedy that does not exist, what the psychologist Jonathan Shay called a "betrayal of 'what's right'" and journalist David Wood calls a "bruise on the soul."[83] Distinct from the novels that depict soldiers struggling to readjust to life in the civilian world described in the previous section, a large group of contemporary works are actually exploring the narrative contours of moral injury. Wood writes: "The symptoms can be similar to those of PTSD: anxiety, depression, sleeplessness, anger. But sorrow, remorse, grief, shame, bitterness, and moral confusion—*What is right?*—signal moral injury, while

"The New Battle"

flashbacks, loss of memory, fear, and a startle complex seem to character-ize PTSD."[84] Moral injury plays a prominent role within the context of so many reintegration narratives in contemporary war fiction. Soldiers who have been to war return home burdened by the weight of their experiences, feeling a sense of remorse or guilt that they find difficult to articulate. These feelings are worsened by a perceived lack of social and societal consequences for what many characters believe to be their own unforgivable actions.

The effect of the American cultural pendulum swing with respect to the reception and treatment of returning war veterans between Vietnam and the wars in Iraq and Afghanistan—from impersonal vilification to casual veneration—has created a social environment in which characters who committed horrible acts of violence seek condemnation from their fellow citizens but find only empty patriotic platitudes. This form of a home front narrative is prominent in a number of contemporary war novels, but plays the most important role in army veteran Kevin Powers's *The Yellow Birds* (2012) and nonveteran Stephen Markley's *Ohio* (2018).

Bearing the emotional weight of his secret complicity in a fellow soldier's death and the murder of an Iraqi civilian, John Bartle in *The Yellow Birds* struggles to reconnect with his friends back home. He hangs back, unable to even muster much of a greeting. He imagines what he would say to them if they asked how he was: "I feel like I'm being eaten from the inside out and I can't tell anyone what's going on because everyone is so grateful to me all the time and I'll feel like I'm ungrateful or something. Or like I'll give away that I don't deserve anyone's gratitude and really they should all hate me for what I've done but everyone loves me for it and it's driving me crazy."[85] Bartle's inability to share the burden of his actions with people who would prefer to give him a hero's welcome manifests itself in an inner monologue, a free association of his trauma, which we pick up mid-stride:

> . . . like you have bottomed out in your spirit but yet a deeper hole is being dug because everybody is so fucking happy to see you, the mur-derer, the fucking accomplice, the at-bare-minimum bearer of some fucking responsibility, and everyone wants to slap you on the back and you start to want to burn the whole goddamn country down, you want to burn every goddamn yellow ribbon in sight, and you can't explain it but it's just, like, Fuck you, but then you signed up to go so

CHAPTER FIVE

it's all your fault, really, because you went on purpose, so you are in the end doubly fucked. . . .[86]

Powers is touching on multiple themes in this passage. Bartle's moral injury and guilt about his complicity in his fellow soldier's death (as well as the murder of an Iraqi civilian witness) is made worse by the patriotic culture to which he returns, a culture that would prefer to praise him for serving without probing the depths of what that service entailed. Like Billy Lynn, who "wishes just once that somebody would call him baby-killer," Bartle seeks some kind of reprimand, an admonishment that acknowledges his heinous actions. Instead, everyone is happy to see him and, implicitly, unconcerned with whatever he did overseas.

Bartle's anger at a society that prefers yellow ribbons and backslaps to moral consequences goes both ways, he realizes. His recognition that his own moral authority rests on shaky ground comes with understanding that he "went on purpose," that he volunteered of his own free will. A draftee could conceivably pin his actions on the whims of a mechanical selection process, but not someone who raised his hand and swore an oath without having been forced to do so. So, in Bartle's own words, he is "doubly fucked."

Bartle isn't the only veteran whose moral injury stems at least partially from society's indifference to his crimes. In Stephen Markley's dark and unflinching novel *Ohio*, the wars in Iraq and Afghanistan mean both nothing and everything to the residents of New Canaan. The tendrils of the September 11, 2001, terrorist attacks — overwhelming the airwaves on an otherwise ordinary Tuesday of the ensemble of characters' junior year in high school — reach into each of their hearts and grab hold of some small piece of their essence, whether they realize it or not.

The war takes the most personal toll on Dan Eaton, another son of New Canaan who carries on the family tradition (his father was a helicopter door gunner in Vietnam) and enlists after high school. Two tours in Iraq and one in Afghanistan later, he returns home on the same fateful night as the other characters, having lost an eye as well as his own sense of moral dignity. Dan can't shake the guilt he has for what he did in the war. He goes to visit Hailey, his high school flame, where she is a nurse caring for Mrs. Bingham, their favorite high school history teacher. Despite Mrs. Bingham's failing health, she recognizes Dan as a former student and tells him how proud she is of him and "all of you who served."[87] She even links Dan's military service to her husband's, who was "headed to the Pacific when Harry Truman dropped the two atom bombs. I always said, you can mourn the devastation, you can mourn all the loss, but I would still thank him for it to this day. That kept my man out of combat, so he could come home and meet me."[88] (This is Paul Fussell's controversial moral argument in *Thank God for the Atom Bomb*).[89] Mrs. Bingham continues and tells Dan, "I had you pegged for some kind of hero back when you were in my class. You were a good, decent boy on his way to a good, decent man."[90] These are the words that Dan has trouble stomaching:

> How he'd come to hate this part of it: the gulf between how people thought of him and how he felt about what he'd done. It brought all the dread back in one vivid constellation: Wiman, his lip pregnant with dip, as he threw an old man to the ground and shattered his arm; Daniel Imana grabbing an ANA soldier and forcing him through a door, telling him to get the fuck in there because these men were their human shields, and some booby trap bomb ripped this guy's entire chest out; backing over an Afghan hut in an MRAP and later finding a whole family inside. What happened after their Humvee was hit on Highway 1, and he crawled out with his M4 ready. He could put that stuff away better than most—except when people got starry-eyed and dreamy about, as Homer put it, where men win glory.[91]

Each of these images contributes something to Dan's moral injury, and his time back home is punctured by memories of his combat tours; they slip in and out of the present tense, either on deliberate recall or as uninvited guests to his thoughts. His personal trauma comes back in memory as well, and we learn the source of his deepest guilt: after the explosion that takes his eye, Dan shoots and kills what he thinks might be a triggerman for the bomb but turns out to be a teenager with a cell phone. Then, for reasons he can neither remember nor explain, he fires his rifle on a crowd of bystanders—including children—and likely also fires the shot that incapacitates his squadmate and leaves him invalided. Like John Bartle in *The Yellow Birds*, Dan's trauma is made worse by the lack of consequences for his actions, which arguably constitute a war crime. "A part of you is sickly

CHAPTER FIVE

impressed with how the enemy orchestrated all this," he thinks to himself. "They got you good this time. You figure your life is over, but the investigation will clear you easily."[92] Dan, in essence, gets away with murder.

The coda to Dan's story comes later, four years after the main storyline set in 2013. Dan is in prison, "serving a year for felony assault after beating a man in a grocery store parking lot."[93] He pleads guilty but is granted a lenient sentence in light of his military service. This is something that "Dan didn't feel he deserved."

> What he'd done in the wars? Yeah, that didn't go unnoticed by God. It required payback. *Depression, PTSD, self-blame,* these were buzzwords, he decided, jargon to describe an ancient human hurt written in the bones, sung in the sinews of muscle, ground out in the anamnesis of cells. And yet Danny still had love in him, which is a kind of bravery.[94]

Redemption may be impossible for either character; they live in an American society that casually lumps their war crimes together with the admirable service of the average veteran, a society that seems generally unwilling to distinguish between the two. Where Bartle ends up in jail for his actions in Iraq, Eaton's prison sentence comes as a result of an unrelated crime for which he was only lightly punished. For Bartle, justice comes from within the military system in the form of an officer from the Criminal Investigation Division at his doorstep on the wisps of a rumor, "the underlying truth of the story long since skewed by the variety of a few boys' memories."[95] Dan's only expectation of justice is a half-hearted gesture toward religion, a belief that his actions "didn't go unnoticed by God" and that his subsequent psychological struggles are all a form of "payback" that he desires as a form of absolution. American society has relieved them both of the burden of responsibility for their actions by refusing to punish them for committing acts that were objectively illegal and morally wrong. The primary form of punishment, it seems, is living with the memory of their experiences.

CHAPTER SIX

"The Other Side of COIN"

Counterinsurgency and the Ethics of Memory

The story of the Vietnam War, as told by most of the American veterans who served there, was almost universally what it was like to be in Vietnam as an American combatant. The Vietnamese people, according to a 1985 conference on the Vietnam experience in American literature, were "the great lost fact of the war."[1] American veteran-authors, preoccupied with trying to understand the war for themselves, had little room in their literary works for the people among whom the war was fought, a "cultural narcissism [that] only reflects the way in which Americans conducted the war itself."[2] These veterans wrote novels about American soldiers fighting a physically demanding and morally confusing battle on behalf of an ungrateful host nation, against an unseen enemy, and without the support of their fellow citizens back home. The Vietnamese themselves are hardly anywhere to be found except as shallow caricatures who merely play a supporting role to the Americans' tragedy.

Such one-dimensional narratives began to lose currency in the late 1980s as globalization and cosmopolitanism encouraged a more multicultural approach to literature. Caren Irr sees the influence of globalization in the emergence of the "world novel" or "geopolitical novel" as distinct literary genres that seek to "make global conditions newly legible to American readers."[3] Cyrus Patell has written about the influence of cosmopolitanism on literature, noting that "cosmopolitanism is best understood . . . as a structure of thought, a perspective that embraces difference and promotes the bridging of cultural gaps."[4] These developments within the literary field challenged many of the dominant cultural narratives in favor of what Patell calls an "emergent literature."[5]

War fiction remained a different animal, though, a subgenre of literary fiction with its own conventions and traditions dating back to the 1920s. Whatever multicultural trends were doing to the rest of American literature

137

in the 1970s and 1980s, war novels resisted. Part of this can be understood as a byproduct of translating the soldier's experience into fiction. As agents of state-sanctioned violence, veterans are the least likely to be pluralistic in their thinking; in many ways they are trained to view the enemy as an Other as part of a dehumanization process that makes killing them less morally questionable, at least in the heat of battle. Jennifer Haytock points to this as a partial explanation for why "the American war story tradition tends to reify the individual soldier's experience over a broader representation of the causes and consequences of violent conflict."[6] So, as other writers were expanding their cultural horizons throughout the 1980s, Vietnam veterans were generally fashioning the materials of their own experience into literary representations that ignored other perspectives.

This has not been the case for contemporary war novels; the evolution of American civil-military relations after Vietnam combined with the tenets of counterinsurgency (often abbreviated as COIN) doctrine have influenced the kinds of characters presented in literary representations of the wars. Many volunteer veteran-authors, trained within a military institution that came to see cultural awareness as a critical component of operational success in Iraq and Afghanistan, have employed narrative strategies designed to introduce a greater degree of moral complexity into their works by rendering the consequences of these conflicts as seen from a non-American point of view. Not only does this approach encourage the reader to empathize with these characters, it enables a more critical assessment of the American involvement in foreign conflicts while also downplaying the authority of the American veteran's experience as central to understanding them.

Critical assessments of contemporary war fiction have been divided on the question of how well the genre has moved beyond American-centric perspectives. Sam Sacks argues that the overarching message of contemporary war fiction is that "the soldier's consciousness is the field of battle."[7] Sacks also links what he sees as similarities between these works to the prevalence of MFA programs: "Nearly all recent war writing has been cultivated in the hothouse of creative-writing programs. No wonder so much of it looks alike." Joseph Darda also addresses the influence of creative writing programs but from a racial perspective, arguing that MFA programs have fed on the experience of a predominantly white male sample of veteran-authors whose stories reinforce a cultural narrative that privileges whiteness as the cultural

"The Other Side of COIN"

center while marginalizing other perspectives.[8] Darda's work builds on Roy Scranton's concept of the "trauma hero," a concept derived at least partially from the perspective that "we allow the psychological suffering endured by those we sent to kill for us displace and erase the innocents killed in our name."[9] That erasure implicitly elevates the American soldier as the true subject of contemporary works of war literature, works that "may portray a loss of innocence that makes the dirty war in Iraq palatable as an individual tragedy, but they only do so by obscuring the connection between American audiences and the millions of Iraqi lives destroyed or shattered since 2003."[10] Each of these assessments contains an implicit critique that contemporary war fiction has failed to move beyond the American soldier's perspective and consider the broader implications of war and conflict through the lens of literary fiction.

In contrast to these views, other scholars have noted a greater and more empathetic focus on other perspectives in contemporary war fiction. Maureen Ryan observes that "the narratives of America's most recent wars include unprecedented observation of, and often unusual respect for, the local nationals (allies and enemies, civilians and combatants) who are thrust into the conflict."[11] Similarly, Jennifer Haytock argues that the multivoiced war novels that include non-American perspectives "disrupt the primacy of the trauma hero narrative," "shift the authority to define values and interpret events away from American soldiers," and "decenter American experiences, link soldiers' voices to those of the other, and open up the question of who matters in war to include civilians, refugees, and other noncombatants."[12] Haytock contextualizes these formal changes alongside the development of multiculturalism—the willingness to embrace and empathize the traditional "Other" places contemporary war writers firmly within modern multicultural trends but in opposition to the vast majority of literary works written about previous conflicts.[13] Brian J. Williams examines the effects of globalization on American war narratives, focusing specifically on what he calls anatopism, or "the presence of items that seem spatially out of place, as foreign to their location as anachronisms are foreign to their times."[14] He argues that these anatopisms disrupt the soldiers' othering of foreign landscapes by confronting them with the familiar objects of home, encouraging them to form more empathetic connections that "are integrally tied to a changing view of the landscape, because by destabilizing the reductive divide between the war and the home front, the combatant comes to locate himself within the perspective of the Other, envisioning his own potential responses to war in a familiar place."[15]

In this chapter, I will argue that critics such as Sacks, Darda, and Scranton have overlooked the trends identified by Ryan, Haytock, and Williams, but my explanation differs in that I draw a link between the civil-military gap, counterinsurgency doctrine, and the dispersion of authority discussed in the previous two chapters. While it's true that not every work, whether authored by a veteran or civilian, embraces a more multicultural narrative form of expression, such critiques miss the empirical trend that veteran-authors of contemporary war novels include well-developed non-American characters (often written from their point of view) at a far higher rate than the writers of Vietnam War novels. In my view, globalization and multicultural trends alone are not sufficient to account for these changes in perspective. Just as the civil-military gap and the emphasis of counterinsurgency doctrine on the avoidance of violence led to a narrative shift from the combat zone to the home front, the counterinsurgency doctrine employed in Iraq and Afghanistan ensured that cultural empathy and awareness would become an integral component of the wartime experience. Veterans seeking to communicate a more inclusive view of that experience to an unburdened civilian population have thus adopted narrative strategies that encourage readers to empathize with characters who are not American.

Veteran-authors who choose to write from a non-American point of view in their novels also subvert the expectation of authority ascribed to their personal experience, breaking with the autobiographical approaches typical of the early phases of a fictional response to a conflict as described in chapter 4. These writers present characters who are unlike themselves and cannot be confused with the author, which challenges the reader's assumption of autobiography in such works. As a professional strategy for a writer looking to enhance their position within the literary field, the conversion of personal experience into a form of cultural capital—what Mark McGurl refers to as "self-commodification"—makes sense strategically.[16] Writing from the perspective of the Other, even when placed next to an autobiographical character, upsets this expectation.

In chapter 4, we examined the idea of authenticity and narrative authority

"The Other Side of COIN"

as it pertained to war fiction authorship. The question boiled down to *who* was writing stories about American conflicts and how that had changed in response to the all-volunteer force. In that case, veteran-authors explicitly ceded their authority via external sources, arguing in op-eds and other secondary texts that personal experience was not the only route to an authentic war story. In chapter 5, we saw how veteran-authors implicitly ceded their authority by writing about the psychological and moral issues on the domestic home front rather than the experience of combat. In this chapter, our focus shifts to the characters of veteran-authored war novels. This is a different kind of dispersion of authority, one by which the veteran-author cedes narrative perspective to another, non-American voice. As acts of communicative memory intended for American audiences largely disconnected from the wars, these novels seek to portray the full range of the wars' consequences.

All five of the authors considered in this chapter served in the American armed forces and deployed to combat zones in Iraq and Afghanistan.[17] Although previous chapters examined works by nonveteran as well as veteran authors, this chapter focuses primarily on the veteran authors for the simple reason that their works, as a group, tend to include these non-American focalizers far more often than nonveterans. There are some exceptions, notably Helen Benedict's *Sand Queen*, half of which is written from the perspective of a young Iraqi woman seeking information about her father and brother who were snatched in the night and sent to an American prison camp for unknown reasons.[18] Of the seven narrators in Joydeep Roy-Bhattacharya's *The Watch*, two are Afghan. Masha Hamilton takes a similar approach in *What Changes Everything*, which includes one Afghan point of view character among an ensemble of five first-person narrators. The second part of Lisa Halliday's *Asymmetry* tells the story of an Iraqi-American man detained at Heathrow Airport en route to find his missing brother in Sulaymaniyah, Iraq. Katey Schulz's short story collection *Flashes of War* includes several stories from the perspective of Iraqis. Overall, though, the narrative strategies of veteran-authors go into far greater depth than nonveterans when it comes to non-American perspectives.[19]

Beginning with a brief assessment of the American fictional response to Vietnam and its exclusion of non-American perspectives from the war's memory, this chapter then reveals how the United States military's approach

141

CHAPTER SIX

to counterinsurgency in Iraq and Afghanistan ushered in a more complex ethics of literary representation that sought formal expression in fiction through the inclusion of non-American characters and points of view.

The "Agonized Solipsism" of Vietnam War Novels

Critical assessments of Vietnam War fiction uniformly identify a recurring formal structure in the literary representations of the war that upholds the primacy of the American perspective.[20] Veteran-authored works tended to focus on the "anguish experienced by the individual American combatant."[21] Vietnamese characters in these novels, if they appeared at all, were flat, one-dimensional, and, from a narratological perspective, rarely written as focalizers. Deployed soldiers' slang and rhetoric—from racial slurs aimed at the people to calling the landscape "Indian Country"—encouraged an othering of the Vietnamese people that found its way into fiction. Literary critics as early as 1980 had observed an undercurrent of cultural bias against other races in published novels about the war that, while not exactly new in the American context, nonetheless had the effect of excluding the Vietnamese from the narrative. "No novelist seems yet to have been willing to confront, directly, the realities of the war, or to have considered it, at least in part, from the Vietnamese point of view—in terms of their suffering rather than ours," as one critic wrote.[22] The cultural awareness needed to think and write that way would have been crowded out by what another literary scholar referred to as "the egregious racism that marked the American presence in Vietnam," a racism that, in his view, is present in most of the novels written about the war:

> We rarely find a fully-realized sympathetic Vietnamese character. Often they exist merely as malign abstractions. In many novels they are presented as dirty, smelly, self-serving, treacherous cowards who don't dare to come out in the open and fight. They're often presented as mere stick figures that place no value on life and speak a stupid-sounding inscrutable language. The narrative voice of the realist novel is usually expressed exclusively from the American point of view.[23]

The attitude toward the "treacherous cowards" who fought a guerrilla war rather than confront American firepower directly merged with characteriza-

142

"The Other Side of COIN"

tions of the local civilian populations, many of whom were eventually considered hostile by default with no consideration for the pressure they would have been under by both the American military and the North Vietnamese or Viet Cong. The differences between the offensive military operations in search of an organized enemy—one that could be fought and killed in tactical battles for control of key terrain—and the occupational nature of the conflict that put American soldiers in close contact with the Vietnamese population led to a kind of narrative tension vying for the spotlight in later fictional representations. Thomas Myers refers to this as the "sequential nature of the war" as well as a "unique historical simultaneity" that "raised narrative problems for the novelists" trying to make sense of "the kind of cultural clash and confusion that offered stories at least as significant as those offered by the military operations."[24] Yet these stories are typically ignored in the majority of fictional works about the war. Traditional military operations—the patrol, the ambush, the attack—take precedence over interacting with and understanding either the enemy or the local population. What little is seen of the enemy in these novels is usually just enough to reinforce the American sense that they simply won't come out and fight in the open as they "should."

The veteran-author's near obsession with his own experience in combat led to a collection of literary works about the Vietnam War that barely mention the Vietnamese. These writers' insufficient cultural sensibility led to what Ross McGregor referred to as the "agonized solipsism of [the] American response," a literature that comes across as "self-absorbed and introspective."[25] Reading imaginative representations about Vietnam leads one to recognize a fundamental disconnect between the reality of who was most harmed by the war and the American-authored novels that followed. McGregor, writing in 1990, sums up the works published to that point as "a narcissistic yet introspective literature in which the portrayal of Vietnam is dominated by the question of what it is to be American."[26] The suffering of the Vietnamese people is either minimized or ignored altogether, and the criticism of most veteran-authors seems aimed at the military institution that deemed their presence in Vietnam necessary to begin with.[27]

What these works lacked was, in a word, empathy. McGregor points out that "American disenchantment with the war is seldom expressed through empathy with the Vietnamese," with veteran-authors instead choosing to vent their frustration and anger on cynical portrayals of the military establishment.[28] Kalí Tal, another literary critic writing in 1990, even goes as far as to say that "the loss of the ability to empathize with or care deeply about other people is a theme in all novels by Vietnam veterans. The conditions of combat demand that the soldier renounce empathy in order to survive."[29] Tal's critique focuses specifically on images of women in veteran-authored novels about Vietnam, arguing that "the combat veteran generates female characters that represent the level of his own alienation. Both Asian and American women appear on the pages of novels by Vietnam veterans, but Asian women compose the most extreme category of objectified images."[30] Her article goes through all the ways that Vietnam War veterans create female characters who are nothing more than a projection of the soldier's objectified fantasy, especially as it pertains to women of another race.

Later works published about the war, foremost among them Elizabeth Scarborough's *The Healer's War* (1988) and Robert Olen Butler's Pulitzer Prize–winning short story collection *A Good Scent from a Strange Mountain* (1993), did seek a more empathetic portrayal of the Vietnamese people, but they were the exceptions that prove the rule. Scarborough served in Vietnam as an army nurse, and her experience forms the basis of a novel that blends the gritty realism of the war zone with an element of science fiction and fantasy that gives the story more symbolic depth. In a pivotal moment, Scarborough creates sympathy for the Vietnamese by showing the many ways in which they have suffered at the hands of the Americans as well as their own people. At the same time, she depicts a graphic scene where the Viet Cong murder women, children, and the elderly in a village that had (presumably) helped the Americans or the South Vietnamese armed forces. The scene is brutal and underscores the difficult situation that the local people faced, torn between two warring sides and punished for choosing the wrong one at the wrong time.

Butler, who had learned to speak Vietnamese as part of his training as a counterintelligence agent and translator with the US Army, wrote *A Good Scent from a Strange Mountain* entirely from the perspectives of various Vietnamese immigrants living in Louisiana. In one story, "The American Couple," the narrator—a Vietnamese woman who had won a trip to Puerto Vallarta on a game show—spots a man at her hotel wearing dog tags whom

"The Other Side of COIN"

she pegs as an army veteran. Later he's wearing a shirt that "had a map of Vietnam and the words I'VE BEEN AND I'M PROUD."[31] The narrator then

> wondered if he'd learned enough about us over there to recognize a Vietnamese when he saw one. I knew he was thinking about it, wondering if Vinh and I were from Vietnam. And after a time I began to worry just a little bit what his attitude might be. The very visible veterans I'd encountered were unpredictable. They seemed to be one extreme or the other about us. We were fascinating and long-suffering and unreal or we were sly and dangerous and unreal.[32]

By presenting this scene from the mind of a Vietnamese woman, Butler inverts the traditional American war story and forces the reader to consider how an American veteran appears from a completely unfamiliar point of view. Having the narrator comment that, in her experience, most American veterans saw the Vietnamese as "unreal" serves as an indirect attack on the cultural stereotypes hurled against the Vietnamese people by soldiers in both combat as well as the subsequent veteran-authored literary fiction. This technique — criticizing aspects of American culture through the voice of a non-American character — flew in the face of more than twenty years of American writing about the Vietnam War but would become far more common in the fictional works about Iraq and Afghanistan.

Counterinsurgency and the Ethics of Remembrance

In the one-page foreword to the army and Marine Corps field manual on counterinsurgency known as FM 3-24, Generals David Petraeus and James Amos write of the challenges facing soldiers and marines tasked with such a mission who must learn to "employ a mix of familiar combat tasks and skills more often associated with nonmilitary agencies." The manual, published to surprising fanfare in 2006,[33] was written as a guidebook for leaders who must be "culturally astute" and "ensure that their Soldiers and Marines are ready to be greeted with either a handshake or a hand grenade."[34]

The emphasis on counterinsurgency in Iraq and Afghanistan did more than shift the defining experience of the wars from combat to coming home, as seen in chapter 5; it also led to a broader recognition that war does not affect combatants alone. Developing a sense of empathy and local knowledge were deemed key ingredients to operational success — counterinsurgency doctrine and best practices encouraged a cultural competence that is generally unnecessary for so-called conventional wars fought between armed adversaries over geographic territory.[35] The counterinsurgency manual emphasizes that "cultural knowledge is essential to waging a successful counterinsurgency"[36] and that "successful conduct of COIN operations depends on thoroughly understanding the society and culture within which they are being conducted."[37] The manual's chapter titled "Intelligence in Counterinsurgency" describes in greater detail the importance of understanding the local population, broken into six categories: society, social structure, culture, language, power and authority, and interests. Even one of the leadership tenets states that leaders should "feel the pulse of the local populace, understand their motivations, and care about what they want and need. Genuine compassion and empathy for the populace provide an effective weapon against insurgents."[38] Understanding the local population among whom the war was fought, as well as those who had actively taken up arms against American and host nation military forces, thus rose to a new prominence for those who served in these conflict zones.[39]

None of this is to imply that every soldier deployed to Iraq or Afghanistan became a doctrinal expert on counterinsurgency or absorbed the intricacies of the local culture, but rather to highlight how the Department of Defense's institutional attitude affected the way soldiers were trained to think about the nature of the conflicts. Deploying units issued their soldiers handbooks that, in the spirit of cultural awareness, described important information about the local populations in Iraq or Afghanistan. Even as early as 2003 — three years before the publication of FM 3-24 — there were leaders on the ground who recognized the importance of cultural competence to their mission. John Batiste, commanding general of the 1st Infantry Division, issued his soldiers a pocket-sized, one-hundred-page "Soldier's Handbook to Iraq" that provided an overview of the Iraqi people, including their history, religion, customs, culture, language, and so on. Batiste's introduction to the manual is worth quoting in its entirety:

> During your deployment to Iraq as a member of the Big Red One
> team, you should be aware of the unique customs and courtesies of

"The Other Side of COIN"

the Iraqi people. This guide provides the basic information on Iraq's culture by offering you an overview of the country, its people and their language, as well as their lifestyle and beliefs.

The First Infantry Division deployment plays a vital role in securing the peace in support of Operation Iraqi Freedom and is pivotal to the reestablishment of a free, democratic Iraq. As a soldier of the First Infantry Division, you are an Infantryman first and a warrior always. Combined with your warrior ethos, a thorough cultural understanding of your environment is a major combat multiplier that makes you all the more lethal on the front lines in the war on terrorism.

On a daily basis you will directly or indirectly contribute to Civil Military Operations (CMO) ongoing in your area of operations. Every encounter with an Iraqi civilian is an opportunity to develop respect and trust in us as professional, educated soldiers who are committed to finishing the job we set out to accomplish. Arming you with a comprehensive knowledge of Iraq's rich and unique traditions, this guide serves as a weapon against ignorance and intolerance that deepens the divide between our forces and the free Iraqi people. My confidence in you as soldiers of this proud division will result in a solid transition of power to the Iraqi people, a safe return home, and a job well done behind us.[40]

It is worth appreciating just how astounding the tone of this document is. From the very first sentence there is an immediate link between the soldiers' combat deployment and Iraqi culture. The second paragraph reintroduces the importance of combat proficiency to the mission but again connects the "warrior ethos" to an understanding of the Iraqi people. Batiste refers to cultural understanding as a "major combat multiplier" for his soldiers that will make them all the more lethal. This metaphor is emphasized explicitly again in the final paragraph; the guidebook will "arm" the soldiers with "a weapon against ignorance and intolerance." The message of the introduction to the deploying infantry soldier is clear: understanding Iraqi culture will make you more effective.

Other units would produce similar guidebooks in the years that followed, but the incorporation of cultural awareness into pre-deployment training also found support within the army's higher echelons. In 2006, the Combat

Studies Institute, a research organization within the army's Training and Doctrine Command, published *Through the Lens of Cultural Awareness: A Primer for US Armed Forces Deploying to Arab and Middle Eastern Countries*, which served as an additional resource for individuals deploying overseas.[41] Sprinkled with case studies and conceptual frameworks for incorporating cultural awareness into tactical unit training models, the document is yet another example of how the American military institution began instilling the importance of understanding the people of these countries into the minds of deploying troops.

Scholars such as Viet Thanh Nguyen and Joseph Darda both view this approach critically, arguing that the military's emphasis on cultural awareness was not intended to create empathy between an occupying force and a local population but rather to make it easier to figure out which people were the "right" ones to label as enemies and kill without remorse. Nguyen worries that empathizing with the enemy could imply that "such a mode of empathy helps us understand our other better in order to control him (or kill him)." He also references the development of the army and Marine Corps' counterinsurgency field manual as an expression of an American fascination with domestic multiculturalism that "finds an overseas corollary via culturally sensitive warfare. In both cases, studying difference and understanding the other are instrumental; they serve the purpose of domesticating others and rendering them harmless."[42]

Darda takes an even harsher stance, arguing that one of the field manual's major theses is that "successful counterinsurgency necessitates the militarization of cultural narrative," a theme that, in his view, "resurfaces in American veteran fiction."[43] His criticism of how counterinsurgency doctrine and American war fiction intersect stems from his reading of veteran-authored literary works about Iraq and Afghanistan as designed to repackage the story of American imperialism as the story of the American soldier's struggle in the complicated operating environments of overseas conflicts. Similar to Roy Scranton's concept of the "trauma hero," which reframes war as an individual endeavor in which "the American veteran [becomes] a sympathetic victim, rather than a perpetrator, of violence,"[44] Darda sees these literary works as intended to convince a domestic population to continue supporting the American "empire of defense" through tax payments and lack of organized antiwar protests: "Counterinsurgency

"The Other Side of COIN"

theorists understand cultural narrative as an instrument for securing consent at home as well, and the vehicle for securing that domestic consent is the counterinsurgent's own story of struggle and sacrifice."[45] In this view, rather than focus on the Iraqi and Afghan civilians whose lives were upended or destroyed by American military operations, war novels encourage the American population to see the wars solely through the eyes of their fellow countrymen and women who fought there.

While Darda's analysis of contemporary American war fiction fits into the larger debate about the memory culture of war and questions of representation, his text selection causes him to miss the empirical trend that contradicts his argument. As mentioned earlier, Darda links veteran-authors' militarization of the cultural narrative to the influence of creative writing programs: "This new generation of MFA-trained veteran-writers has internalized the counterinsurgent's ambition to 'craft' a narrative of white humanitarian sacrifice (counterinsurgency) and Muslim backwardness (insurgency) that reveals whiteness as an enduring condition for the execution of defense."[46] This assessment is not supported by the actual content of these novels or the other veteran-authored works I consider in this chapter, many of which go to great lengths to depict complex, round Muslim characters. Further, his author selection (Kevin Powers, Phil Klay, and Matt Gallagher) is anything but representative of the fictional response to Iraq and Afghanistan as a whole—as we have seen, the totality of contemporary works includes far more nonveterans and women authors. Rather than reframing the conflicts entirely in terms of their American participants, many veteran-authors have deliberately challenged the counterinsurgent's "own story of struggle and sacrifice" by subordinating it to the stories of others, from local nationals caught in the crossfire to enemy combatants.

As acts of communicative and collective memory, war novels serve as objects of cultural importance. The battle for the memory of a war is fought on the field of cultural production, and an author's choice of protagonist is an important revealed preference for what they believe is worth remembering. Selecting a novel's protagonist is one of the most fundamental narrative choices an author will make when writing a novel. That character is granted an authoritative voice and, in a sense, exercises control over the resulting story. Viet Thanh Nguyen refers to this choice as an "ethics" of remembrance in his thought-provoking study of the link between cultural memory and cultural production, *Nothing Ever Dies: Vietnam and the Memory of War* (2016).

Nguyen describes three ethical modes in which fictional representations of war operate: the ethics of remembering one's own (in other words, one's own side of the conflict), the ethics of remembering others, and the ethics of recognition. Remembering one's own is, in Nguyen's view, the "simplest and most explicitly conservative mode [in which] we remember our humanity and the inhumanity of others, while we forget our inhumanity and the humanity of others. This is the ethical mode most conducive to war, patriotism, and jingoism, as it reduces our others to the flattest of enemies." The ethics of remembering others, in contrast, is "more complex" and "operates in two registers, the liberal one where we remember our humanity and the radical one where we remember our inhumanity." Nguyen cautions that this mode tends to devolve toward a reduction of the Other to "an object of our seemingly well-intended pity" by treating them as "only capable of being killed."[47] Nguyen's work is a quest for a "just memory," one that combines the propensity to remember one's own with remembering others to form a more complete recognition of both our, and the other's, capacity to inflict harm and cause violence. "When we recognize our capacity to do harm," Nguyen writes, "we can reconcile with others who we feel have hurt us. This ethics of recognition might be more of an antidote to war and conflict than remembering others, for if we recognize that we can do damage, then perhaps we would go to war less readily and be more open to reconciliation in its aftermath."[48]

Nguyen's approach to the ethics of representation gives us a new way to analyze war fiction, a taxonomy that compares novels according to the kinds of characters depicted in them. The "agonized solipsism" of Vietnam War novels is another way of saying that these novels were overwhelmingly written within the ethics of remembering one's own, as they focus on the depiction of American soldiers while marginalizing others. Novels that include non-American voices may then fall into a broader ethics of representation, one that rejects a purely national perspective as adequate to understand the nature of the conflict.

The inclusion of cultural awareness as an important component of the American-led counterinsurgency operations in Iraq and Afghanistan thus seems to lend itself to an ethics of representation that is more willing to

"The Other Side of COIN"

consider other perspectives. The binary oppositions of "us versus them" and "ally versus enemy" become unstable in a conflict where operational success depends, at least to some extent, on cultural awareness and sensibility. Even if one accepts the criticism that counterinsurgency doctrine implies that cultural knowledge and understanding are valuable only as ways of increasing military effectiveness via killing the "right" people, the "militarization of cultural narrative" is not a proper way to describe the contemporary war novels that include round, complex non-American characters. As I will argue, American veteran-authors writing from the perspective of non-American characters do so as a way to communicate a different kind of experience to the civilian population, an experience that implicitly dethrones the American perspective from the pedestal of narrative centrality.

The Authority of Character:
Non-American Focalizers in Contemporary War Novels

Many veteran-authors of Iraq and Afghanistan have rejected the ethics of remembering one's own in favor of a broader recognition of the importance of other perspectives, reducing the authority of "the soldier's tale" and featuring the voices of characters who have been traditionally flattened or ignored within the American war fiction genre. Having served as part of a counterinsurgent force and with a consciousness of the civil-military gap back home, they cede the authority of the American soldier's perspective in order to present a more holistic view of the wars for an American readership that has become separated from the wars' consequences. They accomplish this through formal narrative structures that incorporate non-American characters as well as by criticizing American foreign policy and Americans' lack of cultural awareness through the eyes of these characters. Including non-American points of view and characters in their novels, or writing from a non-American perspective entirely, disrupts the authority and primacy of the American narrative. Having these characters voice criticism of American interventionist foreign policy and Americans' lack of awareness for other nations' culture heightens the effect and highlights the discrepancy. Iraqi and Afghan characters suffer as a result of the American presence in their countries; seeing this directly from their point of view flips the traditional script of the American liberation narrative and forces the reader to consider what it means that the Americans are thought of as the invaders rather than liberators. The questionable American decision to invade Iraq — treated indirectly as subtext in most contemporary war novels — becomes even more immediate when criticized from the voices of those who experienced its effects firsthand.

Here I consider five novels written by veterans of the wars in Iraq and Afghanistan that include at least one non-American point of view character: Benjamin Buchholz's *One Hundred and One Nights* (2011), Michael Pitre's *Fives and Twenty-Fives* (2014), Elliot Ackerman's *Green on Blue* (2015), Roy Scranton's *War Porn* (2016), and Brian Van Reet's *Spoils* (2017). Each novel develops types of characters that are often excluded from American war narratives, including those who fought against them as well as the people who merely happened to live in the country where the wars were fought. The authors encourage the readers to see them as people with families, lives, emotions, and desires rather than as anonymous fighters or faceless bystanders. The non-American characters in these novels represent a wide range of perspectives: an Iraqi doctor who spent fifteen years in Chicago and returns after the American invasion, believing he can help make his homeland a better place; an Iraqi student who becomes an interpreter for the Americans; an Afghan teenager who joins a US-funded militia to fight the Taliban and avenge his brother; an Iraqi mathematics professor torn between his family and his work during the opening phase of the American invasion; and an Egyptian jihadist whose militant group seizes an opportunity to fight Americans in Iraq. As a narrative strategy, writing from a non-American point of view — whether as a singular narrator or one of multiple — confronts readers with the consequences of American intervention in these nations and presents an indictment of American involvement. There is a moral complexity in these works often missing from the more self-absorbed novels about the Vietnam War.

Structurally, novels such as Buchholz's *One Hundred and One Nights* and Ackerman's *Green on Blue* take this narrative approach the furthest, presenting the story from a single non-American perspective, an Iraqi doctor in Buchholz's case and an Afghan teenager in Ackerman's. Both perform a complete subversion of the veteran-author's privilege in war fiction.[49] The more imaginative and extreme approach comes from Ackerman, whose narrator has no connection to the United States except the fleeting interactions

"The Other Side of COIN"

with a special forces officer destined to play a crucial role in the story. Both novels leverage their first-person narrators to suggest a different way of understanding these conflicts that does not rely on an American viewpoint, with Ackerman's complete rejection of the American perspective and Buchholz's close approximation (his narrator lived in Chicago for fifteen years and shows signs of nostalgia for his adopted homeland).

Green on Blue offers the clearest picture of what an American war novel without Americans looks like. The novel is told entirely from the perspective of a young Afghan named Aziz whose life becomes entangled with the Americans, the Afghan National Army, and the Taliban. Aziz describes what life was like as a civilian torn between the grips of the Americans and various militant groups:

> Militants accused men of being informants and beheaded them in front of their families. Americans accused men of being militants and disappeared them in the night on helicopters. The militants fought to protect us from the Americans and the Americans fought to protect us from the militants, and being so protected, life was very dangerous.[50]

When Aziz's brother, Ali, is critically wounded in an explosion linked to a Taliban leader, he is approached by another Afghan working as a recruiter for the Special Lashkar, a trained militia unit fighting the militants. The recruiter appeals to Aziz's sense of honor (nang) and revenge (badal), two crucial tenets of the ethical code for many tribes in southern Afghanistan and Pakistan known as Pashtunwali. These concepts drive the novel's plot forward, as Aziz's journey to recapture his family's honor is only possible through revenge against those responsible for his brother's wounds. Ackerman employs the language and concepts of Pashtunwali as a way to create empathy with Aziz and encourage the reader to see the Americans as the Other of the novel.

The lone American character in the novel is a mysterious special forces operator known only as Mr. Jack, a name that comes across as more of a caricature than an individual. Ackerman unpacks the series of events that lead Aziz to kill Mr. Jack and two other Afghan warlords. Known as "green on blue" attacks (and giving the novel its title), these incidents are when members of the Afghan military or police turn their weapons on their American or coalition trainers, and they were a common occurrence throughout the last several years of the war in Afghanistan.[51] Because the gunmen are almost always killed immediately afterward, there is rarely a chance to understand what led to those final moments. Ackerman's novel, though, attempts to do exactly this while also revealing the consequences of American actions in the country.

Although Mr. Jack is the only American character to appear directly in the novel, the American presence is felt everywhere. Aziz quickly finds himself caught in a complex web of deception and self-interested profiteering on all sides. What begins as a desire to avenge his parents' deaths and brother's wounds becomes a complicated dance of loyalties in service of the war itself. Much of Ackerman's plot revolves around a plan to build an outpost for the Special Lashkar in Gomal, the border town where they (and the Americans) believe that Gazan — the Taliban leader believed responsible for a string of recent bombings, including the one in Orgun that wounded Ali — is hiding. What seems like a straightforward military need becomes the centerpiece of the war's complex reality, and Aziz slowly realizes that any hopes he might have of clean and simple revenge are lost within the war's bigger picture. Aziz is caught up in the conflict because of a desire to help his brother, a desire that others like Taqbir, the recruiter, and Sabir, the Lashkar's commander, exploit to their own advantage. They give Aziz just enough hope to keep fighting combined with just enough prodding to ensure that he does not forget the object of his revenge while falling deeper into the war's abyss. Aziz comes to understand that the Americans fund the Special Lashkar to fight the Taliban, but Sabir uses some of the money he gets from the Americans to finance Gazan's operations against his own Special Lashkar as well as the mortar attacks on Gomal. Sabir needs an enemy to strengthen himself, all done in the name of profiting from the war.

Ackerman's portrayal of this conflict from the Afghan point of view offers a cynical but realistic view of opportunism, fueling the desire to continue the war and highlighting the Americans' role in sustaining it. In a crucial scene, Aziz challenges Sabir on his own role perpetuating the conflict, noting that Sabir "kept them [the militia members] hungry and you give them just enough be controlled. Food, weapons, an enemy. I know you give all that to them." Sabir, explaining his logic for what he's doing, asks Aziz: "Are you fighting this war to end it. . . . What happens if our war ends?" "I am just

"The Other Side of COIN"

a soldier caught up in this," Aziz replies. "All are caught up in this," Sabir responds:

> The question is whether you'll be a victim or prosper in it. What justice is there for you if Gazan, who crippled your brother, prospers in peace with the Americans? What justice is there if we lose control of him and never build our outpost? Yes, there will be peace for Gomal and Gazan, but us, what of us? *The Americans will no longer need us.* How do we survive then?[52] [emphasis added]

After going with Atal, a powerful local elder, to see the American (while still clandestinely working for Sabir), Aziz asks Atal if the American "seemed upset" after their meeting. Atal says that he was "disappointed" and that Americans "have a different sense of time than us, rushing all things. This often leads to disappointment. . . . He wants his plans to move quicker than they should." Commenting on the intentional distance he is keeping between the Americans and Gazan, Atal says that "the Americans believe that if they give you something they can take everything. That makes them dangerous friends."[53]

Ultimately we come to discover that Mr. Jack's motivations are to bribe Gazan—the Taliban leader responsible for the explosion that wounded Aziz's brother—to switch sides and "provide information . . . about other Taliban and Haqqani militants." He says that he will supply Gazan's men and compensate Gazan himself for whatever intelligence he provides. Atal complains that "if Sabir builds his outpost, all there will be is war." Mr. Jack responds: "Yes, for a time . . . But with Gazan's information and militants flocking to attack a target like the outpost, we'll control much of the fighting."[54] Just as some of the Afghans, like Sabir, appear to fight in order to prosper and have a vested interest in keeping the war going, so too does it seem for the Americans in this moment.

Seizing the opportunity for his revenge, Aziz opens fire during a meeting between Mr. Jack, Gazan, and Atal that takes place inside a Toyota HiLux. Aziz comments: "I'd killed Gazan for my badal. As for Mr. Jack, *another American would surely replace him*. . . . No one would know this killing had been a green on blue" (emphasis added).[55] The conflict continues. Almost immediately, though, Aziz shifts the ultimate blame for his actions away from himself and toward the Americans:

CHAPTER SIX

But as I thought about it [the green on blue], I felt uncertain it was. I no longer wore a uniform. Still, I'd been a member of the Special Lashkar, something the Americans made. I then recalled how Commander Sabir kept Gazan in business, and how the Americans kept Commander Sabir in business. And as I thought of all the ways one could be killed in this war, and of all those who could do it, I couldn't think of a single way to die which wasn't a green on blue. The Americans had a hand in creating all of it.[56]

At its core, *Green on Blue* is a criticism of American involvement in Afghanistan and the seemingly unbreakable cycle of conflict that leaves many broken while others prosper. It is also a good example of an American veteran seeking to explore the moral implications of the war with a critical eye on the United States' role in sustaining the violence.

While *Green on Blue* explicitly rejects the ethics of remembering one's own by focusing entirely on the Afghan side of the story, other novels present a non-American character's point of view alongside that of the more conventional American perspective. Michael Pitre's *Fives and Twenty-Fives*, Roy Scranton's *War Porn*, and Brian Van Reet's *Spoils* all take this approach, inserting non-American characters' points of view into the more traditional multivoiced war novel focused on American soldiers, works such as *Three Soldiers*, *The Naked and the Dead*, *From Here to Eternity*, *Fields of Fire*, and *The 13th Valley*. Both Pitre and Van Reet include non-American characters as first-person narrators, while Scranton's novel employs the third-person limited and focalizes through several Iraqi characters.

The journey of Kateb al-Hariri in *Fives and Twenty-Fives* serves as an indictment of American involvement in Iraq as well as adding a complex, humanizing layer to a local civilian population often rendered invisible in American war fiction. Kateb, one of three focalizing characters that form the narrative structure of Pitre's novel, is an English-speaking Iraqi student who stumbles into becoming an interpreter for the Americans after trying and failing to flee Iraq's sectarian violence with his two young friends. Pitre places Kateb's story next to that of two American marines: Peter Donovan, a lieutenant in charge of a road repair platoon responsible for filling potholes left by roadside bombs, nearly all of which are booby-trapped with explosive devices; and Lester "Doc" Pleasant, the platoon's medic. Kateb

"The Other Side of COIN"

is their interpreter. Pitre tells their stories through the first-person point of view, alternating between them with short italicized sections without narration to divide them. All three narratives are intertwined, with characters appearing in each other's chapters throughout the novel. Pitre also creates two timelines, with the present tense occurring in early 2011 while the primary narrative in Iraq takes place in a sort of linear flashback through the alternating present points of view. This structure anchors the progression of the story while still placing it firmly in the past for the three protagonists. It also sets up a contrast with the before-and-after life of those involved in the main Iraq War narrative.

The narrative shifts evenly between the three characters, but the inclusion of Kateb's point of view counterbalances the typical portrait of American soldiers at war. In the novel's present timeline, Kateb has fled to Tunisia and is watching the opening salvo of the Arab Spring firsthand, while his flashback scenes reveal how he became an interpreter for the Americans. The Americans know him only as Dodge, though he eventually reveals his real name to Doc Pleasant. Unlike Donovan and Doc Pleasant, whose present tense and past tense narratives are easy to identify and whose names change only by the dropping of their military rank, Kateb exists in several simultaneous states owing to the novel's nonlinear structure. Pitre connects Kateb with the two American characters as a way to emphasize the commonality of their experience despite their differences, a revelation hinted through the alliteration of their character names (Donovan, Doc, and Dodge). And Kateb's point of view chapters place his narrative at the same level of importance as Donovan and Doc, reframing the war as something more than just the American experience.

As with *Fives and Twenty-Fives*, Roy Scranton's *War Porn* also places an Iraqi perspective alongside that of two Americans. *War Porn* is unique among the other novels in this chapter as Scranton does not write a non-American character from the first-person point of view but rather from the third-person limited with several focalizers. He weaves several Iraqi voices into the narrative, though he spends the most time with Qasim al-Zabadi, a mathematics professor teaching at a university in Baghdad. Although *War Porn*'s structure is more complicated than the other novels discussed here — the novel jumps back and forth between three primary storylines told in a nonlinear sequence — Qasim's story touches all of them.

CHAPTER SIX

Occupying the middle of the book are around one hundred pages of the March 2003 invasion of Iraq from the eyes of the Iraqis. The early part of the section shows life in Baghdad and Baqubah just before the American invasion. The characters even give a quick summary of life in Iraq from around 1990 to 2003, referencing the first Gulf War as the original disruption to their lives. They all seem to take it for granted that the Americans will come again despite the technical possibility that the government could reach an agreement before the deadline. Scranton paints an impressive and poignant picture of Iraqi life just prior to the expectation of an American attack:

> They'd chat or make phone calls, discussing this or that, what it would be like after, what it was like in the last war, what it was like during the war with Iran, what it was like before the war with Iran, what was good or bad about this CIA guy Chalabi they had on the news, or was America good or bad, or were the Americans better or worse than the British. Then the air-raid sirens would grind up or the AA would cough or something would explode and they'd all jump and run into the living room and it would start all over. It went on and off like that, off and on, all night.[57]

The Iraqis worry about safety as the bombs begin to fall. This is a good perspective of the "other" side of the invasion, a kaleidoscope of characters trying to live their lives with some semblance of normalcy under the looming threat of (American) destruction. The imaginative act paints a picture for readers who likely had never considered what that experience would have been like. There's also an undercurrent of optimism from some of the characters that imported American-style democracy may really be better than life under Saddam Hussein. One Iraqi character wonders, "Will it be worth it?" He pictures a prosperous nation, with skyscrapers and riches and Baghdad rivaling global cities like Berlin, Tokyo, New York, and London. He imagines Iraq becoming "the new economic center of the Arab world," with literature that will "flourish like flowers after the rain." Iraq and Iraqis will have freedom, the freedom to speak their minds without fear of punishment or worse. "And all we have to do is go through a little war, a little trouble."[58] That Scranton puts such optimistic but ultimately misguided hopes into the mind of an Iraqi character complicates the moral question of a war of choice and how harshly we should judge its execution given the myriad political

"The Other Side of COIN"

and military failures that followed the invasion, from the absence of weapons of mass destruction to Iraq's ultimate descent into sectarian violence and insurgency.[59] Not all of the Iraqi characters accept this hopeful view of the war's potential, of course, and Scranton also shows some of them making preparations for the insurgency that we know will follow.

Qasim's story plays out across all three of the novel's major narratives: the invasion of Iraq is told from his point of view; he then appears as an interpreter in the storyline of a junior American soldier named Wilson; and finally, in the novel's other major story about a veteran's tense appearance at a barbecue in small-town Utah, we learn that he was arrested and tortured in a detention camp. That Qasim's presence is the one constant throughout the novel suggests that, in the end, the story is really about him, perhaps as a synecdoche for all of Iraq. Qasim begins the story as a humble Iraqi civilian but is eventually treated as an enemy by American captors despite having risked his life working for them as an interpreter. He is one of the only characters in the novel who comes across as innocent, even if his choices and mistakes ultimately seal his uncertain fate as a prisoner at Abu Ghraib.

Qasim is also the most sympathetic character in the novel, a man who becomes the unfortunate victim of circumstances and choices. The American characters in the novel are naïve, sadistic, or indifferent to suffering in a way that is atypical of most American war fiction; even when these works show Americans engaged in horrific acts of violence against the enemy or local civilians, they are also shown to be victims of the circumstances that put them there in the first place. Blame is spread around to absolve the soldiers of their moral sins. In *War Porn*, however, Scranton deliberately inverts the "trauma hero" narrative so common to American war fiction — the constant use of the term "hadji" throughout Wilson's point of view chapters emphasizes the Iraqis' otherness while Qasim's chapter undercuts this with humanity.[60] The character also stands in stark contrast to the novel's representation of American soldiers, none of whom are portrayed in a positive light. And the American civilians are detached from the war carried out in their name, concerned with trivialities in their lives until Aaron, the veteran, invades their tranquil barbecue space with his personal demons.

Unlike the novels considered so far, Brian Van Reet's *Spoils* includes the only character who, from the very beginning, is an enemy of the United States, confronting the reader with an antithetical perspective to that of the

CHAPTER SIX

American soldier. Abu al-Hool is an Egyptian who had been training with the mujahideen in Afghanistan prior to the September 11, 2001, terrorist attacks. Al-Hool and his band of fighters had nothing to do with the attacks themselves but nevertheless see them as an opportunity to wage war against Americans. "We didn't sign on for this offensive," al-Hool narrates, but he recognizes the untenability of their situation: "Regardless, I suffer no illusions that our ignorance or prior restraint will mitigate what the future holds. Blood must have blood. We are Muslims training in Afghanistan, and for the Americans that will be enough. Only a fool would deny we are now enemies."[61] Van Reet's view of the response to 9/11 comes through clearly; Americans cannot (or will not) form a nuanced view of Muslims from that part of the world.

As if to make this more explicit, Van Reet grants one of Abu al-Hool's fellow mujahideen the foresight to see how the Americans will react to the attacks. Dr. Walid, a charismatic and more militant challenger to al-Hool's leadership, "had been predicting the American invasion of Iraq ever since the weeks immediately following Manhattan." The aging al-Hool reveals himself to be more conservative in his approach to fighting, and, in contrast to Walid, is surprised at the American response: "It had seemed farfetched to me at the time, and it was still hard to believe his prediction was coming correct, their forces massing steadily in Kuwait. That the Americans would be so foolish as to fulfill what I imagined were Sheikh Osama's exact wishes when he had sent those jets smashing into the towers — it seemed too easy, too simple, to trap them in this way."[62] The reference to Osama bin Laden echoes a similar passage in Scranton's *War Porn* in which one of the Iraqi characters speaks about American motivation and intention: "Listen: this has *nothing* to do with democracy. We're under attack from the Zionist crusaders because we stood up against them — because bin Laden stood up against them. It's the same as it was with Kuwait. Someone dares to stand up to America, and they're going to punish whoever they can put their hands on."[63] In both passages, the non-American characters criticize the American response to the 9/11 terrorist attacks as simpleminded and without the ideological motivation with which the war was sold to the world.[64]

In each text, the authors leverage this dramatic irony of historical hindsight to criticize the foreign policy outcome of the American invasion. Just as Dr. Walid predicts the American response to 9/11 in *Spoils*, Qasim in

"The Other Side of COIN"

Scranton's *War Porn* also senses that the Americans will become stuck in his country. While working as an interpreter for the Americans, Qasim has a conversation with Wilson in which he asks if Qasim thinks that Iraq is better now that Saddam is gone. Qasim says: "Some ways better. Other ways more bad. Instead of one Saddam, now too many Saddam. . . . You will be here a long time, I think."[65]

Qasim is innocent of any transgressions against the Americans, but that actually makes him the exception. In the other four novels, the non-American characters are, in one way or another, involved with a plan to attack American forces. Kateb, the English-speaking Iraqi student from a well-connected Sunni family in Michael Pitre's *Fives and Twenty-Fives*, becomes an interpreter for the Americans only after warning them of an impending roadside bomb attack planned by his father and brother, who have joined the resistance. Benjamin Buchholz's Iraqi-American narrator in *One Hundred and One Nights* is enlisted to attack an American convoy as a scheme to blame a rival militia group and bring them to the attention of American forces, who will drive them out. As with *Fives and Twenty-Fives*, the narrator makes known his desire to avoid actually killing any Americans in the attack. In Elliot Ackerman's *Green on Blue*, a young Afghan's journey to support his wounded brother ends with him killing an American special forces soldier inside a truck alongside two other Afghans, collateral damage in a fight for control and agency. And then there is Abu al-Hool in Brian Van Reet's *Spoils*, the only non-American character in these works who is a declared enemy of the United States, working as the leader of a terrorist cell that relocates from Afghanistan to Iraq after 9/11. Al-Hool is the only one of these characters who is ideologically motivated, but even his case resists easy categorization; Van Reet refuses to cast him as a cookie-cutter terrorist villain, instead opting to locate the origins of his ideology in the pre-9/11 era and trace his inner struggle to adapt to the younger, more extreme generation of Islamists. His hands are far from clean in the novel, but the depth of characterization does not allow the reader to imagine yet another faceless terrorist whose actions are more like a machine than a human.

What these works do is remind us that for every attack on American forces in Iraq and Afghanistan, there is a story and a person behind the bombs and bullets. None of these novels seek to excuse their characters' actions or provide them with moral justification; they bring *people* back into the

CHAPTER SIX

wars' calculus. *Green on Blue*, for example, takes an incident that would be reported in the American news as "'Insider Attack' Kills US Service Member in Afghanistan"[66]—a headline that all but erases the identity of the attacker—and completely reframes the story from the attacker's point of view. With a domestic audience in mind for their works, these veterans choose to tell a more complete story of the consequences of American intervention in Iraq and Afghanistan, leveraging the empathetic powers of fiction to channel the cultural awareness they were encouraged to cultivate as soldiers conducting counterinsurgency operations. In contrast to nearly a century of war fiction intended to capture the American soldier's experience at war, many contemporary war novels depict a more global perspective as a way to narrow the gap between those who have been there and those who have not.

CHAPTER SEVEN

"You Volunteered to Get Screwed"

*Public Trust and the Literary Representation
of the Professional Military*

The literary representation of the professional military represents a paradox of civil-military relations. Images of the American veteran in contemporary novels and short stories about the wars in Iraq and Afghanistan have been overwhelmingly negative at a time when public trust in the military as an institution remains high. Collectively, contemporary war novels paint a picture of a legion of traumatized veterans who only volunteered for military service because they had no other choice, and their trauma is a deserved consequence of volunteering in the first place. Such portrayals largely exacerbate the social estrangement that characterizes the relationship between the military and society described in chapters 4 and 5. Despite the progressive influence that the dispersion of the veteran-author's cultural authority has had on the war fiction genre — broadening its authorship and reducing the dominance of the male perspective, shifting the narrative focus from combat violence to home front reintegration, the addition of well-developed non-American characters — the literary representation of the professional military may serve to undermine the public's trust as well as any efforts to bridge the civil-military gap that so many authors seem determined to address.

The stereotypes about the professional military found in many contemporary war novels have their roots in the debates surrounding the end of the draft. When the Department of Defense began studying the possibility of ending conscription and shifting to what they would call an all-volunteer force in the late 1960s and early 1970s, there was considerable fear among policy analysts and government officials that a professional military would not reflect the demographic composition of American society. The Gates Commission, established by President Richard Nixon to advise him on options for ending the draft, had unanimously concluded that "the nation's interest will be better served by an all-volunteer force, supported by an effective standby draft, than by a mixed force of volunteers and conscripts" in early 1970.[1] But this recommendation came on the heels of a heated debate, pitting scholars and analysts from different disciplines against each other in a pitched battle, with cost-focused economists on one side and anxious sociologists on the other, wondering who would serve in a volunteer military.

The economics of an all-volunteer force were sound, but the economists had to concede that the sociologists had a point.[2] As part of their study, the Gates Commission identified a number of logical arguments against the abolition of conscription, including the possibility that "an all-volunteer force would undermine patriotism by weakening the tradition that each citizen has a moral responsibility to serve his country," that draftees provide a safeguard against "the growth of a separate military ethos," that racial and gender inequalities would lead to an overrepresentation of women and African-Americans in the military, and that "an all-volunteer force would consist of mercenaries."[3] Historian William Taylor summarizes the arguments nicely: "Critics contended that the AVF would be either all African American, all poor, all female, or all of the above."[4]

Similar criticism came from academic circles. Samuel Huntington and Morris Janowitz, the two pioneers of early civil-military relations theory in the United States, both considered the consequences of unrepresentative armed forces, with Huntington focused primarily on issues of civilian control while Janowitz worried that a volunteer force would recruit disproportionately from poor, disadvantaged socioeconomic groups and lead to distrust between the military and society. Anticipating the civil-military gap, Janowitz argued in a 1975 article that "the advent of the all-volunteer force weakens the social representativeness of the military, especially through increased self-selection, and is accompanied by internal changes that increase the differentiation of the military establishment from the civilian society." His primary concern was a military with "selective linkages to civilian society, with a strong element of social unrepresentativeness."[5]

Such attitudes have influenced commentary about a professional military ever since. The original criticisms and concerns about the all-volunteer force became accepted into the cultural landscape, repeated for more than forty years by academics, analysts, and amateur commentators alike. Assumptions about the demographic composition of the professional military and

"You Volunteered to Get Screwed"

why someone would choose to join were rooted in the same stereotypes that sociologists had feared decades earlier. Few bothered to challenge these dogmatic notions, even when they have proven false. One team of researchers, for example, conducted an analysis of individual-level demographic data and determined that "in contrast to the accepted wisdom, the U.S. military no longer primarily recruits individuals from the most disadvantaged socio-economic backgrounds. Technological, tactical, operational and doctrinal changes have led to a change in the demand for personnel. As a result, on different metrics such as family income and family wealth as well as cognitive abilities, military personnel are on average like the average American citizen or slightly better."[6] An earlier study by the economist Tim Kane showed that "the volunteer force is already equitable" compared to the rest of American society with respect to the socioeconomic and educational backgrounds of new recruits.[7]

Despite this empirical evidence to the contrary, stereotypes about the professional military have found their way into fictional representations of the all-volunteer force since 9/11, and these representations may challenge the American population's trust in the military as an institution. Notably, contemporary writers of war novels — especially nonveterans — have relied on the very same tropes that have characterized criticisms of the all-volunteer force since 1973 to explain their characters' motivation for joining the military. These novels also use interactions between veterans and civilians on the home front to reflect the paradox of how the civil-military gap simultaneously takes away the volunteer veterans' moral authority over the personal consequences of war while also granting them the authority to pronounce judgment on the wars' justification and progress. This paradox may lead to an instability in Americans' trust in the military in which negative images of veterans in American culture come to overwhelm the abstract, institutional trust that has characterized the civil-military relationship since the end of the draft.

Institutional Trust, Before and After the Draft

A pattern of distrust has characterized the relationship between the military and American society that dates to before the Revolutionary War.[8] Skepticism of large standing armies was built into the American political system

CHAPTER SEVEN

partly as a reaction against British military rule in the colonies. Between the Revolution and the Korean War, the draft had been a governmental tool to fill the military's ranks in times of emergency, and the American armed forces relied heavily on conscription to meet wartime personnel demands, demobilizing the vast majority of these "citizen-soldiers" once the conflict had ended. This changed during the Cold War, when military planners believed a larger peacetime force was necessary to counter potential Soviet aggression. Throughout these years, the draft—known more formally as the Selective Service System—"loomed large and cast the shadow of compulsion across the land," in historian William Taylor's words.[9]

With the exception of during wartime, civilian distrust of the military typically took the form of neglect; military units were concentrated in rural bases, away from major metropolitan areas, easy to forget and easier to ignore. Resentment within the professional military ranks grew, and, as sociologist Morris Janowitz would later observe, "many [soldiers] view themselves as isolated from civilian society and feel morally superior to the business ethic."[10] The journalist Ward Just, writing in 1970, put it even more bluntly: "Society's distrust of soldiers is equaled only by the distrust of soldiers for society."[11]

The end of draft and the shift to an all-volunteer force in 1973 marked a turning point in the relationship between the military and American society. Coming from a conflict in which civil-military relations were fraught at all levels—from the most senior officers and government officials to the most junior soldiers and the civilians around them—the all-volunteer force was an artful solution to ease sociocultural tensions without sacrificing military efficiency. The draft had been a contentious issue during the war; the war's questionable objectives only fanned the flames of a younger generation that protested the possibility of being forced to fight, and possibly die, for no clear purpose. As a political issue, the draft took on even more attention. Nixon pledged to end conscription during the 1968 presidential campaign, and one of his earliest acts as president was the creation of an advisory commission to study the issue in greater depth. The commission was unanimous in its support for the creation of an all-volunteer force despite caveats that such a force could lead to the isolation of the military from the rest of society as well as the insulation of society from the consequences of armed conflict.[12]

"You Volunteered to Get Screwed"

The lingering taste of Vietnam was still too much for some people to regain their trust in the government on matters of war, though. Despite the official end of the conscription, every American man was still required to register for Selective Service upon turning eighteen. Journalist Sebastian Junger, who reached draft age in January 1980, recounts how he refused to sign the draft card he had received in the mail: "The Vietnam War had just ended and every adult I knew had been against it. I had no problem, personally, with fighting a war; I just didn't trust my government to send me to one that was completely necessary."[13]

Flash forward forty years after Junger refused to sign his draft card and the picture has become more complicated; since the end of the draft, Americans' trust in the government and all other institutions has plummeted while trust in the military has risen, reversing the trend that culminated during Vietnam but had once been a staple of American culture.[14] American mistrust and distrust of government—the result, in some sense, of a sustained conservative political campaign that began with Ronald Reagan—does not apply to the military, at least in broad terms. "Supporting a large standing military force in peacetime is no longer a novel practice in American history," sociologist James Burk writes, having now lasted "long enough to seem a hallowed tradition in many quarters and outlasting the forty-year Cold War security crisis that spawned it."[15] In contrast to other institutions that experienced a major decline in Americans' trust in recent decades—religion, Congress, business, and so on—the military remains remarkably resilient.[16] The reasons for this resilience are not well understood, though scholars have pointed to a number of relevant factors that influenced generalized trust such as performance, professionalism, and the perception that the military is an apolitical actor within the broader scope of partisan politics.[17] Fundamentally, though, the shift to a professional military without the threat of conscription simplifies the trust relationship by removing the individual stakes for all except those who volunteer. American men are still required to register for Selective Service (and there is a movement to require women to do the same),[18] but unlike Junger's worry that the government might draft him to fight an unnecessary war, eighteen-year-olds today simply file their paperwork online and dismiss it altogether from their thoughts.

Americans may trust the military as an institution and feel patriotic pride toward those who choose to serve, but that does not translate into engagement in politico-military affairs on behalf of those in uniform — this institutional trust is abstract rather than personal, and a closer look at the social relations between the military and society reveals several indicators of this abstraction. Fewer Americans have interactions with active members of the military or military veterans. An oft-cited survey conducted by the Pew Research Center in 2011 revealed that 91 percent of Americans "felt proud of the soldiers serving in the military," yet less than half would "advise a young person to join the military."[19] The survey also said that nearly six in ten Americans reported having a close friend or family member who had served in the military, though several studies suggest that this may be overstated.[20] Historian James Wright points out that most public engagement with the military comes without personal connection to the people who serve:

> For most Americans, those serving in Iraq and Afghanistan are not the boys — or girls — next door or down the street. Or perhaps even across town. When our citizens do not know many of these young men and women personally, they are more likely to see them and their service as abstractions. Americans warmly salute them, display magnetic ribbons on automobiles affirming support, and applaud their sacrifice, but this has little real impact.[21]

The wars in Iraq and Afghanistan both enjoyed initial popular support that dropped off quickly as early battlefield successes gave way to prolonged counterinsurgency operations.[22] And, while there were some antiwar protests during the early days of the Iraq invasion and subsequent occupation, there was nothing resembling the antiwar movement against American involvement in Vietnam. Even now, more than two decades after the 2001 terrorist attacks that led to the so-called Global War on Terror, the United States military is engaged in more countries than ever before while opposition to the wars rarely rises to a visible level. One could argue that the antiwar protests of the 1960s were, in fact, a form of civilian-military engagement that many lament is lacking today. Of course, those protests took aim at the uniform wearers as well as the government's defense establishment rather than separating policy decisions from those who implement them. Scholars and commentators arguing for a healthier civil-military relationship are not, by and large, advocating for more protests. Yet, despite the lower ratings of

"You Volunteered to Get Screwed"

institutional trust compared with today, the protest movement may have represented the purest form of engagement by a civilian population.

Joining the All-Volunteer Force — in Fiction

In his foundational work on civil-military relations, political scientist Samuel Huntington observed that "changes in the fictional portrayal of any social type usually reflect and help shape more general changes in public attitudes." His observation came from the "more appreciative interpretation of the military in popular fiction" that, in his view, began with Norman Mailer's 1948 novel *The Naked and the Dead* and "represented a distinct change from the main tradition of American literature on military subjects that had carried over into the early postwar years."[23] What Huntington appraised as a shift in public attitude toward the military after World War II also applies to the literary history of the American war fiction genre more generally. Where World War II novels collectively questioned the worth of the conflict as measured in human costs and novels about the Vietnam War exhibited a cynicism toward both the government and the American people, the all-volunteer force itself has become one of the most popular targets of criticism in contemporary war fiction.

And with good reason, as the all-volunteer force represents the most significant difference in the composition of the American armed forces compared with previous wars that relied on a large proportion of draftees to fill the ranks. Major characters in earlier war novels — Billy Pilgrim in *Slaughterhouse-Five*, most of Tim O'Brien's protagonists in *Going After Cacciato* and *The Things They Carried*, as well as other novels about Vietnam by Larry Heinemann, John Del Vecchio, and so on — were often written as draftees, a way to preserve their moral authority to criticize both the wars and the military.[24] For contemporary writers, the only way to achieve a similar effect for wars now fought by professionals is to employ a narrative sleight of hand in which their characters join the military before the terrorist attacks of September 11, 2001, a trick that many authors have used in their works.[25]

So why, in a nation where no one is forced to do so, would anyone choose to join the military? This fundamental question is at the heart of both military sociology as well as many contemporary war novels. Because today's military is comprised entirely of career soldiers, authors who wish to explore the nature of the decision to serve are confronted with a question of motivation. Policy analysts are interested in the same thing, and a 2018 study by the RAND Corporation sought to understand why people choose to enlist in the army.[26] A large proportion were inspired by a family member or relative. The most common response was "to seek out travel, adventure, and new experiences."[27] The desire to serve their country was another frequently cited response. Others joined to escape their prior lives or to earn a level of financial stability. "We also found," the authors wrote, "that soldiers join for a variety of different institutional and occupational reasons. A call to serve and perceptions of honor intermixed with desire for new adventures and considered calculations of benefits and steady paychecks."[28]

While many of these reasons for volunteering find their way into the fictional representation of the professional military, a sense of naïveté lurks beneath the surface of many contemporary war novels, especially those written by nonveterans. Like the recruits surveyed in the RAND study, their characters join the military for a variety of reasons — patriotism, reaction to 9/11, adventure, financial benefits, and so on — but nearly all of them return damaged, scarred, prone to alcoholism and substance abuse, angry at society, and, above all, shocked by the reality of what they volunteered for. In tone, many of these novels are kindred spirits to Stephen Crane's *The Red Badge of Courage* or the disillusioned works of World War I — characters volunteer to serve, seduced by glory and idealism, only to discover emptiness, pain, and loss. Interestingly, one of the biggest predictors of who joins the military — prior service of family members — is noticeably absent from most contemporary war novels.[29]

Of the characters in these novels who are not conscripted through the historical circumstance of joining before 9/11, the stereotype that only those with no other choice would choose to volunteer is one of the most common tropes. In one of the stories in Jon Chopan's collection *Veterans Crisis Hotline* (2018), for example, the seventeen-year-old son of a man deployed to the early days of the Iraq War reflects on telling his classmates stories about his dad:

> Most of the boys I'd told war stories to were going to go off to war soon, not because they wanted to or because their fathers were making them, but because this was what the world had made them for.

They didn't have the privilege to say no. There weren't that many jobs to be had without a college education, and most of them weren't going to go to college. They were blue-collar kids who wanted to stay blue-collar. They really didn't have that many options. This was, in fact, why my father stayed here and did not move us to a suburb. "These are the men you will be serving with," he said. "These are the men we send off to die in our wars."[30]

Taken together with the collection's other stories in which veterans struggle to adapt to civilian life after war, Chopan seems to suggest that those who join the military do so because they can't do anything else. A more considered interpretation could be that socioeconomic structural barriers make the military an attractive career option, but even that becomes complicated by the image of the hard-drinking, aggressive veterans in these stories. Another character even bluntly states, "I'd only joined the army because I didn't have any other options or nothing that was going to get me out of the shithole I'd been born in."[31]

In other works, it isn't the volunteers themselves who echo this sentiment but rather those around them. There's Lauren Clay's ex-boyfriend Shane in *Be Safe I Love You*:

Half the fucking kids from this neighborhood are doing the army 'cause they can't get into college. And after all the bullshit you went through you're going to send yourself to the same place as those white-trash fuckwads.[32]

Or Conrad Farrell's mother Lydia in *Sparta*:

Conrad was an intellectual; how could he choose to enter a totalitarian system? . . . And anyway, weren't the Marines a last resort—for misfits, people who were so violent and misanthropic they couldn't function in the outside world? Weren't they for someone who needed a rigid iron rule to suppress antisocial urges? Conrad wasn't like that. Their family wasn't like that. Their family was bookish and liberal, not martial and authoritarian.[33]

Both Shane's and Lydia's views on who volunteers match closely with the conventional wisdom about the all-volunteer force. The idea of the military as a "last resort" for people whose economic opportunities are otherwise limited evoke the earliest arguments against a professional military. Both characters, though, are described as atypical recruits, people who *have* other options yet—inexplicably, in the minds of those around them—choose to join the military; Lauren Clay is a classically trained singer whose talent transcends the rural military town where she's from (Watertown, New York), while Conrad Farrell is a high-achieving college student who comes from an educated upper-middle class family in a wealthy suburb of New York City. The tone of both novels calls into question the dissonance between the characters' motivations and the authors' inclusion of stereotypes about the volunteer military that undermine the characters' reasons for joining.

Some nonveteran authors use their characters' idealistic expectations and sense of patriotism to make a dramatic counterpoint about what they tend to foreground as the trauma of military experience. In Helen Benedict's polemic novel *Sand Queen*, for example, Kate Brady is enticed by the nobility of service and the respect granted to the volunteer:

> I was sick of being the kind of girl people patted on the head, the Goody Two-shoes who volunteered for bake sales and church bazaars—the girl everybody smiled at but nobody listened to. So when I heard the Army recruiter at school talking about how noble it is to serve your country, I thought it sounded perfect. I wanted to do something impressive like that, something that'd make people sit up and take notice. Anyhow, half the kids in my school were enlisting—the half who got the most respect.[34]

Benedict paints Kate as a wide-eyed high school senior who is easily charmed by the allure of a hollow idea like nobility. Sick of her characterization as a small-town girl next door, Kate is attracted to a choice that affords her the respect of her peers. Benedict also follows the familiar line of criticism about how the all-volunteer force pulls from the underprivileged parts of the population; the subtext of the final comment that "half the kids in my school were enlisting" suggests that, in Benedict's view, Kate isn't the only gullible senior at her high school.

Sand Queen is more interested in what happens to Kate Brady after she joins the army than exploring her motivations for doing so, as are *Be Safe I Love You*,

"You Volunteered to Get Screwed"

Sparta, and many other novels as we saw in chapter 5. These novels thrive on the dichotomy of idealism versus disillusionment; whatever positive images these individuals had of military service before signing their contracts are crushed by the actual experience of wearing the uniform. Kate Brady's parents cheer her for making the decision the join the army ("I'm so proud of you wanting to serve your country, sweetie!" her mother says. "It shows you have a good Christian heart"),[35] but the rest of Benedict's novel serves to undercut this message and render it naïve, ignorant of the sexual harassment and brutal treatment at the hands of her fellow soldiers that would befall Kate during her service. Conrad Farrell's mother, Lydia, in contrast to Kate's, is "mystified" and shocked that her son "was proud of this [decision]" to join the marines. Lydia, who "had grown up in the aftermath of the Vietnam War, when the military was shadowed by disgrace," functions as a representation of the more typical American attitude toward the military after Vietnam.[36] She comes of age during the time of shifting dynamics between the military and society, and her personal relationship to the military reflects the development of the civil-military gap:

> By the time Lydia was a teenager, the draft had ended, and no one she knew enlisted. That whole world receded into vague obscurity for her. The military seemed huge and surreal, like a factory out of Kafka, grinding on endlessly, groaning and rumbling as it produced a vast, dangerous, and incomprehensible product. It was outside the rest of the community, unrelated to civilians or peacetime. Lydia had seldom thought of the military until the spring of Conrad's junior year at Williams, 2001, when he came home to tell them about his plans.[37]

Lydia's experience is relatable for the average American citizen; she has no reason to think about the military until her son chooses to volunteer. Robinson tells both sides of the story—Conrad's idealism and patriotic drive as well as his mother's cynical reaction—but by the end of the novel we are left with the impression that perhaps his mother was right all along. Yes, he joins the marines as an atypical recruit, bucking the primary stereotypes of the volunteer military by leaving his privileged background behind, yet his decision is met with scorn and skepticism rather than applause. Serving the country isn't for people like the Farrells, it seems, a narrative choice that reflects the very real absence of this particular socioeconomic group in the military since the end of the draft.[38] And yet, after all of this, Conrad goes to war and is shocked by its brutality. He is injured physically and morally, and the effects of those injuries nearly drive him to suicide after he resigns his commission and returns home for good. Robinson does not give us Conrad's reasoning for leaving the marines, a narrative thread particularly missing in the novel considering his inability to sever himself from that lifestyle. Like so many other characters in contemporary war fiction, the few scenes we do get of Conrad before he is in uniform present us with a stubborn, headstrong, but potentially naïve boy who wishes to rush the gauntlet toward manhood through the military.

The Paradox of the Veteran's Authority

Conrad Farrell is just one of the many traumatized and troubled veterans scattered throughout the fictional response to Iraq and Afghanistan. As we saw in chapter 5, the "new battle" of post-traumatic stress and the challenges of reintegration have become contemporary war fiction's most dominant themes. Many of these works also explicitly link these consequences of wartime experience to the act of volunteering itself, usually through interactions between veteran and civilian characters within the novels.

As the American population has drifted from its military since the end of the Vietnam War, interactions between military veterans and civilians have become more frequent in war fiction. From Billy Lynn's cynical wonderment at the cluelessness of his fellow citizens, to soldiers' friends and family members pointing out that volunteering to serve is a choice, contemporary war novels have moved beyond simple scapegoats seen in many Vietnam War narratives to highlight the sociocultural complexities of wartime with an all-volunteer military. Where novels about the Vietnam War exhibited an underlying antagonism against the government as well as the American people back home, novels about Iraq and Afghanistan have used interactions between veterans and civilians to probe the complex moral authority of the volunteer soldier, highlighting not only the disparity in the moral burden of contemporary war but also the paradox that American society looks to these veterans for answers while still hanging the consequences of volunteering around their neck.

"You Volunteered to Get Screwed"

Contemporary American war culture has struggled to reconcile the moral burden of war with the responsibilities of civil society. Although volunteers *own* the experience and have little claim to moral authority, the civil-military gap has endowed these volunteers with a unique cultural authority to comment on the wars' justification and progress. Literary scholar Liam Corley even suggests that there is a "trope of the veteran" in contemporary American culture whereby "recognized veteran status confers authority on a person to speak to issues related to military service, foreign policy, and an array of tangential domestic policy issues. This authority to speak, however, comes with a host of expectations and constraints upon what veteran speech will contain."[39] The effect of partisan politics on these expectations also influences this authority.[40] Some military ethics scholars have even argued that the act of volunteering for the armed forces is itself fraught with moral risk. Joining the military means committing oneself to the will of the state, to allow oneself to be employed and deployed as an instrument of state-sanctioned violence. Whether this violence is legitimate or not is, absent an ongoing war, unknowable in advance. This is part of the charge leveled by the adherents of the so-called revisionist critique of just war theory that voluntary enlistment is "morally problematic."[41]

Some of this tension comes from the misplaced rhetoric of war as a defense of American freedom. Joining the military during a national emergency—with the Japanese attack on Pearl Harbor continuing to serve as the canonical example in the American cultural imaginary—carries a sense of honor and pride that comes with a clear moral justification. This kind of rhetoric runs aground, though, when the ideals of military service—serving one's country, defending freedom, and so on—clash with the realities of the conflicts themselves. The wars in Iraq and Afghanistan have challenged any idealistic conception of service. While Afghanistan may have been initially sold as a response to the terrorist attacks of September 11, 2001, the longer the war dragged on, the less clear its objectives became. And, in the absence of any weapons of mass destruction or links to al-Qaeda, the war in Iraq offered little solace to a soldier in search of moral justification. In the 2007 novel *Last One In* by Nicholas Kulish—a journalist who embedded with a marine infantry unit during the invasion of Iraq—an exchange between protagonist Jimmy (like Kulish also an embedded reporter) and a junior marine officer captures this well:

175

CHAPTER SEVEN

"Can you fight without a good reason?" Jimmy asked. "Without the weapons and all that?"

"Orders are orders," [Lieutenant] Larson said, "but it's a whole lot easier to face if you feel like you might be saving your mama or your baby sister's life."[42]

Phrases such as "defending freedom" and "protecting our way of life" that sound good in a recruitment campaign ring hollow for these wars, even if characters like Lieutenant Larson still grasp at them as a way to justify their presence in Iraq. This tension has not escaped unnoticed in other works either. In Stephen Markley's *Ohio*, Bill, a firebrand antiwar character, and Dan, a veteran of both Iraq and Afghanistan, are discussing a mutual friend who was killed serving in Iraq when Bill recalls trying to lecture their friend that "he wasn't fighting for his country or freedom or democracy or anything else. He was going to war so an overstretched superpower could flex nuts and maybe pump a few million more barrels per day onto the world oil markets — that's what I told him. And I was *so fucking right*" (italics in original).[43]

Without the moral certitude of a "just war" or the appeal to the whims of fate that comes with having been drafted, volunteer veterans become burdened with a complex moral authority that, to some extent, robs them of the authority to criticize their experience or lament its consequences as beyond their control. A few novels attempt to work around the complexity of the volunteer's moral authority by either ignoring politics altogether (e.g., Kristin Hannah's *Home Front*) or creating a rhetorical link — however tenuous — between today's wars and World War II (e.g., Ross Ritchell's *The Knife*, Lea Carpenter's *Eleven Days*, Aaron Gwyn's *Wynne's War*). Most novels, though, explore this issue directly. In Whitney Terrell's *The Good Lieutenant*, one veteran's brother explicitly calls her out on her lack of moral authority as a volunteer:

You are all stupid enough to believe that you actually *deserve* something. Because you're good Americans. Because you like to feel that you're morally superior. Hey, I'm a good soldier. Hey, I'm going off to war to save my country! Aren't I awesome! Don't I deserve to be thanked? No! You *volunteered* to get screwed. Okay? And at some level, you know that.[44] [italics in original]

"You Volunteered to Get Screwed"

The idea that the veteran "volunteered to get screwed" is the perfect embodiment of this philosophy, and many variations on that theme appear throughout contemporary war novels. Jesse Goolsby's *I'd Walk with My Friends If I Could Find Them*, for example, uses a conversation between a veteran who just returned from Afghanistan and his father to explore how the professional military fits more broadly into American society. The father is taking a surprisingly cynical view of his son's military service, first calling him "clueless" for "raising your right hand" and taking the oath of enlistment before ranting about the war's absence from Americans' daily life:

> You said no one cares about the wars. I'm agreeing with you. You say we're at war? Where, son? Look around. Who's talking about it? Chicago isn't talking. San Fran? Memphis? We're not a nation at war. We never were. Are you serious? No one cares unless it's someone they know. . . . We don't care because all of you have volunteered to die. If not in war, then when you get home all brain-fucked from an IED some illiterate planted for twenty bucks and his neck. And believe me, I think that's shit. I'm not mad at you. The VA needs to get their shit together, sure. But there are choices. You chose to be a paid rifle. You are all-volunteer.[45]

There is a broad range of emotions in this exchange, but the father's view boils down to the fact that his son had a choice and "chose to be a paid rifle." The passage represents a summary of the civil-military gap issue, with the father's perspective matching that of American society more generally. Comparing a professional soldier (who fights for a nation) to a mercenary (who fights for the highest bidder) may represent an extreme form of cynicism directed at the military institution, but the logical link between signing up for the military during a time of war and the financial benefits of serving in a war zone make it harder to ignore the accusation.[46] Even though soldiers—including draftees—have always been paid for wartime service, contemporary writers frequently emphasize this point in their fiction in a way that previous writers did not. A character on a mission to hunt down Taliban fighters in navy veteran Will Mackin's *Bring out the Dog* wonders, "Do you believe we're getting paid for this?"[47] Here is army veteran David Abrams's *Brave Deeds*: "The starched suits at the Pentagon tell us to go here, we go here; they change their minds and tell us to go *there*, we go there. As long as we get a paycheck, we could give two shits about history and heroes" (italics in original).[48] In *I'd Walk with My Friends If I Could Find Them*, a character tells his girlfriend that he's enlisting in the army and will receive a signing bonus. A brief conversation ensues that encapsulates the issue:

"How much is the bonus?"
"Thirty thousand."
"You're going to the war."
"Is there anything else?"[49]

A scene in Roy Scranton's *War Porn* combines nearly all of the elements just discussed. Mel, a guest at a backyard barbecue party, asks Aaron, a veteran recently returned from Iraq, why he joined the army, alluding to the fact that it was his choice to do so. Aaron says, "College money, patriotism. Service, challenge, honor. Nine-eleven. Same things as anybody else"—all reasons that match the results of the RAND study. Mel continues her pseudo-interrogation, a frustrated tone revealing her political stance against the war; she doesn't buy Aaron's moral reasoning and attempts to reconcile his initial motivation for enlisting with his service in Iraq. Mel's girlfriend Rachel tries to calm her down, but she says, "No, he made a choice. He wasn't drafted. All he had to do was kill people," and then directly to Aaron, "I just can't understand how you can take part in an illegal war that kills thousands of innocent people—*for college money*—and then act like it doesn't matter. Like you didn't choose. That's what seems completely fucked to me" (italics in original).[50] That Scranton, Goolsby, Abrams, and Mackin are all veterans gives these scenes an urgency that calls attention to the dilemma of volunteering to serve in the military during an unpopular, morally questionable war.

Living with the physical, moral, and emotional consequences of these wars affects not only those who served but also their families and friends, and these characters often hold the act of volunteering against them. In Masha Hamilton's *What Changes Everything*, the mother of a soldier who lost his legs in Afghanistan finds herself "fuming that he'd made the choice to go to war; that he'd gotten badly hurt, and now the rest of everything that followed would be changed."[51] Another veteran, named Jolene Zarkades in Kristin Hannah's *Home Front*, falls into a deep depression after returning home, having lost a leg in a helicopter crash. Although she was once outgoing, outspoken, and driven, she now refuses to work with a physical therapist during her hospital stay and also rejects her husband Michael's attempts to reconnect with her. He's pushing her to be the person she once was, but she resists. In a heated conversation, Michael accuses Jolene of "being selfish," saying "*You* wanted to fly. . . . You wanted combat and war and to be all that you could be. Well, you got it, and this is who you are now" (italics in original).[52]

The unintended consequences of choosing to serve in an all-volunteer military during a time of an unpopular war is also a recurring theme in Caleb Cage's short story collection, *Desert Mementos*.[53] In "Proxy War," the narrator tells an embedded journalist that his decision to join the army created even more distance between him and his already estranged father, a man who had protested Vietnam and who tells him over dinner that he thought the Iraq War was also a mistake and that he couldn't support it, not even for his own son. In "Operation Battle Mountain," a soldier's pregnant wife loses one of their unborn twins in the womb, with the other's health questionable. His mother-in-law seems to blame his absence for what happened, and hints that his wife (who won't speak with him) does as well. In "Soldier's Cross," a lieutenant's parents split up after his father has an affair during the deployment. His mother admits that she is "still pretty confused," but is beginning to make peace with it now that he's home. Then she tells him: "I'm still hopeful. I think maybe he was reacting harshly to your leaving, and that this was his only way of dealing with it." The lieutenant becomes "momentarily furious that it had become his fault, but he put it all aside and hugged his mother."[54] In each of these stories there is an undercurrent of judgment against the soldiers who chose to join the army when none of them were forced to do so. The characters who are left behind—a father, a mother-in-law, a wife—can't help linking the emotional dots between the decision that took their soldiers away and the grief they now carry; unlike with a draft, there is no random fate of a lottery to take the brunt of their damnation.

Are We Winning?

The converse of the volunteer veterans' lack of moral authority is the way that Americans still look to them as guides for how and what to think about the conflicts themselves. According to some political scientists, one of the civil-military gap's side effects has been a "troubling level of deference to the military on the side of the civilians and feelings of entitlement on the side of the military."[55] Although civil-military relations scholars typically look at how elite cues influence public support for military and defense issues, these interactions also occur at the individual, interpersonal level.

As with other aspects of the professional military, civilian deference to the volunteer veteran's judgment manifests itself in contemporary war novels through scenes that highlight the civilian-military interactions. In *War Porn*, Scranton uses the barbecue scene introduced earlier to show how the presence of war veteran Aaron disrupts the group's idyllic indifference. At first things are calm; they discuss easy topics like pets, food, the flood of election coverage (this is October 2004, after all), tattoos, and poetry. They tell stories and reminisce. Then Matt, one of the civilians, begins testing how far he can push Aaron to talk about the war, eventually offering his own lack of knowledge as a plea for answers: "I just, you know, I mean, all we know is what they show us on TV, right? I mean, we don't even know. I can't even imagine. We're totally ignorant of this situation, and I'm just wondering, is it really like how they say? Is it bad? Is it getting worse? Is it getting better?"[56] Matt seems genuinely interested and without expectations for Aaron's response, but Aaron rejects any authority to comment on the larger questions about the war: "I don't know, man. . . . I was just a dumb grunt, you know. I don't know what to tell you."[57]

George Saunders satirizes this same dynamic in his short story "Home."[58] Like much of Saunders's fiction, "Home" is full of empathy but also conflicting emotions. The narrator is Mike, a war veteran who has been on the receiving end of a court-martial and other experiences that are only alluded to briefly in passing, with a few stray details that never fully cohere into a picture of what happened to him. Mike carries rage with him, an anger at his circumstance, an aggression he takes out in several instances on those around him, including his mother's new boyfriend and a man sent to collect unpaid rent. His ex-wife has remarried, raising their two children in a posh neighborhood that "was full of castles" compared to the part of town where he grew up, where "the houses were like peasant huts."[59] When he goes to visit his sister and his ex-wife, no one wants to let him in.

At one point, Mike enters a convenience store, where he runs into two kids

"You Volunteered to Get Screwed"

already inside. In a line that echoes Billy Lynn's comment about how "Iraq ages you in dog years," Mike becomes aware of the experiential gap between them when he notices that "They were sweet. Not a line on their faces. When I say they were kids, I mean they were about my age." He tells them he was in the war, and they reflexively thank him for his service and shake his hand:

> "I wasn't for it," the second one said. "But I know it wasn't your deal."
> "Well," I said. "It kind of was."[60]

The simplicity of these sentences contains a clear reference to the all-volunteer force; the civilian offers his political stance on the war and attempts to absolve Mike of his own culpability, which Mike refuses. A moment later, the conversation about the war continues:

> "Is the one you were at still going?" the second one asked me.
> "Yes," I said.
> "Better or worse, do you think?" the first one said. "Like, in your view, are we winning? Oh, what am I doing? I don't actually care, that's what's so funny about it!"
> "Anyway," the second one said, and held out his hand, and I shook it.[61]

Within only a few lines, Saunders presents a scathing assessment of American war culture and civilian political disengagement. Not only are these civilians unaware that their nation is still engaged in an overseas conflict, but they reveal an involuntary impulse to ask the one veteran they encounter for his view on the war before laughing off their own ignorance.

In some of the fictional representations of the war, the civilians who ask veterans about the war's progress or moral justification do so as a way to lend credence to the beliefs they already have. The best example of this comes from *Billy Lynn's Long Halftime Walk* when a rich, conservative older couple looks to Billy for validation and approval of their own opinions about the war in Iraq. The husband first tells Billy about his personal reaction to the combat footage played on the news: "It was cathartic. . . . Seeing yall John Wayne that deal, it's like we finally had something to cheer about. I guess the war'd been depressing me all this time and I didn't even know it, till yall came along. Just a huge morale boost for everybody." The small crowd of like-minded civilians "vigorously agree" before one woman says

CHAPTER SEVEN

to Billy, "You're among friends. You won't find any cut-and-runners here," implicitly assuming that Billy and his fellow soldiers adhere to the conservative politics that coined the phrase "cut-and-runners" as a jab against Democrats who wished to pull out of Iraq. Then the man asks Billy, "Is it gettin' better?" to which Billy—a nineteen-year-old specialist—hedges in response: "I think so, sir. In certain areas, yeah, definitely. We're working hard to make it better."[62]

This happens again and again to Billy. "Then someone asks are we winning and that opens the floor for discussion about the war, and Billy gets passed around like everybody's favorite bong."[63] Throughout the football game, seated on the aisle at what he calls "the Bravo-citizen interface," Billy describes his interactions with the civilians who come to him for answers:

> Yes sir, thank you sir. Yes ma'am having a great time, absolutely. Billy
> passes programs down the row for everybody to autograph and has
> to make conversation while they come back. *It's getting better, don't you
> think? It was worth it, don't you think? We had to do it, don't you think?* He
> wishes that just once somebody would call him baby-killer, but this
> doesn't seem to occur to them, that babies have been killed. Instead
> they talk about *democracy, development, dubya em dees.* They want badly
> to believe, he'll give them that much, they are as fervent as children
> insisting Santa Claus is real because once you stop believing, well,
> what then, maybe he doesn't come anymore?[64] [italics in original]

In a theme that recurs throughout the novel, no one really wants to hear the truth from Billy; they only want to assure themselves that the war is justified. They grant him a conditional authority so long as he conforms to their preconceived narrative.

While most contemporary war novels depict actual civilian-military interactions, Brian Van Reet addresses this question of authority and expectation through a layer of symbolism that highlights the performative dimension of the relationship. In *Spoils*, a junior soldier named Sleed has a recurring dream after his unit shoots up a truck with a family of four Iraqi civilians during a checkpoint stop gone wrong. The dream, however, isn't what one might expect:

"You Volunteered to Get Screwed"

But the dreams weren't about what I'd seen, the man and his wife, the two kids, the sick-looking girl and the little boy with the messed up arm. I thought of them all the time but they never made it into my dreams. No blood and gore, no dead bodies snapping back to life, like the ones that bother guilty people in the movies. Instead, I started having this dream where I was onstage under bright lights. There was a huge audience out there, most of them dressed in tuxedos and fancy gowns, and everybody was waiting for me to say something, to deliver a final line they wanted to hear, so they could get up and go home, but I had no idea what I was supposed to say.[65]

The symbolism of Sleed's dreams suggests that civilians, in their role as audience and spectators to the veteran onstage, are seeking moral absolution from the military as symbolized in the "final line they wanted to hear." Just like the throngs of people in *Billy Lynn's Long Halftime Walk* who constantly look to Billy and his squad for answers to the question "How are we doing over there?," Sleed's dream audience grants him the ultimate authority to "deliver a final line they wanted to hear, so they could get up and go home." His speechlessness undercuts that authority, implying that either he can't find the right words to please them, or that it was never his role to do so in the first place.

A person unfamiliar with the modern military or the experience of a volunteer soldier in Iraq and Afghanistan who looks to literary representations for answers will come away with an almost universally negative view of military service as well as those who choose to serve. The narrative choices in these works—from nonveteran authors reaffirming the beliefs that those who join come from underprivileged backgrounds and have no other choice, to veterans directing their cynicism and ire at the institution itself—form a projection of stereotypes that merely reinforce many of the divisions between the military and society that drive the civil-military gap in the first place.

In a democracy, the moral responsibility of war is a complex question. Soldiers become representatives of state-sanctioned violence; citizens remain beholden to their choice of political leaders who ultimately choose whether to send those soldiers to war. Since the end of the draft and the shift to an all-volunteer force, though, American citizens have played little meaningful role in that decision-making process, and little to no sacrifice has been asked of them during times of war. Although the American cultural response to the contemporary conflicts has not fallen back on the Vietnam-era attitude that often equated blame for the war with those who fought, the nature of the all-volunteer military has made some kinds of criticism unavoidable.

The lack of social contact between veterans and most civilians is one of the greatest challenges to post-9/11 civil-military relations. Hugh Liebert and Jim Golby argue that "the emerging civil-military divide has unique, and uniquely troubling, features," and that "the most significant problem is not the number of citizens who serve in the military or have close contact to those who do, but how service and contact are distributed throughout the nation." One of the most pressing concerns, then, is that the military will become "completely foreign to certain Americans in particular areas around the country."[66] As the military becomes less familiar to the vast majority of Americans, images of the military in American society become susceptible to the misperceptions and oversimplifying narratives. The cultural frame of the trauma hero described in chapters 3 and 6 persists at least in part because of these kinds of representations, oscillating between images of heroes and victims with little room for nuance in between.

The media also plays a role in presenting specific images of military veterans. A 2015 study by Meredith Kleykamp and Crosby Hipes showed that the media frames veterans as "damaged by their service but deserving of government benefits and social assistance."[67] Another study that examined American attitudes toward soldiers who had returned home from combat tours in Iraq found that veterans are "stereotyped" but "not stigmatized." According to their analysis, "members of the public are not surprised to learn that men who went to a war zone behave according to stereotypes that imply that such men have problems with mental health, substance abuse, and violent behavior. Yet they do not discriminate against these men." Veterans, it turns out, "benefit from symbolic capital, which outweighs the effect of stereotypes on discrimination."[68] A quantitative analysis of media representation of veterans on Twitter also suggested that "U.S. news consumers are provided a narrow representation of what it means to be a veteran,"

"You Volunteered to Get Screwed"

finding that stories about veterans fall into three primary narratives: hero, victim, and charity case.[69] These narratives tend to ignore veterans as complicated individuals with a wide range of experiences and instead reduce them to metonymic archetypes within American memory culture.[70]

Placed alongside what Americans see on the news and social media, the literary representation of the professional military predominantly reinforces the existing images and stereotypes of veterans in American culture. How, then, has public trust in the military remained so resilient? At first glance, Americans' high levels of trust in the military since the transition to an all-volunteer force would seem to be a positive development, a way to separate the politics of foreign policy from the violent instruments of implementation. But this trust becomes more complicated when we peek under the hood to see how political polarization has introduced a partisan gap as well. Recent civil-military relations research has shown that a large element of the increased public trust in the military is driven by Republican support, and that the differences between Republicans' and Democrats' views of the military diverge significantly.[71] Democrats are less likely to agree that the military shares their values, that the military is diverse, and that most of the military are heroes. (Republicans are more likely to agree to all of those.) Tellingly, Democrats are more likely to believe that most military veterans suffer from post-traumatic stress disorder. Partisan politics also seem to drive the difference in perception for why someone would choose to enlist, while some politicians have begun to probe the limits of the military's presumed apolitical orientation as yet another way to curry favor with certain base constituencies.[72]

The trauma hero narrative and the persistent myths about the professional military thus offer a little something for everyone, regardless of their political persuasions.[73] Although literary fiction is but one pillar of cultural production, the picture that the fictional response to the wars paints of the military and military veterans largely confirms these existing beliefs. Most of the soldiers in these novels are white men. Few of them act heroically, at least in the traditional sense that one might imagine from Americans' cultural memory of the Second World War. And, as we have seen, struggles with post-traumatic stress and moral injury are primary themes that run across the fictional response to Iraq and Afghanistan.

The combination of the literary representation of the all-volunteer force with media narratives that conform to stereotypes and political views leads to an instability in the story of American trust in the military. The dispersion of the veteran's cultural and narrative authority that came with the end of the draft has broken down some of the war fiction genre's conventions in recent years, but unless writers—veterans as well as nonveterans—look beyond the well-trodden ground of trauma and recovery, the gap between the military and American society is unlikely to close anytime soon.

APPENDIX

The American Novels of Iraq and
Afghanistan through 2020

THE FOLLOWING LIST is compiled from a variety of sources, including Peter Molin's incomparable *Time Now* blog as well as my own additions. While I hope that I have collected as many relevant works as possible, there may be others that I have inadvertently missed. Any errors are mine alone.

Authors listed with an asterisk (*) are military veterans who served in either Iraq or Afghanistan while in uniform. Those with a circumflex (ˆ) are insiders who spent time in Iraq or Afghanistan as either journalists or government civilians.

* Abrams, David. *Brave Deeds* (2017)
* Abrams, David. *Fobbit* (2012)
* Ackerman, Elliot. *Green on Blue* (2015)
* Ackerman, Elliot. *Waiting for Eden* (2018)
   Baxter, Greg. *The Apartment* (2013)
   Benedict, Helen. *Sand Queen* (2011)
   Benedict, Helen. *Wolf Season* (2017)
   Bennett, Eric. *A Big Enough Lie* (2015)
* Buchholz, Benjamin. *One Hundred and One Nights* (2011)
* Cage, Caleb S. *Desert Mementos: Stories of Iraq and Nevada* (2017)
* Caro, Brandon. *Old Silk Road* (2015)
   Carpenter, Lea. *Eleven Days* (2013)
   Chopan, Jon. *Veterans Crisis Hotline* (2018)
   Dau, Stephen. *The Book of Jonas* (2012)
   Doten, Mark. *The Infernal* (2015)
   Fallon, Siobhan. *You Know When the Men Are Gone* (2012)
* Farria, Dewaine. *Revolutions of All Colors* (2020)
   Fountain, Ben. *Billy Lynn's Long Halftime Walk* (2012)
* Freedman, Mike. *King of the Mississippi* (2019)
* Gallagher, Matt. *Youngblood* (2016)

APPENDIX

* Goolsby, Jesse. *I'd Walk with My Friends If I Could Find Them* (2015)

Gwyn, Aaron. *Wynne's War* (2014)

Halliday, Lisa. *Asymmetry* (2018)

^ Hamilton, Masha. *What Changes Everything* (2013)

Hannah, Kristin. *Home Front* (2012)

* Hefti, Matthew J. *A Hard and Heavy Thing* (2016)

Hoffman, Cara. *Be Safe I Love You* (2014)

Hutson, Raymond. *Finding Sgt. Kent* (2018)

* Klay, Phil. *Redeployment* (2014)

* Klay, Phil. *Missionaries* (2020)

* Kovac, Adam. *The Surge* (2019)

^ Kulish, Nicholas. *Last One In* (2007)

* Lindsey, Odie. *We Come to Our Senses* (2016)

* Lindsey, Odie. *Some Go Home* (2020)

* Mackin, Will. *Bring Out the Dog: Stories* (2018)

Markley, Stephen. *Ohio* (2018)

Marro, Elizabeth. *Casualties* (2016)

McBride, Laura. *We Are Called to Rise* (2014)

^ McInnis, Kathleen J. *The Heart of War: Misadventures in the Pentagon* (2018)

* McPadden, Ray. *And the Whole Mountain Burned* (2018)

Miller, Derek. *The Girl in Green* (2016)

^ Mogelson, Luke. *These Heroic, Happy Dead: Stories* (2016)

Oates, Joyce Carol. *Carthage* (2014)

* O'Brien, Perry. *Fire in the Blood* (2020)

* Pitre, Michael. *Fives and Twenty-Fives* (2014)

Plum, Hilary. *They Dragged Them through the Streets* (2013)

Plum, Hilary. *Strawberry Fields* (2018)

* Powers, Kevin. *The Yellow Birds* (2012)

* Renehan, John. *The Valley* (2015)

* Ritchell, Ross. *The Knife* (2015)

Robinson, Roxana. *Sparta* (2013)

Rogan, Charlotte. *Now and Again* (2016)

Roy-Bhattacharya, Joydeep. *The Watch* (2012)

Schultz, Katey. *Flashes of War* (2013)

Schultz, Katey. *Still Come Home* (2019)

* Scranton, Roy. *War Porn* (2016)

The American Novels of Iraq and Afghanistan through 2020

Stark, Sarah. *Out There* (2014)
Tedrowe, Emily. *Blue Stars* (2015)
^ Terrell, Whitney. *The Good Lieutenant* (2016)
Tsetsi, Kristen. *Pretty Much True* (2012)
* Van Reet, Brian. *Spoils* (2017)
Vandenburg, Margaret. *The Home Front* (2015)
Vandenburg, Margaret. *Weapons of Mass Destruction* (2015)
Vlautin, Willy. *The Free* (2014)
Waldman, Amy. *A Door in the Earth* (2019)
* Walker, Nico. *Cherry* (2018)
Zimmerman, David. *The Sandbox* (2010)

ACKNOWLEDGMENTS

THIS BOOK BEGAN as a doctoral dissertation with the research training group on authority and trust (GKAT) at the Heidelberg Center for American Studies. My profound gratitude to Manfred Berg, Ulrike Gerhard, Sebastian Harnisch, Günter Leypoldt, and the other GKAT faculty members who took a chance on someone with a background in astrophysics and political science but who wanted to do a doctoral project in literary and cultural studies. Above all, I want to thank my advisor, Margit Peterfy, whose unwavering support, guidance, and encouragement were a blessing for my entire time in Heidelberg. I could not have imagined a better supervisor.

Throughout this project I was fortunate to have a great number of friends and colleagues in Heidelberg and beyond who helped make this book possible, including Mike Bishop, Thomas Bjerre, Elizabeth Corrao-Billeter, Birgit Däwes, Annika Elstermann, Claudia Jetter, Steve Leech, Desirée Link, Julia Nohle, Jennifer Orth-Veillon, Lauren Rever, Aline Schmidt, Linnea Stadler, Sebastian Tants-Boestad, and Georg Wolff. I also wish to thank my former colleagues at the Institute for Defense Analyses, especially Jim Ayers, Dan Chiu, Mike Fitzsimmons, and Tony Johnson.

The limited archival work in this project would not have been possible without the efforts of Sarah Seraphin and John Baky (Connelly Library, La Salle University), Tim Noakes (Department of Special Collections, Stanford University), and Denise Anderson (Special Collections Department, University of Iowa Libraries). I am also grateful to Sam Cohen, Meredith Stabel, and the entire University of Iowa Press team, as well as Eric Bennett for kind words and insightful suggestions on an earlier draft of the manuscript.

To my parents, Steven Eisler and Betty-Jo Frank, for a lifetime of encouragement no matter what I decided to do next or how far it took me from home. And to my sister, Rachel, for her creativity and humor.

Finally, thank you to Verena for all your support over the years and for our two wonderful children, Noah and Emilia, to whom I dedicate this book.

NOTES

Introduction

1. Matt Gallagher, "You Don't Have to Be a Veteran to Write about War," LitHub, February 2, 2016, https://lithub.com/you-dont-have-to-be-a-veteran-to-write-about-war/.
2. On the symbolic capital of experience, see John B. Thompson, *Merchants of Culture: The Publishing Business in the Twenty-First Century* (Cambridge: Polity, 2010), 9.
3. Quoted in Jackson J. Benson, *Wallace Stegner: His Life and Work*, reprint ed. (Lincoln: University of Nebraska Press, 2009), 162.
4. Ernest Hemingway, *Green Hills of Africa* (New York: Charles Scribner's Sons, 1935), 70.
5. William Broyles, "Why Men Love War." *Esquire*, November 1, 1984.
6. See the appendix for a complete list of texts and their authors, as well as which authors are veterans and which are not.
7. Tony Judt, *Reappraisals: Reflections on the Forgotten Twentieth Century* (New York: Penguin Books, 2008), 6–7.
8. Mary L. Dudziak, "Death and the War Power," *Yale Journal of Law and Humanities* 30 (2018): 25.
9. Dudziak, "Death and the War Power," 60.
10. For a general overview, see Lindsay Cohn, "The Evolution of the Civil-Military 'Gap' Debate," paper prepared for the TISS Project on the gap between the military and civilian society, 1999. Andrew Bacevich discusses the evolution of civil-military relations in *Breach of Trust: How Americans Failed Their Soldiers and Their Country* (New York: Metropolitan Books, 2013). Although there are some inconsistencies in the application of the term *civil-military gap*, I am using it to refer to the social gap between the military and American society rather than, for example, civilian and military elites. See Jon Rahbek-Clemmensen et al., "Conceptualizing the Civil-Military Gap: A Research Note," *Armed Forces and Society* 38, no. 4 (2012): 669–78.
11. Samuel Huntington, *The Soldier and the State* (Cambridge, MA: Harvard University Press, 1957); Morris Janowitz, *The Professional Soldier* (New York: Free Press, 1960).
12. For a more detailed discussion and criticism of these theories, see, for example, James Burk, "Theories of Democratic Civil-Military Relations," *Armed Forces and Society* 29, no. 1 (2002): 7–29.
13. Thomas E. Ricks, "The Widening Gap between Military and Society," *The Atlantic*, July 1997.

Notes to Pages 6–10

14. Richard D. Hooker, "Soldiers of the State: Reconsidering American Civil-Military Relations," *Parameters* 23, no. 4 (Winter 2003–2004): 4–17.

15. James Mattis and Kori Schake, eds., *Warriors and Citizens: American Views of Our Military* (Stanford, CA: Hoover Institution Press, 2016), 287.

16. Among Bacevich's relevant works are *The New American Militarism: How Americans Are Seduced by War* (New York: Oxford University Press, 2005), *Washington Rules: America's Path to Permanent War* (New York: Metropolitan Books, 2010), and *Breach of Trust: How Americans Failed Their Soldiers and Their Country* (New York: Metropolitan Books, 2013).

17. Karl Eikenberry, "Reassessing the All-Volunteer Force," in *The Modern American Military*, ed. David M. Kennedy (New York: Oxford University Press, 2013); Hugh Liebert and James Golby, "Midlife Crisis? The All-Volunteer Force at 40," *Armed Forces and Society* 43, no. 1 (2017): 115–38.

18. Cohn, "The Evolution of the Civil-Military 'Gap' Debate." See also Crispin Burke, "How Veterans Can Help Bridge the Civil-Military Divide," *The Atlantic*, November 13, 2017, https://www.theatlantic.com/amp/article/545669/.

19. Astrid Erll, *Memory in Culture* (New York: Palgrave Macmillan, 2011), 163–64. See also Astrid Erll, "Reading Literature as Collective Texts: German and English War Novels of the 1920s as Media of Cultural and Communicative Memory," in *Anglistentag München 2003: Proceedings*, ed. Christoph Bode, Sebastian Domsch and Hans Sauer (Trier: Wissenschaftlicher Verlag Tier, 2004), 335–54.

20. Norman Mailer, *Advertisements for Myself* (Cambridge, MA: Harvard University Press, 1992), 28.

21. Roxana Robinson, "The Right to Write." *New York Times*, June 28, 2014, https://opinionator.blogs.nytimes.com/2014/06/28/the-right-to-write/.

22. Jennifer Haytock, *The Routledge Introduction to American War Literature* (New York: Routledge, 2018), 3.

23. Haytock, *The Routledge Introduction to American War Literature*, 3.

24. Kate McLoughlin, *Authoring War: The Literary Representation of War from the Iliad to Iraq* (Cambridge: Cambridge University Press, 2011), 22.

25. McLoughlin, *Authoring War*, 42. Italics in original.

26. Aaron B. O'Connell, "Review of Stacey Peebles, *Welcome to the Suck: Narrating the American Soldier's Experience in Iraq* (2011)," *Journal of American Studies* 47, no. 3 (2013).

27. James Campbell, "Combat Gnosticism: The Ideology of First World War Poetry Criticism," *New Literary History* 30, no. 1 (Winter 1999): 203–15.

28. These include Jon Robert Adams, *Male Armor: The Soldier-Hero in Contemporary American Culture* (Charlottesville: University of Virginia Press, 2008); David Buchanan, *Going Scapegoat: Post-9/11 War Literature, Language and Culture* (Jefferson, NC: McFarland, 2016); Susan Farrell, *Imagining Home: American War Fiction from Hemingway to 9/11* (Rochester, NY: Camden House, 2017); Keith Gandal, *The Gun and the Pen: Hemingway, Fitzgerald, Faulkner, and the Fiction of Mobilization* (New

Notes to Pages 10–17

York: Oxford University Press, 2008); and Roy Scranton, *Total Mobilization: World War II and American Literature* (Chicago: Chicago University Press, 2019). Only Buchanan considers the veteran's authority as a focal point of his analysis, while the others either mention it in passing or implicitly.

29. Yuval Noah Harari, *The Ultimate Experience: Battlefield Revelations and the Making of Modern War Culture, 1450–2000* (New York: Palgrave Macmillan, 2008).

30. John Newman, *Vietnam War Literature: An Annotated Bibliography of Imaginative Works about Americans Fighting in Vietnam*, 3rd ed. (Lanham, MD: Scarecrow Press, 1996).

31. See "A Note from Bobbie Ann Mason" in the 2005 edition of *In Country* (New York: Harper Perennial).

32. "In Country" [review], *Kirkus Reviews*, August 15, 1985, https://www.kirkus reviews.com/book-reviews/bobbie-ann-mason-2/in-country/.

33. Linda Martín Alcoff, "The Problem of Speaking for Others," in *Who Can Speak? Authority and Critical Identity*, ed. Judith Roof and Robyn Wiegman (Urbana: University of Illinois Press, 1995), 97–119.

34. Linda Wagner-Martin, *A History of American Literature, 1950 to the Present* (Malden, MA: Wiley-Blackwell, 2015), 177–78.

35. This is especially important as they relate to issues of representation within the mostly white publishing industry. A 2019 survey on diversity in publishing found the industry to be 76 percent white. "Where Is the Diversity in Publishing? The 2019 Diversity Baseline Survey Results," Lee & Low Books, January 2020. https://blog.leeandlow.com/2020/01/28/2019diversitybaselinesurvey. Clayton Childress points out that book editors "are at least partially selecting manuscripts based on works that match their own tastes, sensibilities, and experiences," and he identifies the lack of racial diversity within editorial staffs as an issue that affects the kinds of novels that do get published. Clayton Childress, *Under the Cover: The Creation, Production, and Reception of a Novel* (Princeton, NJ: Princeton University Press, 2017), 95–96.

36. See Rebecca Alter, "Why Is Everyone Arguing about American Dirt?" *Vulture*, February 7, 2020, https://www.vulture.com/article/american-dirt-book -controversy-explained.html.

37. Mark McGurl, *The Program Era: Postwar Fiction and the Rise of Creative Writing* (Cambridge, MA: Harvard University Press, 2009).

38. See for example Frank Usbeck, "Writing Yourself Home: US Veterans, Creative Writing, and Social Activism," *European Journal of American Studies* 13, no. 2 (2018).

39. Joseph Darda, *Empire of Defense: Race and the Cultural Politics of Permanent War* (Chicago: University of Chicago Press, 2019), 172–73.

40. Sam Sacks, "First-Person Shooters," *Harper's*, August 2015, https://harpers.org /archive/2015/08/first-person-shooters-2/.

41. Birgit Däwes, *Ground Zero Fiction: History, Memory, and Representation in the*

Notes to Pages 21–24

American 9/11 Novel (Heidelberg: Universitätsverlag Winter, 2011), 89–91. See also Alexander Manshel, "The Rise of the Recent Historical Novel," *Post45* 29 (2017).

Chapter One

1. Campbell, "Combat Gnosticism," 203.
2. Paul Fussell, *The Great War and Modern Memory*, new ed. (New York: Oxford University Press, 2013), 95.
3. McLoughlin, *Authoring War*, 43. Italics in original.
4. Haytock, *The Routledge Introduction to American War Literature*, 9.
5. Buchanan, *Going Scapegoat*, 30.
6. See, for example, Buchanan, *Going Scapegoat*; Farrell, *Imagining Home*; Lynne Hanley, *Writing War: Fiction, Gender, and Memory* (Amherst: University of Massachusetts Press, 1991); McLoughlin, *Authoring War*.
7. Philip Hager and Desmond Taylor, *The Novels of World War I: An Annotated Bibliography* (New York: Garland Publishing, 1981). To be included in the authors' bibliography, the novel must "use the World War I conflict either as a substantial part of the action or those whose plot is set wholly or in part against the 1914–1918 war period. . . . The work of fiction must deal in some significant and substantial way with an aspect of the war, or with its impact on people on the battlefields and on the home fronts. Naturally, there is some subjectivity involved in the selection process" (x).
8. These numbers are derived from Hager and Taylor's *The Novels of World War I*. Hager and Taylor included the publishing data for every First World War novel published in English between 1914 and 1980. I then compiled these entries into a dataset and, using publicly available documents and information, determined each author's nationality and gender and whether or not they had served in the war or witnessed it firsthand in some capacity, for example, as a war correspondent or a civilian living near the battlefields. For some cases, I was unable to determine the author's gender or whether or not they had witnessed the war. These cases are categorized as "Unknown" and included in the data accordingly.
9. Jeffrey Walsh, *American War Literature, 1914 to Vietnam* (London: Macmillan, 1982), 12.
10. On readers' preferences after World War I, see Kimberly J. Lamay Licursi, *Remembering World War I in America* (Lincoln: University of Nebraska Press, 2018), 93–94. On the publishing industry's preference for sentimentality, see Alex Vernon, *Soldiers Once and Still: Ernest Hemingway, James Salter, and Tim O'Brien* (Iowa City: University of Iowa Press, 2004), 44, and Michael W. Schaefer, "Civil War," in *Encyclopedia of American War Literature*, ed. Philip K. Jason and Mark Graves (Westport, CT: Greenwood, 2001), 66–67. Vernon writes that "Those

Notes to Pages 24–27

who wished to write truthfully and nonromantically about the war confronted a literary taste that preferred lighter, more conventional fare. Editors and publishers catered to that taste; writers who wanted to be published and read also catered to that taste." On censorship, see Hazel Hutchison, *The War That Used Up Words: American Writers and the First World War* (New Haven, CT: Yale University Press, 2015), 20–21.

11. Similar statistics apply to writers in the United Kingdom during the same time frame. From 1914 to 1920, 135 British, Irish, and Scottish writers published 208 novels about the war. Of these, 35 authors were either veterans or witnesses, compared with 100 nonwitnesses—a slightly higher proportion (24 percent) than in the American case (13 percent).

12. Licursi, *Remembering World War I in America*, 46.

13. "Frederick Palmer's Wartime Romance," *New York Times*, December 24, 1916, 21, accessed online at https://timesmachine.nytimes.com/timesmachine/1916/12/24/101576227.pdf.

14. "A Hospital Romance," *The Independent*, January 1, 1917, 30, accessed online at https://archive.org/details/independen89v9onewy/page/n41.

15. *The New Republic*, December 30, 1916, 248.

16. Hager and Taylor, *The Novels of World War I*, 39.

17. *The Sewanee Review* 25, no. 1 (January 1917): 120, accessed online at https://www.jstor.org/stable/pdf/27532984.pdf.

18. "Current Fiction." *The Nation*, December 28, 1916, 610, accessed online at https://www.unz.com/print/Nation-1916dec28-00610/.

19. Hutchison, *The War That Used Up Words*, 159. See also Cynthia Wachtell's introduction to Ellen La Motte, *The Backwash of War: An Extraordinary American Nurse in World War I* (Baltimore: Johns Hopkins University Press, 2019), 6–13.

20. Robert Lynd, "The Backwash of War," *Publishers' Weekly*, September 16, 1916, 850.

21. "Mrs. Wharton's Story of the Marne," *New York Times*, December 8, 1918, section 7, 1.

22. Frederic Taber Cooper, "A Clear-Cut Gem of War Fiction," *Publishers' Weekly*, December 28, 1918, 2033.

23. *The New York Times Review of Books*, March 16, 1919, 82.

24. American Library Association, "The Booklist: A Guide to the Best New Books," vol. 15, no. 1, October 1918, 264, accessed online at https://babel.hathitrust.org/cgi/pt?id=mdp.39015036942541.

25. *The Outlook*, April 16, 1919, 668, accessed online at https://www.unz.com/print/Outlook-1919apr16-00668/.

26. *Wisconsin Library Bulletin* 15 (March 1919): 79, accessed online at https://babel.hathitrust.org/cgi/pt?id=uc1.b2920334;view=1up;seq=87.

27. Rebecca Deming Moore, "Hans Andersen Up to Date," *Publishers' Weekly* 95 (January 18, 1919): 182, accessed online at https://babel.hathitrust.org/cgi/pt?id=mdp.39015033468813.

Notes to Pages 28–32

28. *The Nation*, June 7, 1919, 920, accessed online at https://www.unz.com/print/Nation-1919jun07-00920/.

29. John Walcott, "Current Taste in Fiction: A Quarterly Survey," *The Bookman*, January 1920, 457.

30. On the competing visions of the war in American collective memory, see G. Kurt Piehler, *Remembering War the American Way* (Washington, DC: Smithsonian Books, 2004), and Steven Trout, *On the Battlefield of Memory: The First World War and American Remembrance, 1919–1941* (Tuscaloosa: University of Alabama Press, 2010).

31. Trout, *On the Battlefield*, 3.

32. William E. Matsen, *The Great War and the American Novel: Versions of Reality and the Writer's Craft in Selected Fiction of the First World War* (New York: Peter Lang Publishing, 1993), 55. See also John Rohrkemper, "Mr. Dos Passos' War," *Modern Fiction Studies* 30, no. 1, Special Issue: Modern War Fiction (Spring 1984): 37–51. Rohrkemper says of *One Man's Initiation*, "although not as weak or inconsequential as some critics have argued, [it] is limited in both artistic vision and sociopolitical understanding."

33. John Dos Passos, *Three Soldiers*, Sentry ed. (Boston: Houghton Mifflin, 1949).

34. Barry Maine, ed., *Dos Passos: The Critical Heritage* (London: Routledge, 1988), 5.

35. Linda W. Wagner, *Dos Passos: Artist as American* (Austin: University of Texas Press, 1979), 18.

36. Owen W. Gilman, "John Dos Passos's 'Three Soldiers' and Thoreau," *Modern Fiction Studies* 26, no. 3, Special Issue: John Dos Passos (Autumn 1980): 471. Gilman reads Andrews's story somewhat differently than many critics, seeing a "positive counter-message" in his ultimate resistance to the Army through his desertion. Andrews knows he will likely be caught and punished for his decision, and this acceptance for his act of civil disobedience, in Gilman's view, elevates Andrews's moral conscience above the institution and the government against which he has rebelled.

37. Sidney Howard, "Review of *Three Soldiers*," *Survey*, November 5, 1921, 221–22.

38. Nancy Gentile Ford, *The Great War and America: Civil-Military Relations during World War I* (Westport, CT: Praeger Security International, 2008), 56–57.

39. Coningsby Dawson, "Insulting the Army," *New York Times Book Review*, October 2, 1921, 1.

40. H. L. Mencken, *Smart Set* 66 (December 1921): 143–44. Quoted in Maine, *Dos Passos*, 51.

41. John Peale Bishop, *Vanity Fair*, October 1921, 9. Quoted in Maine, *Dos Passos*, 32.

42. Dawson, "Insulting the Army."

43. "Harold Norman Denny," *Annals of Iowa* 27 (1945): 165–66, https://doi.org/10.17077/0003-4827.6426

44. Harold Norman Denny, "One Soldier on 'Three Soldiers,'" *New York Times*, October 16, 1921, Section 3, 1, 22.

Notes to Pages 33–37

45. Gandal, *The Gun and the Pen*, 31–32.
46. Phil McArdle, "Sidney Howard: From Berkeley to Broadway and Hollywood," *Berkeley Daily Planet*, December 18, 2007, http://www.berkeleydailyplanet.com /issue/2007-12-18/article/28760.
47. Howard, "Review of *Three Soldiers*," 222.
48. John Rohrkemper points out that "the only common characteristic of the reviews — and it is an important one — was that hardly any of the reviewers addressed themselves in any detail to the art of the novel; their reactions were almost entirely to the content." John Rohrkemper, *John Dos Passos: A Reference Guide* (Boston: G. K. Hall & Co., 1980), vii.
49. Licursi, *Remembering World War I in America*, 120–21.
50. Kimberly Licursi notes that "Dos Passos was selling a virulent antiwar message, a new phenomenon at a time when the public was apathetic to almost anything war related." Licursi, *Remembering World War I in America*, 121.
51. *The New Republic*, December 30, 1916, 248.
52. Matsen, *The Great War and the American Novel*, 75. This process was taken to the extreme by the French combat veteran Jean Norton Cru in his 1929 book *Témoins* ("Witnesses," but later translated into English as *War Books*), in which he systemically compared the narrative content of more than three hundred works of war literature with the war experiences of their authors. Cyril Falls, a British war veteran, published a similar book (also titled *War Books*) in 1930 that focused on war literature published in English.
53. Matsen, *The Great War and the American Novel*, 76.
54. David Sanders, "Lies and the System: Enduring Themes in Dos Passos's Early Novels," *South Atlantic Quarterly* 65 (1966): 215–28.
55. Wayne Miller, *An Armed America, Its Face in Fiction: A History of the American Military Novel* (New York: New York University Press, 1970), 109.
56. Walsh, *American War Literature*, 69, 77.
57. Haytock, *The Routledge Introduction to American War Literature*, 80–81.
58. Charles A. Fenton, "A Literary Fracture of World War I," *American Quarterly* 12, no. 2, Part I (Summer 1960).
59. Matsen, *The Great War and the American Novel*, 48.
60. Steven Trout, *Memorial Fictions: Willa Cather and the First World War* (Lincoln: University of Nebraska Press, 2002), 6.
61. NPR, "'Wonderful Words' in Willa Cather's No-Longer-Secret Letters." April 30, 2013. Accessed online at https://www.npr.org/2013/04/30/178647158 /wonderful-words-in-willa-cathers-no-longer-secret-letters.
62. Trout, *Memorial Fictions*, 37, 114.
63. Trout, *Memorial Fictions*, 3.
64. Trout, *Memorial Fictions*.
65. Margaret Anne O'Connor, ed., *Willa Cather: The Contemporary Reviews* (Cambridge: Cambridge University Press, 2001), xx.

Notes to Pages 37–40

66. Based on a count found in collected volumes of their reviews, specifically John Rohrkemper's *John Dos Passos* and Margaret Anne O'Connor's *Willa Cather*. Rohrkemper includes eighteen contemporary reviews of *Three Soldiers*, while O'Connor has forty reviews of *One of Ours*.

67. Licursi, *Remembering World War I in America*, 96–102. According to Licursi's work, *One of Ours* debuted at number seven on the bestseller lists and eventually peaked at number six. In total, it remained on the bestseller lists for twenty-eight weeks. Hemingway's *A Farewell to Arms* lasted for only twenty weeks, though it would later outsell *One of Ours* by a wide margin.

68. Trout, *Memorial Fictions*, 109–10.

69. Caroline H. Walker, letter to Willa Cather, October 10, 1922, Nebraska State Historical Society, Willa Cather Pioneer Memorial Collection, Red Cloud. Quoted in Trout, *Memorial Fictions*, 110.

70. O'Connor, *Willa Cather*.

71. Carlos Baker, ed., *Ernest Hemingway: Selected Letters 1917–1961* (New York: Charles Scribner's Sons, 1981), 105.

72. Hemingway did criticize Cather publicly in his 1926 satirical novella *The Torrents of Spring*. "Nobody had any damn business to write about it [war], though, that didn't at least know about it from hearsay. Literature has too strong an effect on people's minds. Like this American writer Willa Cather, who wrote a book about the war where all the last part of it was taken from the action in 'Birth of a Nation,' and ex-servicemen wrote to her from all over America to tell her how much they liked it." Quoted in David M. Kennedy, *Over Here: The First World War and American Society* (New York: Oxford University Press, 1980), 219. For references to Hemingway's "Catherized," see, at least, O'Connor, *Willa Cather* (2001); Frederick T. Griffiths, "The Woman Warrior: Willa Cather and *One of Ours*," *Women's Studies* 11 (1984); Jean Schwind, "The 'Beautiful' War in *One of Ours*," *Modern Fiction Studies* 30, no. 1 (Spring 1984): 53–71; James Dawes, *The Language of War: Literature and Culture in the U.S. from the Civil War through World War II* (Cambridge, MA: Harvard University Press, 2002); Steven Trout, "Antithetical Icons? Willa Cather, Ernest Hemingway, and the First World War," *Cather Studies* 7 (2007); Buchanan, *Going Scapegoat*; Licursi, *Remembering World War I in America* (2018); Rebecca Onion, introduction to the reprint edition of *One of Ours* (Cleveland: Belt Publishing, 2019); Alex Ross, "Willa Cather's Quietly Shattering War Novel," *New Yorker*, July 7, 2020. There are likely others.

73. Quoted in James Schroeter, ed., *Willa Cather and Her Critics* (Ithaca, NY: Cornell University Press, 1967), 12.

74. Quoted in Schroeter, *Willa Cather and Her Critics*, 32.

75. Quoted in Schroeter, *Willa Cather and Her Critics*, 32–33.

76. Quoted in Schroeter, *Willa Cather and Her Critics*, 12.

77. Sidney Howard, "Miss Cather Goes to War," *The Bookman*, October 1922, 217, https://www.unz.com/print/Bookman-1922oct-00217/

Notes to Pages 40–44

78. Howard, "Miss Cather Goes to War," 218.
79. Howard, "Miss Cather Goes to War," 218.
80. Kimberly Licursi summarizes the critical response as a gender issue, noting that "much of the criticism was a backlash against Cather's rejection of the prevailing idea among the literary set that John Dos Passos's version of the war in *Three Soldiers* was correct and Cather's was hopelessly outdated. . . . Critics effectively discredited her interpretation of the war by suggesting that a woman had no perspective from which to judge the situation accurately." *Remembering World War I in America*, 104.
81. Quoted in Schroeter, *Willa Cather and Her Critics*, 143.
82. Stanley Cooperman, *World War I and the American Novel* (Baltimore: Johns Hopkins University Press, 1967), 129. One wonders how closely Cooperman read the novel, as he gets certain details about the plot wrong, including saying that Claude's wife, Enid, travels to Africa as a missionary when she very clearly goes to China to tend to her sick sister (133).
83. Cooperman, *World War I and the American Novel*, 136.
84. Trout, *Memorial Fictions*, 4. Italics in original.
85. Licursi, *Remembering World War I in America*, 106. See also Trout, *Memorial Fictions*; Griffiths, "The Woman Warrior"; Schwind, "The 'Beautiful' War in *One of Ours*"; Onion, "Introduction"; Ross, "Willa Cather's Quietly Shattering War Novel."
86. Trout, *Memorial Fictions*, 6.
87. Dawes, *The Language of War*, 145.
88. Haytock, *The Routledge Introduction to American War Literature*, 74–75; Licursi, *Remembering World War I in America*, 103.
89. Miller, *An Armed America*, 117.
90. Hager and Taylor, *The Novels of World War I*, 158.
91. Bobbie Ann Mason, *In Country* (1985); Ben Fountain, *Billy Lynn's Long Halftime Walk* (2012); Helen Benedict, *Sand Queen* (2011); Roxana Robinson, *Sparta* (2013); Cara Hoffman, *Be Safe I Love You* (2014).
92. For more on the relationship between Hemingway and Dos Passos, see James McGrath Morris, *The Ambulance Drivers: Hemingway, Dos Passos, and a Friendship Made and Lost in War* (Boston: Da Capo Press, 2017). On Hemingway's own war experiences, see for example, Keith Gandal, *The Gun and the Pen* as well as William E. Matsen, *The Great War and the American Novel*. Matsen notes that Hemingway's actual combat experience was far less than authors like Thomas Boyd or William March. "One thing that is strikingly evident about Hemingway's war experience in Italy during the summer of 1918 is that it was distressingly brief: distressing for both Hemingway and those critics who insisted the experiences of Frederic Henry in *A Farewell to Arms* were based on the author's own in Italy" (57).

Notes to Pages 45–50

Chapter Two

1. On Hall's classroom experience, see David O. Dowling, *A Delicate Aggression: Savagery and Survival in the Iowa Writers' Workshop* (New Haven, CT: Yale University Press, 2019), 123.
2. Ken Kesey, "Remember This: Write What You Don't Know," *New York Times*, December 31, 1989, section 7, 1, https://www.nytimes.com/1989/12/31/books /remember-this-write-what-you-don-t-know.html.
3. In *Facing the Abyss: American Literature and Culture in the 1940s* (New York: Columbia University Press, 2018), George Hutchinson writes that "studies of modern American literature and culture tend to end or begin at 1945, and they tend therefore to focus on what preceded or followed the 1940s. . . . While hundreds of books have covered the political, social, cinematic, and military history of the United States during the 1940s, that decade has been the black hole of American literary history" (1–2). He also argues that "major overviews of American literary history . . . [tend] to exaggerate a sense of total transformation identified with 1945" (2).
4. Elizabeth Tallent, "The Big X: Unravelling Mysteries in a Workshop for Fine Writing," *Stanford Today*, March/April 1996. http://stanford.edu/dept/news /stanfordtoday/ed/9603/9603bigx.html
5. Wallace Stegner, "Writing as Graduate Study," *College English*, 11, no. 8 (May 1950): 429–32.
6. Quoted in Jackson J. Benson, *Wallace Stegner: His Life and Work*, reprint ed. (Lincoln: University of Nebraska Press, 2009), 162.
7. Tallent, "The Big X."
8. McGurl, *The Program Era*, 60–61, 175–76.
9. McGurl, *The Program Era*, 175–76.
10. McGurl, *The Program Era*, 186.
11. What Stegner told his students at Harvard in 1940: "You need to write what you know about . . . and the next thing you need to understand is that all of you sitting there are somewhere between 19 and 22 years of age, and you really don't know enough about what it is you want to say until you are at least 30" (quoted in Benson, *Wallace Stegner*, 116–17).
12. McGurl, *The Program Era*, 94–95.
13. Astrid Erll, *Gedächtnisromane: Literatur über den Ersten Weltkrieg als Medium englischer und deutscher Erinnerungskulturen in den 1920er Jahren* (Trier: Wissenschaftlicher Verlag Trier, 2003). Working with British and German war novels of the 1920s, Erll distinguishes four modes: experiential, monumental, antagonistic, and reflexive. See also Astrid Erll, *Memory in Culture* (New York: Palgrave Macmillan, 2011), 158.
14. Alex Vernon, *Soldiers Once and Still: Ernest Hemingway, James Salter, and Tim O'Brien* (University of Iowa Press, 2004), 47. Italics in original.

Notes to Pages 50–53

15. Vernon, *Soldiers Once and Still*, 47.

16. Haytock, *The Routledge Introduction to American War Literature*, 109.

17. McGurl, *The Program Era*, 61. Italics in original.

18. The Stanford University Library provided me with a list of ninety-three Stegner Fellowship recipients from 1947 through 1956, but unfortunately does not have a complete list of program graduates for the 1940s and 1950s (it is unclear how many students attended the program without a fellowship). The Special Collections Department of University of Iowa Library provided me with a list of ninety-one workshop graduates from 1945 through 1955. Using these as a starting point, I searched for publicly available information about each graduate, including their military service (if any) and subsequent careers. Many graduates left little traceable information, leading me to conclude that they most likely did not become professional writers. In quite a few cases, though, I found book reviews, university website listings, and, sadly, many obituaries. A more detailed analysis of each graduate could be possible by going through government service records and university archives, but such data collection was beyond the scope of this project. For military service records, I reasoned that anyone who had served during World War II was likely to mention that fact in their biography, either as a writer or in their obituary. Although I cannot rule out exceptions, I believe that the sample I was able to obtain represents a reasonable set from which to base these conclusions about the general trajectory of graduates' post-workshop lives and careers.

19. *The Monterey Herald*, May 22, 2007, https://www.legacy.com/obituaries/monterey herald/obituary.aspx?n=robert-waring-hinwood&pid=88242276.

20. "'Acropolis' Tells Story of WW II Vets at Vassar College, Community Impact," *Poughkeepsie Journal*, January 3, 2018, https://eu.poughkeepsiejournal.com /story/life/2018/01/03/acropolis-tells-story-ww-ii-vets-vassar-college -community-impact/999585001/.

21. One crucial exception to this was African American veterans of the war, many of whom were denied any GI Bill benefits. The bill was structured in such a way that individual states retained discretion over how the benefits were awarded, all but ensuring that African American veterans would find it nearly impossible to use the benefits at colleges across the country that would deny them admission. For more, see Steven White, *World War II and American Racial Politics: Public Opinion, the Presidency, and Civil Rights Advocacy* (New York: Cambridge University Press, 2019), 184; Robert Levinson, "Many Black World War II Veterans Were Denied Their GI Bill Benefits. Time to Fix That," *War on the Rocks*, September 11, 2020, https://warontherocks.com/2020/09/many-black-world -war-ii-veterans-were-denied-their-gi-bill-benefits-time-to-fix-that; Alexis Clark, "Returning from War, Returning to Racism," *New York Times*, July 30, 2020, https://www.nytimes.com/2020/07/30/magazine/black-soldiers-wwii -racism.html.

Notes to Pages 54–60

22. Joseph Darda, "The Philosophy of Creative Writing," *LA Review of Books*, February 25, 2019, https://lareviewofbooks.org/article/philosophy-creative-writing/.

23. Vernon, *Soldiers Once and Still*, 23.

24. Roy Scranton, "The Trauma Hero: From Wilfred Owen to *Redeployment* and *American Sniper*," *Los Angeles Review of Books*, January 25, 2015, www.lareview ofbooks.org/essay/trauma-hero-wilfred-owen-redeployment-american-sniper.

25. Matthew J. Bruccoli, ed., with Judith S. Baughman, *Hemingway and the Mechanism of Fame* (Columbia: University of South Carolina Press, 2006), xxiv–xxv.

26. Hemingway, *Green Hills of Africa*, 70.

27. Bruccoli, xxii. Italics in original.

28. Ernest Hemingway, ed., Introduction to *Men at War* (New York: Bramhall House, 1955), xiv.

29. Eric Bennett, "Ernest Hemingway and the Discipline of Creative Writing, Or, Shark Liver Oil," *Modern Fiction Studies* 56, no. 3 (Fall 2010): 545.

30. Hemingway, *Men at War*, xi.

31. Hemingway, *Men at War*, xii.

32. Hemingway, *Men at War*, xiii.

33. Hemingway, *Men at War*, xiii.

34. Hemingway, *Men at War*, xv.

35. For more on the relationship between Hemingway and Dos Passos, see Donald Pizer, "The Hemingway-Dos Passos Relationship," *Journal of Modern Literature* 13, no. 1 (March 1986): 111–28; Dan Piepenbring, "Good Hearted Naiveté," *Paris Review*, January 14, 2015; James McGrath Morris, *The Ambulance Drivers* (2017).

36. Laurence W. Mazzeno, *The Critics and Hemingway, 1924–2014: Shaping an American Literary Icon* (Rochester, NY: Camden House, 2015), 40.

37. Howard Mumford Jones, *Saturday Review of Literature* 25, December 12, 1942, 11.

38. Benjamin Kirbach, "Institutional Itinerancy: Malcolm Cowley and the Domestication of Cosmopolitanism," in *After the Program Era: The Past, Present, and Future of Creative Writing in the University*, Loren Glass, ed. (Iowa City: University of Iowa Press, 2016), 44.

39. In 1946, Cowley edited the next Portable installment, which focused on William Faulkner. *The Portable Faulkner* revived Faulkner's reputation and is widely credited with leading to his winning the Nobel Prize three years later.

40. Kirbach, 45.

41. Malcolm Cowley, "Hemingway's Wound — and Its Consequences for American Literature," *Georgia Review* 38, no. 2 (Summer 1984): 223.

42. Cowley, "Hemingway's Wound," 238. Italics in original.

43. Eric Bennett, *Workshops of Empire: Stegner, Engle, and American Creative Writing during the Cold War* (Iowa City: University of Iowa Press, 2015), 12. Italics in original.

44. Bennett, "Ernest Hemingway and the Discipline of Creative Writing," 551.

45. Bennett, *Workshops of Empire*, 143.

Notes to Pages 68–70

46. John Barth, *Further Fridays: Essays, Lectures, and Other Nonfiction 1984–1994* (Boston: Little, Brown & Company, 1995), 95. Quoted in Bennett, *Workshops of Empire*, 143.

47. McGurl notes that "Hemingway's conversion of war trauma into graceful literary understatement would prove a powerful example" for creative writing students—war veterans chiefly among them—modeling a process of "'softening,' a subtle transition from the silent suffering of trauma into the controlled pathos of literary recollection." *Program Era*, 60–61.

48. Malcolm Cowley, "War Novels: After Two Wars," in *The Literary Situation* (New York: Viking Press, 1958), 23.

49. Malcolm Cowley, "War Novels," 34.

50. Malcolm Cowley, "War Novels," 34.

51. Malcolm Cowley, "War Novels," 36.

52. Malcolm Cowley, "War Novels," 36.

53. Malcolm Cowley, "War Novels," 25.

54. Hemingway, *Men at War*, xiv.

55. Desmond Taylor, *The Novels of World War II: An Annotated Bibliography, Volumes 1 and 2* (New York: Garland 1993).

56. Roy Scranton argues that readers and literary scholars have reduced the canon of American World War II to novels to a "handful of misrepresentative texts," namely Joseph Heller's *Catch-22* (1961), Kurt Vonnegut's *Slaughterhouse-Five* (1969), and Thomas Pynchon's *Gravity's Rainbow* (1973). Scranton, *Total Mobilization*, 14.

Chapter Three

1. John M. Del Vecchio, *The 13th Valley* (New York: Bantam Books, 1982), 414–16.

2. Timothy Lomperis, *"Reading the Wind": The Literature of the Vietnam War* (Durham, NC: Duke University Press, 1987), 120.

3. Linda Hutcheon, *A Poetics of Postmodernism: History, Theory, Fiction* (New York: Routledge, 1988), 89.

4. Tim O'Brien, *The Things They Carried* (New York: Penguin Books, 1990), 78; Kurt Vonnegut, *Slaughterhouse-Five* (New York: Dell Publishing, 1969).

5. Robert A. Wright, "'History's Heavy Attrition': Literature, Historical Consciousness, and the Impact of Vietnam," *Canadian Review of American Studies* 17, no. 3 (Fall 1986): 303. Italics in original.

6. Michael Herr, *Dispatches* (New York: Vintage, 1977), 49.

7. John Carlos Rowe, "Eye-Witness: Documentary Styles in the American Representations of Vietnam," *Cultural Critique*, no. 3, American Representations of Vietnam (Spring 1986): 126–50.

8. Mark Baker, *Nam: The Vietnam War in the Words of the Men and Women Who Fought There* (New York: Berkley Books, 1981), 24.

9. Paul Budra analyzes the tension between the authority derived from the

Notes to Pages 70–72

first-person presentation of the narratives (i.e., the oral history component) and the way that "the authority of orality is paradoxically heightened by Baker's refusal to name the vets who are speaking." Budra, "Concatenation and History in Nam," in *Soldier Talk: The Vietnam War in Oral Narrative*, ed. Paul Budra and Michael Zeitlin (Bloomington: Indiana University Press, 2004), 52–61.

10. Rowe, "Eye-witness," 136.

11. Pearl K. Bell, "Writing about Vietnam," *Commentary* (October 1978): 65–66.

12. Philip Beidler, *American Literature and the Experience of Vietnam* (Athens: University of Georgia Press, 1982), xiv.

13. Donald Ringnalda, "Fighting and Writing: America's Vietnam War Literature," *Journal of American Studies* 22, no. 1, Civil Rights and Student Protest (April 1988): 26. First and foremost, Ringnalda argues that Vietnam was unique because "it is the first war America ever lost. This was (and is) a monumental blow to a nation's hubris, to a nation's narrative in which the story has always been the same: we are righteous winners."

14. Gregory A. Daddis, "Mansplaining Vietnam: Male Veterans and America's Popular Image of the Vietnam War," *Journal of Military History* 82, no. 1 (2018): 185. Interestingly, the political scientist Adam Berinsky identifies World War II as the unique event in American history: "World War II was the only war in the last two centuries in which Americans were directly attacked by another nation before becoming engaged in active combat." Berinsky, *In Time of War: Understanding American Public Opinion from World War II to Iraq* (Chicago: University of Chicago Press, 2009), 3–4. There is some irony to this statement, as World War II has been the primary example for US defense planning requirements ever since.

15. Michiko Kakutani, "Novelists and Vietnam: The War Goes On," *New York Times Book Review*, April 15, 1984. Kakutani continues her assessment: "In novel after novel, a variation of the following true-to-life sequence occurs: the naive or gung-ho hero's initiation into military life at boot camp; his arrival in Southeast Asia; his encounters with suffering, pain and death; his attempts to escape the realities of war by drinking, whoring and fantasizing; and his return to an indifferent America."

16. Wright, "History's Heavy Attrition," 310. Italics in original.

17. Timothy Lomperis's *"Reading the Wind"* describes the comments of Bill Pelfrey, a Vietnam veteran who "admitted that war novelists do not write for other combat veterans but really more for the historical record. Like the World War I literature, the Vietnam War literature provides the veteran his distinctive perspective in the larger context of his generation. The literature gives a record of the veteran's emotions, a record, Bill feels, that can come only through fiction" (45). Keith Beattie also writes that "The unique war, it was argued, needed a form of representation capable of revealing the truth of the war. The result of this conception was the denigration of conventional written histories, which

Notes to Pages 73–79

were deemed incapable of adequately representing the war. This conclusion reflected the exclusionary notion that only those who experienced the war could adequately describe its truth." Keith Beattie, *The Scar That Binds: American Culture and the Vietnam War* (New York: New York University Press, 1998), 8.

18. Larry Heinemann, *Close Quarters* (New York: Vintage, 1974), 53–54.
19. Del Vecchio, *The 13th Valley*, 132.
20. Beidler, *American Literature*, 6.
21. Beidler, *American Literature*, 6.
22. O'Brien, *The Things They Carried*, 57.
23. Gustav Hasford, *The Short-Timers* (1979).
24. One example of where the idea of uniqueness breaks down is with the reception of Vietnam War veterans. John Wood writes that "Authors who fought in Vietnam suggest that their postwar troubles were unique because previous generations of soldiers supposedly had few readjustment troubles and were welcomed home as heroes. Historical scholarship and other sources reveal, however, that veterans of pre-Vietnam conflicts did not always have wonderful, trouble-free homecomings." John A. Wood, *Veteran Narratives and the Collective Memory of the Vietnam War* (Athens: Ohio University Press, 2016).
25. Broyles, "Why Men Love War."
26. "Public Trust in Government Remains Near Historic Lows as Partisan Attitudes Shift," Pew Research Center, May 2017, https://www.people-press.org /2019/04/11/public-trust-in-government-1958-2019/.
27. Marc Leepson, "Vietnam Voices," *New York Times*, May 17, 1981.
28. Philip H. Melling, *Vietnam in American Literature* (Boston: Twayne, 1990), 53–54.
29. Beattie, *The Scar That Binds*, 91–95.
30. Melling, *Vietnam*, 51, 55.
31. Rowe, "Eye-Witness," 135.
32. Daddis, "Mansplaining Vietnam," 187.
33. John S. Baky, "Vietnam War Fiction," *Articles and Conference Papers*, 1994.
34. This follows the line of argument in Yuval Noah Harari's *The Ultimate Experience*.
35. Harari, *The Ultimate Experience*, 22.
36. Harari, "Scholars, Eyewitnesses, and Flesh-Witnesses of War: A Tense Relationship," *Partial Answers* 7, no. 2 (2009): 231–32.
37. Harari, "Scholars, Eyewitnesses, and Flesh-Witnesses of War," 217. See also Harari, "Armchairs, Coffee, and Authority: Eye-Witnesses and Flesh-Witnesses Speak about War, 1100–2000," *Journal of Military History* 74 (January 2010): 62–63.
38. Harari, "Scholars, Eyewitnesses, and Flesh-Witnesses of War," 222.
39. In *The Other Side of Grief: The Home Front and the Aftermath in American Narratives of the Vietnam War* (Amherst: University of Massachusetts Press, 2008), Maureen Ryan makes a similar argument: "You had to be there. If there is a single theme

Notes to Pages 79–80

that echoes most loudly throughout the Vietnam 'aftermath' texts and combat novels of the past generation, it is the notion that only the soldiers who directly engaged this singular, complex war can ever understand it. It is this concept that privileges firsthand accounts of the grunts who survived the jungles of Vietnam, and, paradoxically, that accounts for the massive and endless testimony that they offer us. You had to be there. Most of you weren't, so you can't understand. But we'll try nonetheless — over and over — to explain" (17). Italics in original.

40. Harari writes that eyewitnesses are also "interested in authority, but in order to gain authority the eyewitness must provide the audience with factual knowledge. Hearing an eyewitness narrative is an equal exchange which simultaneously empowers both the author and the audience. Flesh-witnesses, in contrast, gain authority without providing the audience with knowledge. Hearing a flesh-witness narrative is consequently a rather one-sided exchange which empowers the witness while often disempowering the audience." Harari, "Scholars, Eyewitnesses, and Flesh-Witnesses of War," 222.

41. According to Harari, the turning point of the war veteran's image in society was the early nineteenth century, after which three competing images came to define the soldier: hero, criminal, and victim. "Throughout history, the image of common soldier was built around a basic tension between heroism and criminality. The soldier was half-hero, half-criminal, who stood apart and above from normal civilian society. All societies made huge efforts to reward and strengthen the heroic half and to discourage the criminal part. The campaigns of 1812 and of Sebastopol marked a turning point in military history, when this simple tension became a complex three-way struggle. To the heroic and the criminal soldier was now added the victimized soldier. By the late twentieth century, this image became dominant in the minds of civilians, so that, for example, Vietnam War veterans came to be seen in the United States as the chief victims of the war. Even when Vietnam veterans were accused of heinous crimes, the dominant tendency was to absolve them from responsibility to these crimes. The soldier's crimes were really the fault of the generals and politicians who victimized him and placed him in an impossible situation." *The Ultimate Experience*, 189. Italics in original.

42. The particular form of trauma that the war veteran experiences is distinct from other traumas, though. "Because they were traumatized by a sublime experience — and not by a merely awful experience such as child abuse — traumatized soldiers often appear in Western culture as 'holy fools,' bearers of a potent and sacred wisdom." Harari, *The Ultimate Experience*, 205.

43. Scranton, *Total Mobilization*, 3–4.

44. Aleksandra Musiał, *Victimhood in American Narratives of the War in Vietnam* (New York: Routledge, 2020).

Notes to Pages 81–90

45. For a critique of this, see Parul Sehgal, "The Case against the Trauma Plot," *New Yorker*, December 27, 2021.
46. Avishai Margalit, *The Ethics of Memory* (Cambridge, MA: Harvard University Press, 2002), 178.
47. Heinemann, *Close Quarters*, 282.

Chapter Four

1. For a summary of this issue, see Jerome de Groot, *The Historical Novel* (London: Routledge, 2009); Andrew James Johnston and Kai Wiegandt, eds., *The Return of the Historical Novel? Thinking about Fiction and History after Historiographic Metafiction* (Heidelberg: Universitätsverlag Winter, 2017).
2. Tatiana Prorokova, *Docu-Fictions of War: U.S. Interventionism in Film and Literature* (Lincoln: University of Nebraska Press, 2019).
3. In this case, I'm equating direct experience of the war with battle and combat. See Mary Dudziak, *War Time: An Idea, Its History, Its Consequences* (Oxford: Oxford University Press, 2012) for an alternate view on when wars actually end. Dudziak shows how ambiguities surrounding the question of when a war ends (or begins, for that matter) have profound legal implications.
4. See Vincent Trott, *Publishers, Readers and the Great War: Literature and Memory since 1918* (London: Bloomsbury, 2017). Trott explores the power possessed by publishers with respect to the literary response to the First World War during the 1920s. He argues that "the publishing industry played an integral role in shaping the memory of First World War throughout the 1920s," at first by downplaying war themes when marketing books but later, after the themes of disillusionment become more widespread, by promoting them vigorously once they had become commercially viable (49).
5. Lomperis, *"Reading the Wind,"* 47.
6. Lomperis, *"Reading the Wind,"* 45.
7. Erll, *Memory in Culture*, 165–66.
8. Erll, *Gedächtnisromane.*
9. Jerome de Groot discusses these attributes in *The Historical Novel*. He looks at war novels specifically as "historical fiction marketed at men" with a focus on the factual details of violence and battle (78–79).
10. Ben Fountain, "Soldiers on the Fault Line: War, Rhetoric, and Reality," *War, Literature, and the Arts*, 2013: 7.
11. Phil Klay, *Redeployment* (New York: Penguin, 2014), 259.
12. Erll, *Memory in Culture*, 166.
13. Hayden White, *The Practical Past* (Evanston, IL: Northwestern University Press, 2014), 23. Italics in original.
14. White, *The Practical Past*, 29.

Notes to Pages 90–94

15. White, *The Practical Past*, 32. Italics in original.
16. White's focus in this particular essay is the representation of the Holocaust and the individual experience of the concentration camp, in many cases captured in witness testimony after the fact, but the theory behind it is generalizable to other historical events, including war.
17. John Bodnar, *The "Good War" in American Memory* (Baltimore: Johns Hopkins University Press, 2010), 26.
18. Hutchinson, *Facing the Abyss*, 146.
19. Bodnar, *The "Good War,"* 217–25. See also Elizabeth Samet, *Looking for the Good War: American Amnesia and the Violent Pursuit of Happiness* (New York: Farrar, Straus & Giroux, 2021).
20. Astrid Erll, "Wars We Have Seen: Literature as a Medium of Collective Memory in the 'Age of Extremes,'" in *Memories and Representations of War: The Case of World War I and World War II*, ed. Elena Lamberti and Vita Fortunati (Amsterdam: Rodopi, 2009), 31.
21. Paul Fussell, *Wartime: Understanding and Behavior in the Second World War* (New York: Oxford University Press, 1989), 142–43.
22. Roy Scranton details the negative critical reactions to Fussell's *Wartime* in *Total Mobilization*, 229–32.
23. Consider the following taken from a review of the novel on NPR: "In his debut novel, *Matterhorn*, Vietnam combat veteran Karl Marlantes attempts to transport his readers to 1969, in a jungle near Laos, just south of the Vietnamese Demilitarized Zone where a company of young U.S. Marines are fighting for their lives in a war none of them really understands. And while no one who didn't serve in Vietnam can really grasp what life in that time, that place, was like, Marlantes comes closer than any American writer ever has to capturing the unrelenting terror and enormity of one of the saddest chapters in recent world history. . . . It's the rare kind of masterpiece that enriches not just American literature but American history as well." Michael Schaub, "*Matterhorn*: A Beautiful, Brutal Vietnam War Epic," NPR, April 22, 2010, https://www.npr .org/2010/04/22/126170933/matterhorn-a-beautiful-brutal-vietnam-war-epic. The veteran war correspondent Sebastian Junger penned the review for the *New York Times*, saying that "Chapter after chapter, battle after battle, Marlantes pushes you through what may be one of the most profound and devastating novels ever to come out of Vietnam — or any war. It's not a book so much as a deployment, and you will not return unaltered." Sebastian Junger, "The Vietnam Wars: *Matterhorn*," *New York Times*, April 1, 2010, https://www.nytimes .com/2010/04/04/books/review/Junger-t.html.
24. Quoted in Lomperis, "*Reading the Wind*," 54.
25. Today, all writers who wish to have their books published in the "traditional" manner (that is, not self-published) need a literary agent. There are some

Notes to Pages 94–96

subtleties to this process; while certain writers may be able to secure representation from a literary agent without having already published a novel, most will have to query literary agents with a completed manuscript before finding an agent willing to represent them. An author who has already published a novel will, in most cases, already have an agent. See Clayton Childress, *Under the Cover: The Creation, Production, and Reception of a Novel* (Princeton, NJ: Princeton University Press, 2017), 65–88. For more on how literary agents shape both the form and content of contemporary fiction, see Laura B. McGrath, "Literary Agency," *American Literary History* 33, no. 2 (2021): 350–70.

26. Michael Bourne, "'A Right Fit': Navigating the World of Literary Agents," *The Millions*, August 15, 2012, https://themillions.com/2012/08/a-right-fit-navigating -the-world-of-literary-agents.html.

27. Childress, *Under the Cover*, 72–73. See also McGrath, "Literary Agency," 352–61.

28. Childress, *Under the Cover*, 42.

29. Childress, *Under the Cover*, 274n4. Italics in original.

30. Childress, *Under the Cover*, 158, 274n4.

31. While Childress refers to these as secondary texts, Gérard Genette's concept of "paratext" is also applicable here.

32. For example, Roxana Robinson's "The Right to Write," *New York Times*, June 28, 2014; Cara Hoffman, "The Things She Carried," *New York Times*, March 31, 2014; Emily Gray Tedrowe, "Who Has the Right to Write about War?" *Daily Beast*, July 12, 2014.

33. Barbara Fisher, "A Tale of Two Women in Iraq—a Civilian and a Soldier," *Boston Globe*, August 29, 2011, http://archive.boston.com/ae/books/articles /2011/08/29/a_tale_of_two_women_in_iraq_a_civilian_and_a_soldier/.

34. The focus on single-authored works removes from the sample two coauthored novels, *War of the Encyclopaedists* (2015) by Christopher Robinson and Gavin Kovite, and *The Chords of War* (2017) by Christopher Meeks and Samuel Gonzalez. One reason for excluding these two works is that in both cases one author is a veteran and the other is not. Since an important point of comparison is the number of novels authored by veterans versus nonveterans, including coauthored works such as these give a false impression of authorship. The same applies to the two anthologies of veteran-authored short fiction (2013's *Fire and Forget: Short Stories from the Long War* and 2017's *The Road Ahead: Fiction from the Forever War*), both of which were coedited by veterans. For simplicity, I will use the term "novels" to apply to collections of short stories as well.

35. Authors who have published multiple works about the war are David Abrams (*Fobbit, Brave Deeds*), Elliot Ackerman (*Green on Blue, Waiting for Eden*), Helen Benedict (*Sand Queen, Wolf Season*), Phil Klay (*Redeployment, Missionaries*), Odie Lindsey (*We Come to Our Senses, Some Go Home*), Hilary Plum (*They Dragged Them through the Streets, Strawberry Fields*), Katey Schultz (*Flashes of War, Still Come*

Notes to Pages 96–99

Home), and Margaret Vandenburg (*The Home Front, Weapons of Mass Destruction*). Abrams, Ackerman, Klay, and Lindsey are veterans, while Benedict, Plum, Schultz, and Vandenburg are not.

36. Three of these five authors have personal experience in Iraq or Afghanistan as journalists, and two were deployed to Afghanistan as civil servants working for the US government. Nicholas Kulish (*Last One In*) and Whitney Terrell (*The Good Lieutenant*) both spent short amounts of time in Iraq as embedded journalists. Luke Mogelson (*These Heroic, Happy Dead*) enlisted as a medic in the Army National Guard, but never deployed as a soldier. Later he spent three years living in Kabul as a journalist. Masha Hamilton (*What Changes Everything*) worked at the US embassy in Afghanistan for sixteen months as the director of communications and public diplomacy. Kathleen McInnis (*The Heart of War*) worked as a civil servant in the Office of the Secretary of Defense (Policy) and spent time in Afghanistan with the Department of Defense. One other borderline case should be noted here as well. Odie Lindsey (*We Come to Our Senses*) is a combat veteran of the Persian Gulf War, and his story collection includes both that war as well as the 2003 Iraq War. I've chosen to treat him as a veteran within this dataset because the book's publisher prominently identifies Lindsey as a veteran, and many of the reviews focus on his military experience as a source for the book's material. Putting him in the "observer" category seems less fitting.

37. There are some subtleties to characterizing authors. How should we think of authors such as Atticus Lish, who served in the military but not in war? Or Siobhan Fallon, an Army spouse? While each of these authors has privileged access to information and experiences that may serve as the basis for their fiction, the distinction lies with Harari's concept of the flesh-witness; none of these authors personally experienced war and therefore cannot claim the authority of the flesh-witness that the veteran can.

38. Erll, *Memory in Culture*, 56. See also Jan Assmann, *Cultural Memory and Early Civilization* (Cambridge: Cambridge University Press, 2012) on the distinction between "communicative" and "cultural" memory.

39. Amy Schafer, "Generations of War: The Rise of the Warrior Caste and the All-Volunteer Force," Center for a New American Security, May 2017.

40. Jay Teachman, "A Note on Disappearing Veterans," *Armed Forces and Society* 39, no. 4 (October 2013): 740–50; Phillip Carter, Amy Schafer, Katherine Kidder, and Moira Fagan, "Lost in Translation: The Civil-Military Divide and Veteran Employment," Center for a New American Security, June 2017.

41. For a contrasting view that examines the "institutional presence" of the military in American society, see James Burk, "The Military's Presence in American Society, 1950–2000," in *Soldiers and Civilians: The Civil-Military Gap and American National Security*, ed. Peter D. Feaver and Richard H. Kohn (Cambridge, MA: MIT Press, 2001). Burk's concept of institutional presence rests on "the social

Notes to Pages 99–105

significance of an institution in society" and has both a material and a moral dimension. While Burk's framework remains valid, his conclusion that the military is a "highly salient" and "central institution" in American society relies too heavily on defense spending as a material indicator, missing the social factors determined more by interpersonal relationships.

42. "Survey of Young Americans' Attitudes toward Politics and Public Service," 28th ed., Harvard University Institute of Politics, December 10, 2015, https://iop.harvard.edu/survey/details/harvard-iop-fall-2015-poll.

43. Schafer, "Generations of War."

44. Kennedy, *The Modern American Military*, 4.

45. These dimensions are cultural, demographic, policy preference, and institutional. See Rahbek-Clemmensen et al., "Conceptualizing the Civil-Military Gap: A Research Note," 669–78.

46. Sebastian Junger, *Tribe: On Homecoming and Belonging* (New York: Twelve Books, 2016), 111.

47. Robert D. Putnam, *Bowling Alone: The Collapse and Revival of American Community* (New York: Simon & Schuster, 2000).

48. Owen Gilman, *The Hell of War Comes Home: Imaginative Texts from the Conflicts in Iraq and Afghanistan* (Jackson: University Press of Mississippi, 2018), 5.

49. Fountain, "Soldiers on the Fault Line," 3.

50. William A. Taylor, *Military Service and American Democracy: From World War II to the Iraq and Afghanistan Wars* (Lawrence: University Press of Kansas, 2016), 171–79. See also Sarah Kreps, *Taxing Wars: The American Way of War Finance and the Decline of Democracy* (New York: Oxford University Press, 2018).

51. Ben Fountain, *Beautiful Country Burn Again: Democracy, Rebellion, and Revolution* (New York: HarperCollins, 2018), 165–66.

52. Meredith Kleykamp and Crosby Hipes, "Coverage of Veterans of the Wars in Iraq and Afghanistan in the U.S. Media," *Sociological Forum* 30, no. 2 (June 2015); Scott Parrott, David L. Albright, Caitlin Dyche, and Hailey Grace Steele, "Hero, Charity Case, and Victim: How U.S. News Media Frame Military Veterans on Twitter," *Armed Forces and Society* 45, no. 4 (2019): 702–22; Caleb Cage, *War Narratives: Shaping Beliefs, Blurring Truths in the Middle East* (College Station: Texas A&M University Press, 2019).

53. Buchanan, *Going Scapegoat*, 44.

54. Buchanan, *Going Scapegoat*, 68.

55. "Conversation: Kevin Powers, Author of *The Yellow Birds*." PBS NewsHour, October 4, 2012. https://www.pbs.org/newshour/arts/conversation-kevin-powers-author-of-the-yellow-birds.

56. David Buchanan argues that Fountain's satiric style leads to "a loss of effectiveness and emotional resonance due to what I see as a somewhat frantic attempt to establish authenticity and authority on the topic of war in fiction written by a civilian. Or, to put it another way, Fountain often panders to the

Notes to Pages 105–10

demands of combat gnosticism, stylistically and thematically" (*Going Scape-goat*, 107). I see no evidence in the text for such a reading. On the contrary, Billy Lynn constantly wrestles with the meaning of his "knowledge" and the fact that having experienced combat does not make him any wiser on the subject of war. Fountain's primary concern in the novel is how Billy's fellow citizens seem more interested in projecting their own thoughts and opinions onto him rather than getting to know him as a human being, as something more than the symbolic reduction of the medals for valor he wears on his uniform.

57. See, for example, Dana Milbank, "It's Time to Cut and Run From 'Cut and Run,'" *Washington Post*, June 21, 2006, https://www.washingtonpost.com /wp-dyn/content/article/2006/06/20/AR2006062001343.html.

58. John Williams, "Writing Differently about the War, but Drawing from the Same Rich Vein," *New York Times*, November 13, 2012, https://www.nytimes .com/2012/11/13/books/kevin-powers-and-ben-fountain-national-book-award -nominees.html.

59. Phil Klay, "After War, a Failure of the Imagination," *New York Times*, February 8, 2014, https://www.nytimes.com/2014/02/09/opinion/sunday/after-war-a-failure -of-the-imagination.html.

60. Gallagher, "You Don't Have to Be a Veteran."

61. Brian Van Reet, "The Red and the Blue: Writing War in a Divided America," https://brianvanreet.com/2019/01/11/the-red-and-the-blue-writing-war-in-a -divided-america/.

62. Matthew Komatsu, "Review of Jon Chopan's *Veterans Crisis Hotline*," *Wrath-Bearing Tree*, April 1, 2019, https://www.wrath-bearingtree.com/2019/04 /review-of-jon-chopans-veterans-crisis-hotline/.

63. Cage, *War Narratives*, 5.

64. Scranton, *Total Mobilization*, 224–25.

Chapter Five

1. "Moral Injury Is the 'Signature Wound' of Today's Veterans," NPR, November 11, 2014, https://www.npr.org/2014/11/11/363288341/moral-injury-is-the -signature-wound-of-today-s-veterans.

2. Jim Golby, Lindsay P. Cohn, and Peter D. Feaver, "Thanks for Your Service: Civilian and Veteran Attitudes after Fifteen Years of War," in *Warriors and Citizens: American Views of Our Military*, ed. Jim Mattis and Kori Schake (Stanford, CA: Hoover Institution Press, 2016), 126–27. The authors of this study used a new set of YouGov survey data that examined respondents' social contact with the military. They observe that "demographic trends make the decline in the number of Americans with some kind of military connection inexorable," and also note that "25 percent to 30 percent of the nonveteran masses consistently chose not to give an answer when the YouGov survey asked them a question

Notes to Pages 110–13

about the military," a result that they interpret as potentially related to the lack of social contact mentioned earlier.

3. "The Nexus between Engaged in Combat with the Enemy and Post-Traumatic Stress Disorder in an Era of Changing Warfare Tactics," hearing before the Subcommittee on Disability Assistance and Memorial Affairs of the House Committee on Veterans' Affairs, 111th Congress, March 24, 2009, https://www .govinfo.gov/content/pkg/CHRG-111hhrg48423/html/CHRG-111hhrg48423 .htm.

4. "The Nexus between Engaged in Combat."

5. For a detailed account of the invasion of Iraq and subsequent deterioration of the occupation, see Michael R. Gordon and Bernard E. Trainor, *Cobra II: The Inside Story of the Invasion and Occupation of Iraq* (New York: Pantheon Books, 2006).

6. *United States Government Counterinsurgency Guide*, January 2009, 2, https://2009-2017.state.gov/documents/organization/119629.pdf.

7. David Kilcullen, *Counterinsurgency* (Melbourne: Scribe, 2010), 4.

8. Field Manual 3-24, 5-3, 2006. For more on metrics and measuring success in a counterinsurgency campaign, see Jason Campbell, Michael O'Hanlon, and Jeremy Shapiro, "How to Measure the War," *Policy Review*, no. 117 (October/November 2009); and Ben Connable, *Embracing the Fog of War: Assessment and Metrics in Counterinsurgency* (Santa Monica, CA: RAND Corporation, 2012).

9. "Recent Trends in Active-Duty Military Deaths," *Congressional Research Service*, report IF10899, May 20, 2019, https://crsreports.congress.gov/product/pdf/IF /IF10899.

10. A 2015 study of veterans who served in Iraq during different time periods (i.e., during the invasion, during the insurgency, or during the surge) found that "the use of asymmetric or guerilla-style tactics by enemy fighters may result in higher rates of PTSD among U.S. military personnel than the use of symmetric tactics, which mirror tactics used by U.S. forces." Jonathan D. Green et al., "The Effect of Enemy Combat Tactics on PTSD Prevalence Rates: A Comparison of Operation Iraqi Freedom Deployment Phases in a Sample of Male and Female Veterans," *Psychological Trauma* 8, no. 5 (2016): 634–40, doi: 10.1037 /tra0000086.

11. "American War and Military Operations Casualties: Lists and Statistics," *Congressional Research Service*, report RL32492, updated September 24, 2019; Jennie W. Wenger, Caolionn O'Connell, and Linda Cottrell, "Examination of Recent Deployment Experience across the Services and Components," *RAND Corporation*, report RR-1928-A, 2018. In a working paper on comparing casualty survival rates from Vietnam to Iraq, Matthew Goldberg uses a unit of measurement called a "troop-year," which is "the equivalent of a single soldier serving for a period of a year." He then compares the number of troops wounded and killed in action per 100,000 troop-years between Vietnam and Iraq both before and during the "Surge" in 2007 as well for a single army brigade combat

Notes to Pages 113–15

team (BCT) that "apparently faced more intense combat than most of the other 19 BCTs that were present during the surge." Even in that extreme case, the number of wounded in action in Vietnam (per 100,000 troop-years) was nearly double that of Iraq, and the number of killed in action was more than triple. Matthew S. Goldberg, "Updated Death and Injury Rates of U.S. Military Personnel during the Conflicts in Iraq and Afghanistan," *Congressional Budget Office*, Working Paper 2014-08 (December 2014), 6–9, https://www.cbo.gov /sites/default/files/113th-congress-2013-2014/workingpaper/49837-Casualties _WorkingPaper-2014-08_1.pdf.

12. Andrew F. Krepinevich, *The Army and Vietnam* (Baltimore: Johns Hopkins University Press, 1988). For a dissenting view that argues against Vietnam as primarily a counterinsurgency, see Harry G. Summers, *On Strategy: A Critical Analysis of the Vietnam War* (New York: Presidio Press, 1982).

13. Examples of book-length works of criticism that focus on combat as the primary element of war literature include Wayne Miller, *An Armed America* (1970); Paul Fussell, *The Great War and Modern Memory* (1975); Peter G. Jones, *War and the Novelist: Appraising the American War Novel* (1976); Philip Beidler, *American Literature and the Experience of Vietnam* (1982); Jeffrey Walsh, *American War Literature: 1914 to Vietnam* (1982); William Matsen, *The Great War and the American Novel* (1993); John Limon, *Writing after War: American War Fiction from Realism to Postmodernism* (1994); Kate McLoughlin, *Authoring War: The Literary Representation of War from the Iliad to Iraq* (2011); and Tatiana Prorokova, *Docu-Fictions of War: U.S. Interventionism in Film and Literature* (2019).

14. Wallis Sanborn III, *The American Novel of War: A Critical Analysis and Classification System* (Jefferson, NC: McFarland, 2012), 12.

15. Sanborn, *The American Novel of War*, 11. He mentions the following noteworthy, excluded novels by name: Willa Cather's *One of Ours*, Hemingway's *A Farewell to Arms*, James Jones's *From Here to Eternity*, Kurt Vonnegut's *Slaughterhouse-Five*, James Webb's *Fields of Fire*, Robert Stone's *Dog Soldiers*, Bobbie Ann Mason's *In Country*, and Ben Fountain's *Billy Lynn's Long Halftime Walk*, among others.

16. In his study on the fictional texts about the conflicts in Iraq and Afghanistan, Owen Gilman comes to a similar conclusion: "The most startling revelation from these most recent American experiences with war as represented in diverse imaginative texts involves the way the hell of war becomes the hell of home." Owen W. Gilman Jr., *The Hell of War Comes Home: Imaginative Texts from the Conflicts in Iraq and Afghanistan* (Jackson: University Press of Mississippi, 2018), 6.

17. Harari, *The Ultimate Experience*, 7.

18. James Wright, *Those Who Have Borne the Battle: A History of America's Wars and Those Who Fought Them* (New York: Public Affairs, 2012), 200.

19. Wright, *Those Who Have Borne the Battle*, 199.

Notes to Pages 115–17

20. Thomas Myers argues that representations of Vietnam veterans in popular culture repeatedly reinforced this idea of veterans as scapegoats. He writes that "the Vietnam veteran returned home to find he was still surrounded by enemies, and his new mythic status as scapegoat achieved prominence through the conduits of popular culture." Thomas Myers, *Walking Point: American Narratives of Vietnam* (New York: Oxford University Press, 1988), 189.

21. Hasford, *The Short-Timers*, 151.

22. Gates Commission, *The Report of the President's Commission on an All-Volunteer Armed Force* (Washington, DC: Government Printing Office, 1970), 164–65.

23. Berinsky, Adam J., *In Time of War: Understanding American Public Opinion from World War II to Iraq*, 18–21.

24. Loren Baritz, *Backfire: A History of How American Culture Led Us into Vietnam and Made Us Fight the Way We Did* (Baltimore: Johns Hopkins University Press, 1985), 181.

25. "Rather than the garlanded symbol of national goodness," Thomas Myers writes in *Walking Point*, "the Vietnam veteran often became the despised and feared Other, the scapegoat for a variety of ills, the greatest of which was the failure to secure the familiar, unambiguous historical closure that is called victory. . . . The Vietnam veterans, feeling that they had performed as required, found dark new tabulations at home rather than gratitude or under-standing" (189). Philip Melling's assessment in *Vietnam in American Literature* is similar: "In the early seventies the Vietnam veteran was the object rather than the agent of censure—the problem rather than the victim of the war. In the period 1970–1974 he was regarded as public enemy number one in the nation's media. . . . By a process of extension the veteran was rejected along with the war in which he had served. The problem of rejection both by the media and by the antiwar movement came to animate much of the writing by Vietnam veterans in the later 1970s" (50).

26. Many historians and literary scholars comment on the general image of Viet-nam veterans in film and literature during the 1970s. See, for example, Piehler, *Remembering War the American Way*, 168; Melling, *Vietnam in American Literature*, 50; Myers, *Walking Point*, 189.

27. Maureen Ryan, *The Other Side of Grief*, 14.

28. Ryan, *The Other Side of Grief*, 37.

29. Ryan, *The Other Side of Grief*, 59.

30. Wright, *Those Who Have Borne the Battle*, 203.

31. Jerry Lembcke's *The Spitting Image: Myth, Memory, and the Legacy of Vietnam* (New York: New York University Press, 1998) was the first significant study to criti-cize the spat-upon Vietnam veteran as a myth, arguing that the image "gained prominence during the fall of 1990, when the [George H. W.] Bush admin-istration used it to rally support for the Persian Gulf War" (2). Others have continued to disagree, though. A good summary of the issue as well as the

Notes to Pages 117–25

works that have addressed it can be found in Heather Vlieg, "Were They Spat On? Understanding the Homecoming Experience of Vietnam Veterans," *Grand Valley Journal of History* 7, no. 1, article 3 (2019).

32. Karl Marlantes, *What It Is Like to Go to War* (New York: Atlantic Monthly Press, 2011).

33. Marlantes, *What It Is Like*, 177.

34. Gilman, *The Hell of War Comes Home*, 8.

35. Beverly P. Bergman, Howard J. Burdett, and Neil Greenberg, "Service Life and Beyond—Institution or Culture?" *RUSI Journal* 159, no. 5 (2014): 60–68.

36. Klay, *Redeployment*, 11.

37. Fountain, *Billy Lynn*, 219.

38. Golby et al., "Thanks for Your Service," 126.

39. Golby et al., "Thanks for Your Service," 127–28.

40. Department of Defense policy allows deployed service members up to fifteen days of "R&R" (rest and recuperation) once during a year-long tour. This typically occurs near the halfway point of the deployment, though not always. Nonetheless the colloquial term is "mid-tour leave" or simply "R&R." "Leave and Liberty Policy and Procedures," Department of Defense Instruction 1327.06, May 19, 2016.

41. Siobhan Fallon, *You Know When the Men Are Gone* (New York: G. P. Putnam's Sons, 2011), 53–54.

42. Fallon, *You Know When the Men Are Gone*, 54.

43. Stephen Markley, *Ohio* (New York: Simon & Schuster, 2018), 313.

44. Roy Scranton, *War Porn* (New York: Soho Press, 2016), 235–36.

45. Scranton, *War Porn*, 238.

46. Cara Hoffman, *Be Safe I Love You* (New York: Simon & Schuster, 2014), 159.

47. Roxana Robinson, *Sparta* (New York: Picador, 2013), 145.

48. Robinson, *Sparta*, 145–46.

49. Robinson, *Sparta*, 242.

50. Michael Pitre, *Fives and Twenty-Fives* (New York: Bloomsbury, 2014), 367.

51. Pitre, *Fives and Twenty-Fives*.

52. Fountain, *Billy Lynn*, 22.

53. Fountain, *Billy Lynn*, 86, 155.

54. Fountain, *Billy Lynn*, 45–46.

55. Rebecca Rapp, "Bravo! Ben Fountain Scores a Touchdown on Reality," *The Wrath-Bearing Tree*, August 2020, https://www.wrath-bearingtree.com/2020/08/bravo-fountain-scores-touchdown-on-reality/.

56. Fountain, *Billy Lynn*, 28.

57. Fountain, *Billy Lynn*, 40.

58. Carol Giacomo, "Suicide Has Been Deadlier Than Combat for the Military," *New York Times*, November 1, 2019, https://www.nytimes.com/2019/11/01/opinion/military-suicides.html. The number of troops killed by hostile fire

Notes to Pages 125–29

excludes those killed in accidents or other "non-hostile" incidents as categorized by the Department of Defense. The total number of troops killed in action includes those killed during all named operations since 2001 (e.g., Operation Iraqi Freedom, Operation Enduring Freedom, Operation New Dawn, and so on). *Department of Defense Press Release on Casualty Status*, August 31, 2020, https://www.defense.gov/casualty.pdf.

59. The classic study on veteran reintegration is Jonathan Shay's *Odysseus in America: Combat Trauma and the Trials of Homecoming* (New York: Scribner, 2002). For a more technical and policy-oriented approach to the same psychological issues, see Terri Tanielian and Lisa H. Jaycox, eds., *Invisible Wounds of War: Psychological and Cognitive Injuries, Their Consequences, and Services to Assist Recovery* (Santa Monica: RAND Corporation, 2008).

60. Junger, *Tribe*, 124.

61. Surveys in which veterans are asked about whether they had traumatic experiences tend to overstate the proportion of PTSD compared with clinical studies. According to one survey, 47 percent of post-9/11 veterans reported having "emotionally traumatic or distressing experiences," with 36 percent saying that had suffered from post-traumatic stress. In 2015, the Department of Veterans Affairs commissioned a study that looked at combined data on PTSD rates and estimated the average value to be 23 percent of Iraq and Afghanistan veterans. This is higher than the estimated 15 percent of Vietnam veterans diagnosed with PTSD, according to the National Vietnam Veterans Readjustment Study in the late 1980s. "The American Veteran Experience and the Post-9/11 Generation," Pew Research Center, September 2019; Jessica J. Fulton, Patrick S. Calhoun, H. Ryan Wagner, Amie R. Schry, Lauren P. Hair, Nicole Feeling, Eric Elbogen, and Jean C. Beckham, "The Prevalence of Posttraumatic Stress Disorder in Operation Enduring Freedom/Operation Iraqi Freedom (OEF/OIF) Veterans: A Meta-analysis," *Journal of Anxiety Disorders* 31 (April 2015): 98–107.

62. Junger, *Tribe*, 90. Italics in original.

63. Beidler, *American Literature and the Experience of Vietnam*, 88. Beidler mentions Robert Stone's 1974 novel *Dog Soldiers* as his example and refers to this period as the "middle range" of Vietnam writing between 1970 and 1975.

64. Matthew Hefti, *A Hard and Heavy Thing* (Blue Ash, OH: Tyrus Books, 2015), 6.

65. Nico Walker, *Cherry* (New York: Knopf, 2018), 261.

66. Walker, *Cherry*, 263.

67. Walker, *Cherry*, 196.

68. Robinson, *Sparta*, 3–4.

69. Robinson, *Sparta*, 9.

70. Tanielian and Jaycox, *Invisible Wounds of War*.

71. Hoffman, *Be Safe*, 9.

72. Hoffman, *Be Safe*, 12.

73. Hoffman, *Be Safe*, 41.

Notes to Pages 129–36

74. Hoffman, *Be Safe*.
75. Hoffman, *Be Safe*, 42. Soldiers (and government civilians) deploying to combat zones are required to complete a health assessment before and after their overseas tours. This process included a consultation with a physician and a psychologist, as well as a self-assessment form that asks questions such as whether the respondent had been in physical danger, encountered dead bodies, or engaged in direct combat, in addition to asking about other physical symptoms and ailments. The comment that Lauren had "no red flags" means that her answers to this questionnaire did not give the impression of psychological trauma. Given what we learn about Lauren later in the novel, it is probable that she lied in her responses. For DoD policy, see DoD Instruction 6490.03 ("Deployment Health"), June 19, 2019, as well as Department of Defense Form 2900 ("Post-Deployment Health Re-Assessment"), October 2015.
76. Robinson, *Sparta*, 172.
77. Robinson, *Sparta*, 172.
78. Robinson, *Sparta*, 173.
79. Hoffman, *Be Safe*, 72–73.
80. Robinson, *Sparta*, 243.
81. Hoffman, *Be Safe*, 267.
82. Hoffman, *Be Safe*, 268–69.
83. Jonathan Shay, *Achilles in Vietnam: Combat Trauma and the Undoing of Character* (New York: Scribner, 1994); David Wood, *What Have We Done? The Moral Injury of Our Longest Wars* (New York: Little, Brown and Company, 2016). On the neurological distinction between PTSD and moral injury, see Haleigh A. Barnes, Robin A. Hurley, and Katherine Taber, "Moral Injury and PTSD: Often Co-Occurring Yet Mechanistically Different," *Journal of Neuropsychiatry and Clinical Neurosciences* 31, no. 2 (Spring 2019): A4–103, https://doi.org/10.1176/appi.neuro psych.19020036.
84. Wood, *What Have We Done*, 17. Italics in original.
85. Kevin Powers, *The Yellow Birds* (New York: Little, Brown and Company, 2012), 144.
86. Powers, *The Yellow Birds*, 145.
87. Markley, *Ohio*, 324.
88. Markley, *Ohio*.
89. For a rebuttal to Fussell's argument, see Roy Scranton, *Total Mobilization*, 222–25.
90. Markley, *Ohio*, 324.
91. Markley, *Ohio*, 324.
92. Markley, *Ohio*, 358.
93. Markley, *Ohio*, 472.
94. Markley, *Ohio*, 473. Italics in original.
95. Powers, 186.

Notes to Pages 137–41

Chapter Six

1. Lomperis, "Reading the Wind," 5.
2. Lomperis, "Reading the Wind,"63–64.
3. Caren Irr, "Toward the World Novel: Genre Shifts in Twenty-First-Century Expatriate Fiction," *American Literary History* 23, no. 3 (2011): 660. See also Caren Irr, *Toward the Geopolitical Novel: U.S. Fiction in the Twenty-First Century* (New York: Columbia University Press, 2014).
4. Cyrus Patell, *Cosmopolitanism and the Literary Imagination* (New York: Palgrave Macmillan, 2015), 8.
5. Cyrus Patell, *Emergent U.S. Literatures: From Multiculturalism to Cosmopolitanism in the Late Twentieth Century* (New York: New York University Press, 2014).
6. Jennifer Haytock, "Reframing War Stories: Multivoiced Novels of the Wars in Iraq and Afghanistan," *Modern Fiction Studies* 63, no. 2 (Summer 2017): 337.
7. Sam Sacks, "First-Person Shooters," *Harper's* (August 2015).
8. Darda, *Empire of Defense*, 159.
9. Scranton, "The Trauma Hero."
10. Scranton, "The Trauma Hero."
11. Maureen Ryan, "Intraspecies Communication: Memory, Story-Telling, and Football in American Fiction of the Iraq and Afghanistan Wars," *War, Literature, and the Arts* 28 (2016): 18.
12. Haytock, "Reframing War Stories," 338.
13. Haytock, "Reframing War Stories," 337.
14. Brian J. Williams, "The Desert of Anatopism: War in the Age of Globalization," *American Literature* 87, no. 2 (June 2015): 360.
15. Williams, "The Desert of Anatopism," 376.
16. McGurl, *The Program Era*, 337–38.
17. Benjamin Buchholz was an officer in the Army National Guard, Michael Pitre and Elliot Ackerman were officers in the United States Marine Corps, and Roy Scranton and Brian Van Reet were enlisted soldiers in the United States Army.
18. The same character appears in Benedict's later novel, *Wolf Season* (2017).
19. I'm also focused on sustained point of view characters, not brief appearances that occur in *The Good Lieutenant*, *The Valley*, and *The Knife*. I have also chosen not to include sympathetic portrayals of Iraqis and Afghans in novels that are otherwise about Americans (e.g., *Youngblood*, *Wynne's War*). In those cases, the story is focalized through American characters, and the portrayal of non-American characters, while noteworthy, is still a minor element of the narrative. I have also excluded novels that portray non-American characters but who aren't from the wars, for example Atticus Lish's *Preparation for the Next Life* (a Chinese immigrant) and Laura McBride's *We Are Called to Rise* (the young son of Albanian refugees).

Notes to Pages 142–45

20. Book-length works that address this aspect of Vietnam War literature include Philip Beidler, *American Literature and the Experience of Vietnam* (1982); Loren Baritz, *Backfire: A History of American Culture Led Us into Vietnam and Made Us Fight the Way We Did* (1985); Timothy Lomperis, *"Reading the Wind"* (1987); Thomas Myers, *Walking Point: American Narratives of Vietnam* (1988); Ross McGregor, *A Terrible Irony: American Response to the Vietnam War in Fiction* (1990); Philip Melling, *Vietnam in American Literature* (1990); Katherine Kinney, *Friendly Fire: American Images of the Vietnam War* (2000); Viet Thanh Nguyen, *Nothing Ever Dies: Vietnam and the Memory of War* (2016); and Aleksandra Musiał, *Victimhood in American Narratives of the War in Vietnam* (2020).

21. Brenda Boyle, ed., *The Vietnam War: Topics in Contemporary North American Literature* (New York: Bloomsbury Academic, 2015), 8.

22. Peter Marin, "Coming to Terms with Vietnam," *Harper's*, December 1980, 53.

23. Donald Ringnalda, "Fighting and Writing: America's Vietnam War Literature," 33.

24. Myers, *Walking Point*, 25.

25. Ross McGregor, *A Terrible Irony: American Response to the Vietnam War in Fiction* (Trier: Wissenschaftlicher Verlag Trier, 1990), 5, 34.

26. McGregor, *A Terrible Irony*, 5. McGregor argues that "Lacking sufficient knowledge of the Vietnamese to feel comfortable in characterizing them, the novelists merely sketch them, preferring to concentrate on the American tragedy" (34).

27. McGregor's analysis is unsparing and harsh: "An overview of the American novels leaves the reader surprised when he confronts the statistics of the war. Surprised that less than 60,000 Americans died, and that the Vietnamese suffering was so much greater. An estimated 1.9 million (other estimates say 3 million) Vietnamese were killed during America's involvement in the war, 4.5 million were wounded and 9 million became refugees, but in the novels this appalling suffering remains indistinct background to the central American passion." McGregor, *A Terrible Irony*, 36.

28. McGregor, *A Terrible Irony*, 47.

29. Kalí Tal, "The Mind at War: Images of Women in Vietnam Novels by Combat Veterans," *Contemporary Literature* 31, no. 1 (1990): 77.

30. Tal, "The Mind at War," 77.

31. Robert Olen Butler, *A Good Scent from a Strange Mountain* (New York: Grove Press, 1992), 203.

32. Butler, *A Good Scent from a Strange Mountain*, 205.

33. The manual received national media coverage far beyond what one might expect for the publication of new military doctrine, including reviews in the *New York Times* and *Foreign Affairs*. It was also downloaded more than 1.5 million times in its first month alone and was later republished with new introductory material by the University of Chicago Press and sold in commercial

Notes to Pages 145–50

bookstores. Raphael S. Cohen, "A Tale of Two Manuals," PRISM 2, no. 1 (December 2010): 87–100, https://cco.ndu.edu/Portals/96/Documents/prism/prism_2-1/Prism_87-100_Cohen.pdf.

34. FM 3-24, *Counterinsurgency* (2006). Page numbers are given as they appear in the manual.

35. FM 3-24, 1–23. "In most COIN operations in which U.S. forces participate, insurgents hold a distinct advantage in their level of local knowledge. They speak the language, move easily within the society, and are more likely to understand the population's interests. Thus, effective COIN operations require a greater emphasis on certain skills, such as language and cultural understanding, than does conventional warfare. The interconnected, politico-military nature of insurgency and COIN requires immersion in the people and their lives to achieve victory."

36. FM 3-24, 1–15.

37. FM 3-24, 1–22.

38. FM 3-24, 7–2.

39. After Vietnam there was a debate over how the army and Marine Corps had fought and whether there had been too much or too little emphasis on counterinsurgency as an operational approach. Although there were programs, such as the Strategic Hamlet Program and the Civil Operations and Revolutionary Development Support (CORDS), that emphasized a more nuanced approach to cultural awareness, they were never the main military effort. For more on this debate, see Krepinevich, *The Army and Vietnam*, as well as Summers, *On Strategy*.

40. 1st Infantry Division, "Soldier's Handbook to Iraq," https://nsarchive2.gwu.edu//IMG/soldiershandbookiraq.pdf.

41. William D. Wunderle, *Through the Lens of Cultural Awareness: A Primer for US Armed Forces Deploying to Arab and Middle Eastern Countries* (Ft. Leavenworth, KS: Combat Studies Institute Press, 2006), https://www.armyupress.army.mil/Portals/7/Primer-on-Urban-Operation/Documents/Through-the-lens.pdf.

42. Viet Thanh Nguyen, *Nothing Ever Dies: Vietnam and the Memory of War* (Cambridge, MA: Harvard University Press, 2016), 83.

43. Darda, *Empire of Defense*, 169. Darda's main argument is that the United States has been "waging defense" since the end of World War II by promoting American values as a quest for justice, a policy often couched in racial terms: "Defense is the idea with which the state assigns value to some forms of being and denies it to others. Some are worth defending; some are worth saving; and some must be abolished" (8).

44. Scranton, *Total Mobilization*, 3.

45. Darda, *Empire of Defense*, 170.

46. Darda, *Empire of Defense*, 172–73.

47. Nguyen, *Nothing Ever Dies*, 96–97.

Notes to Pages 150–62

48. Nguyen, *Nothing Ever Dies*, 73.

49. This may be one reason why Buchholz's novel, which by my count was the first veteran-authored novel published about the wars, went mostly unnoticed upon its publication in 2011.

50. Elliot Ackerman, *Green on Blue* (New York: Scribner, 2015), 12.

51. Between 2011 and 2013, green-on-blue attacks targeting US and Coalition forces increased significantly, accounting for 15 percent of all Coalition forces killed in action in 2012. Bill Roggio and Lisa Lundquist, "Green-on-Blue Attacks in Afghanistan: The Data," *Real Clear Defense*, March 21, 2017, https://www.realcleardefense.com/articles/2017/03/21/green-on-blue_attacks_in_afghanistan_the_data_111015.html. See also *Operation Freedom's Sentinel: Lead Inspector General Report to the United States Congress*, May 19, 2020.

52. Ackerman, *Green on Blue*, 202.

53. Ackerman, *Green on Blue*, 210.

54. Ackerman, *Green on Blue*, 224.

55. Ackerman, *Green on Blue*, 226.

56. Ackerman, *Green on Blue*, 226.

57. Scranton, *War Porn*, 207.

58. Scranton, *War Porn*, 209–10.

59. For an analysis of the political decisions that led to the post-invasion insurgency in Iraq, see Daniel Byman, "An Autopsy of the Iraq Debacle: Policy Failure or Bridge Too Far?" *Security Studies* 17, no. 4 (2008): 599–643.

60. David Buchanan points out that the term "hajji" (his spelling) is just the latest iteration of the American soldier's epithets for enemy combatants. Yet he also argues that the word takes on much more symbolic power as a scapegoating function in contemporary American war fiction. Part of the issue is that the word originally serves as an honorific for Muslims who have made the pilgrimage (hajj) to Mecca. The word becomes a title, a gesture of respect, often taking the place of a person's first name. The American soldiers' use of the term as a pejorative for any Iraqi (or Afghan) makes a straightforward etymological reading of the word problematic. Buchanan, *Going Scapegoat*, 156–94.

61. Brian Van Reet, *Spoils* (New York: Back Bay Books, 2017), 32.

62. Van Reet, *Spoils*, 66.

63. Scranton, *War Porn*, 178. Italics in original.

64. For historical accounts of the events leading up to the Iraq War, see Michael Isikoff and David Corn, *Hubris: The Inside Story of Spin, Scandal, and the Selling of the Iraq War* (New York: Crown, 2006), as well as Thomas E. Ricks, *Fiasco: The American Military Adventure in Iraq* (New York: Penguin, 2006).

65. Scranton, *War Porn*, 247.

66. "'Insider Attack' Kills US Service Member in Afghanistan," *New York Times*, July 7, 2018, https://www.nytimes.com/2018/07/07/world/middleeast/insider-attack-kills-us-service-member-in-afghanistan.html. A search through just

Notes to Pages 164–67

the *New York Times* archives reveals many similar headlines over the years, including "Second Insider Attack Kills Service Member in Afghanistan" (September 3, 2018), "7 U.S. Soldiers Wounded in Insider Attack in Afghanistan" (June 17, 2017), "3 U.S. Soldiers Are Killed and a 4th Is Wounded by an Afghan Soldier" (June 10, 2017), and so on.

Chapter Seven

1. Gates Commission, *The Report of the President's Commission on an All-Volunteer Armed Force* (Washington, DC: Government Printing Office, 1970), 5–6.
2. On the analytic studies in support of the Gates Commission, see Bernard Rotsker, *I Want You! The Evolution of the All-Volunteer Force* (Santa Monica, CA: RAND Corporation, 2006), 112–20.
3. These arguments are paraphrases of the original report made in Rostker, *I Want You*, 79.
4. Taylor, *Military Service and American Democracy*, 141.
5. Morris Janowitz, "The All-Volunteer Military as a 'Sociopolitical' Problem." *Social Problems* 22, no. 3 (February 1975): 448.
6. Andrea Asoni, Andrea Gilli, Mauro Gilli, and Tino Sanandaji, "A Mercenary Army of the Poor? Technological Change and the Demographic Composition of the Post-9/11 U.S. Military," *Journal of Strategic Studies*, 2020, doi: 10.1080/01402390.2019.1692660.
7. Tim Kane, "Who Bears the Burden? Demographic Characteristics of U.S. Military Recruits before and after 9/11," The Heritage Center for Data Analysis, November 2005.
8. This pattern is described in Russel F. Weigley, "The American Civil-Military Cultural Gap: A Historical Perspective, Colonial Times to the Present," in *Soldiers and Civilians: The Civil-Military Gap and American National Security*, ed. Peter D. Feaver and Richard H. Kohn (Cambridge, MA: MIT Press, 2001), 215–46. See also Arthur Ekirch, *The Civilian and the Military: A History of the American Anti-Militarist Tradition* (New York: Oxford University Press, 1956).
9. Taylor, *Military Service and American Democracy*, 13.
10. Morris Janowitz, *The Professional Soldier: A Social and Political Portrait* (New York: Free Press, 1960), 252–53.
11. Ward Just, *Military Men* (New York: Michael Joseph, 1970), 5. "The thing that binds military men together in 1970," Just continues a few sentences later, "is the belief that the country is falling to pieces and the military is the only place where duty, honor, and country are put above self."
12. For a comprehensive history of the all-volunteer force, see Bernard Rostker, *I Want You!*, and Beth Bailey, *America's Army: Making the All-Volunteer Force* (Cambridge, MA: Harvard University Press, 2009).
13. Junger, *Tribe*, 36.

Notes to Pages 167–69

14. Jean M. Twenge, W. Keith Campbell, and Nathan T. Carter, "Declines in Trust in Others and Confidence in Institutions among American Adults and Late Adolescents, 1972–2012," *Psychological Science* 25, no. 10 (2014): 1914–23. See also Lee Rainie, Scott Keeter, and Andrew Perrin, "Trust and Distrust in America," Pew Research Center, July 2019.
15. Burk, "The Military's Presence in American Society," 247.
16. See Gallup's "Confidence in Institutions," http://www.gallup.com/poll/1597/confidence-institutions.aspx, and "Most Americans Trust the Military and Scientists to Act in the Public's Interest," Pew Research Center, October 18, 2016, http://www.pewresearch.org/fact-tank/2016/10/18/most-americans-trust-the-military-and-scientists-to-act-in-the-publics-interest/.
17. On the relationship between generalized trust and trust in institutions, see Bo Rothstein and Dietlind Stolle, "The State and Social Capital: An Institutional Theory of Generalized Trust," *Comparative Politics* 40, no. 4 (July 2008): 441–59. For more specific analyses of trust and the American military, see David T. Burbach, "Gaining Trust while Losing Wars: Confidence in the U.S. Military after Iraq and Afghanistan," *Foreign Policy Research Institute*, February 15, 2017; David T. Burbach, "Partisan Dimensions of Confidence in the U.S. Military, 1973–2016," *Armed Forces and Society* 45, no. 2 (2019): 211–33; Hugh Liebert and James Golby, "Midlife Crisis? The All-Volunteer Force at 40," *Armed Forces and Society* 43, no. 1 (2017): 116.
18. In February 2019, a federal judge ruled that the Selective Service System was unconstitutional because it discriminated on the basis of gender. In March 2020, the National Commission on Military, National, and Public Service published a report that recommended maintaining the Selective Service System for use in national emergencies, and that registration requirements should be extended to women as well. In December 2021, a provision to extend these requirements to women was dropped from the annual defense budget legislation, and as of June 2022 there have been no official changes to the system's registration policy.
19. "The Military-Civilian Gap: War and Sacrifice in the Post-9/11 Era," Pew Research Center, October 2011, 60.
20. Hugh Liebert and James Golby, "National Service and the All-Volunteer Force: A Response to Hauser's 'Why America Should Restore the Draft,'" *Armed Forces and Society* 44, no. 1 (2018); Amy Schafer, "Generations of War." Liebert and Golby also comment on the statistical correlation between having military connections and likelihood of joining the military (118).
21. Wright, *Those Who Have Borne the Battle*, 275.
22. Berinsky, *In Time of War*, 28–32.
23. Samuel Huntington, *The Soldier and the State* (Cambridge, MA: Belknap Press, 1957), 461.

Notes to Pages 169–75

24. Notable exceptions include some of the best-known works from World War I such as John Andrews in John Dos Passos's *Three Soldiers* and Frederic Henry in Ernest Hemingway's *A Farewell to Arms*.

25. Works that have characters who explicitly join the military before 9/11 include Roxana Robinson's *Sparta*, Cara Hoffman's *Be Safe I Love You*, Helen Benedict's *Sand Queen*, Kristin Hannah's *Home Front*, Elliot Ackerman's *Waiting for Eden*, Jesse Goolsby's *I'd Walk with My Friends If I Could Find Them*, and Brian Van Reet's *Spoils*. A handful of others have their characters join because of 9/11: Siobhan Fallon's *You Know When the Men Are Gone*, Ross Ritchell's *The Knife*, Stephen Markley's *Ohio*, and Lea Carpenter's *Eleven Days*.

26. Todd Helmus, S. Zimmerman, Marek Posard, Jasmine Wheeler, Cordaye Ogletree, Quinton Stroud, and Margaret Harrell, *Life as a Private: A Study of the Motivations and Experiences of Junior Enlisted Personnel in the U.S. Army* (Santa Monica, CA: RAND Corporation, 2018).

27. Helmus et al., *Life as a Private*, 28.

28. Helmus et al., *Life as a Private*, 33.

29. Schafer, "Generations of War." There are a few minor exceptions. Dan Eaton in Stephen Markley's *Ohio* (2018) decides to enlist in the Army rather than go to college, possibly because his father had served as a helicopter door gunner in Vietnam, though it's never completely clear. And two characters in Odie Lindsey's short story collection *We Come to Our Senses* (2016) are shown to be linked as family. "Colleen" tells the story of a woman who served during the invasion of Iraq, while her mother, Janette, served with the Army National Guard during Operation Desert Storm.

30. Jon Chopan, *Veterans Crisis Line* (Amherst: University of Massachusetts Press, 2018), 170.

31. Chopan, *Veterans Crisis Hotline*, 47.

32. Hoffman, *Be Safe*, 11.

33. Robinson, *Sparta*, 22.

34. Benedict, *Sand Queen*, 38.

35. Benedict, *Sand Queen*, 40.

36. Robinson, *Sparta*, 17.

37. Robinson, *Sparta*, 18.

38. See, for example, Kathy Roth-Douquet and Frank Schaeffer, *AWOL: The Unexcused Absence of the America's Upper Classes from Military Service — and How It Hurts Our Country* (New York: HarperCollins, 2006).

39. Liam Corley, "Epistemological Interference and the Trope of the Veteran," *Journal of Veterans Studies* 2, no. 1 (Spring 2017).

40. See Berinsky, *In Time of War*, 100–111.

41. For a good overview of the debate, see "The Moral Responsibility of Volunteer Soldiers," *Boston Review*, November 6, 2013.

Notes to Pages 176–82

42. Nicholas Kulish, *Last One In* (New York: Harper Perennial, 2007), 155.

43. Markley, *Ohio*, 309.

44. Whitney Terrell, *The Good Lieutenant* (New York: Farrar, Straus and Giroux, 2016), 227.

45. Jesse Goolsby, *I'd Walk with My Friends If I Could Find Them* (Boston: Houghton Mifflin Harcourt, 2015), 119.

46. Service members are eligible for a number of financial benefits during overseas deployments, including hostile fire pay, imminent danger pay, and a tax break on all income earned for any month or part of a month of service in a designated combat zone. A 2011 study by the Institute for Defense Analyses showed, however, that "there is only a weak relationship between the risk faced by personnel and the combat-related compensation they receive." Saul Pleeter, Alexander Gallo, Brandon Gould, Maggie Li, Shirley Liu, Curtis Simon, Carl Witschonke, and Stanley Horowitz, "Risk and Combat Compensation," Institute for Defense Analyses, paper P-4747, August 2011, https://www.ida.org/-/media/feature/publications/i/id/ida-p-4747-risk-and-combat-compensation/ida-document-p-4747.ashx.

47. Will Mackin, *Bring Out the Dog* (New York: Random House, 2018), 119.

48. David Abrams, *Brave Deeds* (New York: Black Cat, 2017), 25.

49. Goolsby, *I'd Walk*, 29.

50. Scranton, *War Porn*, 30–31.

51. Masha Hamilton, *What Changes Everything* (Lakewood, CO: Unbridled Books, 2013), 158.

52. Kristin Hannah, *Home Front* (New York: St. Martin's Griffin, 2012), 264. Italics in original.

53. Portions of this section were originally published, in slightly different form, in *Michigan War Studies Review*, 2019-063 (July 2019).

54. Cage, *Desert Mementos*, 111.

55. Golby et al., "Thanks for Your Service," 134.

56. Scranton, *War Porn*, 28.

57. Scranton, *War Porn*, 28. The line echoes a famous quote from Tim O'Brien's memoir, *If I Die in a Combat Zone, Box Me Up and Ship Me Home* (1973): "Can the foot soldier teach anything important about war, merely for having been there? I think not. He can tell war stories."

58. George Saunders, "Home," in *Tenth of December* (New York: Random House, 2013).

59. Saunders, "Home," 188.

60. Saunders, "Home," 184.

61. Saunders, "Home," 185.

62. Fountain, *Billy Lynn*, 193.

63. Fountain, *Billy Lynn*, 202.

64. Fountain, *Billy Lynn*, 219.

Notes to Pages 183–85

65. Van Reet, *Spoils*, 217.

66. Liebert and Golby, "Midlife Crisis?" 116.

67. Meredith Kleykamp and Crosby Hipes, "Coverage of Veterans of the Wars in Iraq and Afghanistan in the U.S. Media," *Sociological Forum* 30, no. 2 (June 2015).

68. Alair MacLean and Meredith Kleykamp, "Coming Home: Attitudes toward U.S. Veterans Returning from Iraq," *Social Problems* 61, no. 1 (2014).

69. Parrott et al., "Hero, Charity Case, and Victim."

70. Lance Brendan Young argues that veterans are "discursively objectified through the elevation of hero talk and the instrumental use of military rhetoric for commercial and political ends." Objectification comes through social obligation, and "The cultural directive to 'thank a veteran' is emblematic of a dominant social discourse, which idealizes veteran identities while marginalizing veterans' individual voices." Lance Brendan Young, "'Thank a Veteran': The Elevation and Instrumentation of U.S. Military Veterans," *Journal of Veterans Studies* 2, no. 2 (2017): 58–75.

71. Burbach, "Partisan Dimensions of Confidence in the U.S. Military," 211–33.

72. Ronald R. Krebs and Robert Ralston, "Patriotism or Paychecks: Who Believes What about Why Soldiers Serve," *Armed Forces and Society* 48, no. 1 (2022); Risa Brooks, "Paradoxes of Professionalism: Rethinking Civil-Military Relations in the United States," *International Security* 44, no. 4 (Spring 2020): 9.

73. Caleb Cage also sees evidence of the narrative split into heroes and victims. He argues that the hero and victim narratives "represent America's divided political culture. The hero narrative is the dominant narrative of the political right, an ideology that promotes a strong national defense and appreciates military service to promote it. The victim narrative, conversely, is largely the view of the political left, factions of which have historically critiqued the nation's wars and military service. Both sides of the political spectrum have also been willing to appropriate both narratives to manipulate the public for political gain." Cage, *War Narratives*, 79.

BIBLIOGRAPHY

Adams, Jon Robert. *Male Armor: The Soldier-Hero in Contemporary American Culture.* Charlottesville: University of Virginia Press, 2008.

Asoni, Andrea, Andrea Gilli, Mauro Gilli, and Tino Sanandaji. "A Mercenary Army of the Poor? Technological Change and the Demographic Composition of the Post-9/11 U.S. Military." *Journal of Strategic Studies*, January 30, 2020, 1–47. https://doi.org/10.1080/01402390.2019.1692660.

Assmann, Jan. *Cultural Memory and Early Civilization: Writing, Remembrance, and Political Imagination.* New York: Cambridge University Press, 2012.

Bacevich, Andrew J. *Breach of Trust: How Americans Failed Their Soldiers and Their Country.* 1st ed. New York: Metropolitan Books, 2013.

Bailey, Beth. *America's Army: Making the All-Volunteer Force.* Cambridge, MA: Harvard University Press, 2009.

Baker, Carlos, ed. *Ernest Hemingway: Selected Letters 1917–1961.* New York: Charles Scribner's Sons, 1981.

Baker, Mark. *Nam: The Vietnam War in the Words of the Men and Women Who Fought There.* New York: Berkley Books, 1981.

Baky, John S. "Vietnam War Fiction." Articles and Conference Papers, 1994. https://digitalcommons.lasalle.edu/vietnam_papers/2/.

Baritz, Loren. *Backfire: A History of How American Culture Led Us into Vietnam and Made Us Fight the Way We Did.* Baltimore: Johns Hopkins University Press, 1985.

Baughman, Judith S., and Matthew Joseph Bruccoli. *Hemingway and the Mechanism of Fame: Statements, Public Letters, Introductions, Forewords, Prefaces, Blurbs, Reviews, and Endorsements.* Columbia: University of South Carolina Press, 2006.

Beidler, Philip D. *American Literature and the Experience of Vietnam.* Athens: University of Georgia Press, 1982.

Bennett, Eric. "Ernest Hemingway and the Discipline of Creative Writing, Or, Shark Liver Oil." *Modern Fiction Studies* 56, no. 3 (2010): 544–67. https://doi.org/10.1353/mfs.2010.0003.

———. *Workshops of Empire: Stegner, Engle, and American Creative Writing during the Cold War.* 1st ed. Iowa City: University of Iowa Press, 2015.

Benson, Jackson J. *Wallace Stegner: His Life and Work.* Lincoln: University of Nebraska Press, 1996.

Bergman, Beverly P., Howard J. Burdett, and Neil Greenberg. "Service Life and Beyond—Institution or Culture?" *RUSI Journal* 159, no. 5 (2014): 60–68. https://doi.org/10.1080/03071847.2014.969946.

Berinsky, Adam J. *In Time of War: Understanding American Public Opinion from World War II to Iraq.* Chicago: University of Chicago Press, 2009.

Bibliography

Bodnar, John. *The "Good War" in American Memory*. Baltimore: Johns Hopkins University Press, 2010.

Boyle, Brenda M., ed. *The Vietnam War: Topics in Contemporary North American Literature*. New York: Bloomsbury Academic, 2015.

Broyles, William. "Why Men Love War." *Esquire*, November 1, 1984.

Bruccoli, Matthew J. (Ed.) with Judith S. Baughman. *Hemingway and the Mechanism of Fame*. Columbia: University of South Carolina Press, 2006.

Buchanan, David A. *Going Scapegoat: Post-9/11 War Literature, Language and Culture*. Jefferson: McFarland, 2016.

Budra, Paul, and Michael Zeitlin, eds. *Soldier Talk: The Vietnam War in Oral Narrative*. Bloomington: Indiana University Press, 2004.

Burbach, David T. "Gaining Trust While Losing Wars: Confidence in the U.S. Military after Iraq and Afghanistan." *Armed Forces and Society* 45, no. 2 (2019): 154–71. https://doi.org/10.1016/j.orbis.2017.02.001.

———. "Partisan Dimensions of Confidence in the U.S. Military, 1973–2016." *Armed Forces and Society* 45, no. 2 (April 2019): 211–33. https://doi.org/10.1177/0095327 X17747205.

Burk, James. "The Military's Presence in American Society, 1950–2000." In *Soldiers and Civilians: The Civil-Military Gap and American National Security*, edited by Peter D. Feaver and Richard H. Kohn. Cambridge, MA: MIT Press, 2001.

———. "Theories of Democratic Civil-Military Relations." *Armed Forces and Society* 29, no. 1 (Fall 2002): 7–29.

Burke, Crispin. "How Veterans Can Help Bridge the Civil-Military Divide." *The Atlantic*, November 13, 2017. https://www.theatlantic.com/politics/archive/2017/11 /how-veterans-can-help-bridge-the-civilian-military-divide/545669/.

Butler, Robert Olen. *A Good Scent from a Strange Mountain: Stories*. New York: Grove Press, 1992.

Byman, Daniel. "An Autopsy of the Iraq Debacle: Policy Failure or Bridge Too Far?" *Security Studies* 17, no. 4 (December 9, 2008): 599–643. https://doi.org/10 .1080/09636410802507974.

Cage, Caleb S. *War Narratives: Shaping Beliefs, Blurring Truths in the Middle East*. College Station: Texas A&M University Press, 2019.

Campbell, James. "Combat Gnosticism: The Ideology of First World War Poetry Criticism." *New Literary History* 30, no. 1 (1999): 203–15.

Cather, Willa. *One of Ours*. London: Hamilton, 1965 [1922].

Childress, Clayton. *Under the Cover: The Creation, Production, and Reception of a Novel*. Princeton, NJ: Princeton University Press, 2017.

Cohen, Raphael S. "A Tale of Two Manuals." *PRISM* 2, no. 1 (December 2010): 87–100.

Cohn, Lindsay. "The Evolution of the Civil-Military 'Gap' Debate." Paper prepared for the TISS Project on the gap between the military and civilian society, 1999.

Bibliography

Cooperman, Stanley. *World War I and the American Novel*. Baltimore: Johns Hopkins University Press, 1967.

Corley, Liam. "Epistemological Interference and the Trope of the Veteran." *Journal of Veterans Studies* 2, no. 1 (2017): 69. https://doi.org/10.21061/jvs.29.

Cowley, Malcolm. "Hemingway's Wound—and Its Consequences for American Literature." *Georgia Review* 38, no. 2 (Summer 1984): 223–39.

———. *The Literary Situation*. New York: Viking Press, 1954.

Daddis, Gregory A. "Mansplaining Vietnam: Male Veterans and America's Popular Image of the Vietnam War." *Journal of Military History* 82, no. 1 (2018): 181–207.

Darda, Joseph. *Empire of Defense: Race and the Cultural Politics of Permanent War*. Chicago: University of Chicago Press, 2019.

———. "The Philosophy of Creative Writing." *Los Angeles Review of Books*, February 25, 2019. https://lareviewofbooks.org/article/philosophy-creative-writing/.

Däwes, Birgit. *Ground Zero Fiction: History, Memory, and Representation in the American 9/11 Novel*. Heidelberg: Universitätsverlag Winter, 2011.

Dawes, James. *The Language of War: Literature and Culture in the U.S. from the Civil War through World War II*. Cambridge, MA: Harvard University Press, 2002.

De Groot, Jerome. *The Historical Novel*. London: Routledge, 2009.

DeBruyne, Nese F. "American War and Military Operations Casualties: Lists and Statistics." *Congressional Research Service*, September 24, 2019.

Del Vecchio, John M. *The 13th Valley*. New York: Bantam Books, 1982.

Dos Passos, John. *Three Soldiers*. Sentry ed. Boston: Houghton Mifflin, 1949.

Dowling, David O. *A Delicate Aggression: Savagery and Survival in the Iowa Writers' Workshop*. New Haven, CT: Yale University Press, 2019.

Dudziak, Mary L. "Death and the War Power." *Yale Journal of Law and the Humanities* 30, no. 1 (2018). https://doi.org/10.2139/ssrn.3004292.

———. *War Time: An Idea, Its History, Its Consequences*. Oxford: Oxford University Press, 2012.

Eikenberry, Karl. "Reassessing the All-Volunteer Force." In *The Modern American Military*, edited by David M. Kennedy. New York: Oxford University Press, 2013.

Erll, Astrid. *Gedächtnisromane: Literatur über den Ersten Weltkrieg als Medium englischer und deutscher Erinnerungskulturen in den 1920er Jahren*. Trier: Wissenschaftlicher Verlag Trier, 2003.

———. *Memory in Culture*. New York: Palgrave Macmillan, 2011.

———. "Reading Literature As Collective Texts." In *Anglistentag München 2003: Proceedings*, edited by Christoph Bode, Sebastian Domsch, and Hans Sauer, 335–54. Trier: Wissenschaftlicher Verlag Trier, 2004.

———. "Wars We Have Seen: Literature as a Medium of Collective Memory in the 'Age of Extremes.'" In *Memories and Representations of War: The Case of World War I and World War II*, edited by Elena Lamberti and Vita Fortunati. Amsterdam: Rodopi, 2009.

Bibliography

Farrell, Susan. *Imagining Home: American War Fiction from Hemingway to 9/11*. Rochester: Camden House, 2017.

Fenton, Charles A. "A Literary Fracture of World War I." *American Quarterly* 12, no. 2 (1960): 119–32.

Field Manual 3-24, *Counterinsurgency*. Department of the Army, 2006.

Field Manual 3-24, *Insurgencies and Countering Insurgencies*. Department of the Army, May 2014.

Ford, Nancy Gentile. *The Great War and America: Civil-Military Relations during World War I*. Westport, CT: Praeger Security International, 2008.

Fountain, Ben. *Beautiful Country Burn Again: Democracy, Rebellion, and Revolution*. New York: HarperCollins, 2018.

———. "Soldiers on the Fault Line: War, Rhetoric, and Reality." *War, Literature, and the Arts*, 2013. https://www.wlajournal.com/wlaarchive/25_1/fountain.pdf.

Fussell, Paul. *The Great War and Modern Memory*. New ed. New York: Oxford University Press, 2013 [1975].

———. *Wartime: Understanding and Behavior in the Second World War*. New York: Oxford University Press, 1989.

Gallagher, Matt. "You Don't Have to Be a Veteran to Write about War." LitHub, February 2, 2016. https://lithub.com/you-dont-have-to-be-a-veteran-to-write -about-war/.

Gandal, Keith. *The Gun and the Pen: Hemingway, Fitzgerald, Faulkner, and the Fiction of Mobilization*. New York: Oxford University Press, 2008.

Gates Commission. *The Report of the President's Commission on an All-Volunteer Armed Force*. Washington, DC: Government Printing Office, 1970.

Gilman, Owen W., Jr. *The Hell of War Comes Home: Imaginative Texts from the Conflicts in Afghanistan and Iraq*. Jackson: University Press of Mississippi, 2018.

———. "John Dos Passos: 'Three Soldiers' and Thoreau." *Modern Fiction Studies* 26, no. 3 (Autumn 1980): 470–81.

Golby, James, Lindsay Cohn, and Peter D. Feaver. "Thanks for Your Service: Civilian and Veteran Attitudes after Fifteen Years of War." In *Warriors and Citizens: American Views of Our Military*, edited by Jim Mattis and Kori Schake. Stanford, CA: Hoover Institution Press, 2016.

Goldberg, Matthew. "Updated Death and Injury Rates of U.S. Military Personnel during the Conflicts in Iraq and Afghanistan." Congressional Budget Office, December 2014. www.cbo.gov/sites/default/files/113th-congress-2013-2014 /workingpaper/49837-Casualties_WorkingPaper-2014-08_1.pdf.

Green, Jonathan D., Michelle J. Bovin, Sarah E. Erb, Mark Lachowicz, Kaitlyn R. Gorman, Raymond C. Rosen, Terence M. Keane, and Brian P. Marx. "The Effect of Enemy Combat Tactics on PTSD Prevalence Rates: A Comparison of Operation Iraqi Freedom Deployment Phases in a Sample of Male and Female Veterans." *Psychological Trauma: Theory, Research, Practice, and Policy* 8, no. 5 (2016): 634–40. https://doi.org/10.1037/tra0000086.

Bibliography

Griffiths, Frederick T. "The Woman Warrior: Willa Cather and *One of Ours.*" *Women's Studies* 11, no. 3 (1984): 261–85. https://doi.org/10.1080/00497878.1984.9978616.

Hager, Philip, and Desmond Taylor. *The Novels of World War I: An Annotated Bibliography.* New York: Garland Publishing, 1981.

Hanley, Lynne. *Writing War: Fiction, Gender, and Memory.* Amherst: University of Massachusetts Press, 1991.

Harari, Yuval Noah. "Armchairs, Coffee, and Authority: Eye-Witnesses and Flesh-Witnesses Speak about War, 1100–2000." *Journal of Military History* 74, no. 1 (January 2010): 53–78.

———. "Scholars, Eyewitnesses, and Flesh-Witnesses of War: A Tense Relationship." *Partial Answers: Journal of Literature and the History of Ideas* 7, no. 2 (2009): 213–28. https://doi.org/10.1353/pan.0.0147.

———. *The Ultimate Experience: Battlefield Revelations and the Making of Modern War Culture, 1450–2000.* New York: Palgrave Macmillan, 2008.

Hasford, Gustav. *The Short-Timers.* New York: Bantam Books, 1979.

Haytock, Jennifer. "Reframing War Stories: Multivoiced Novels of the Wars in Iraq and Afghanistan." *Modern Fiction Studies* 63, no. 2 (2017): 336–54. https://doi.org/10.1353/mfs.2017.0025.

———. *The Routledge Introduction to American War Literature.* New York: Routledge, 2018.

Heinemann, Larry. *Close Quarters.* New York: Vintage, 1974.

———. *Paco's Story.* New York: Vintage, 1986.

Helmus, Todd, S. Zimmerman, Marek Posard, Jasmine Wheeler, Cordaye Ogletree, Quinton Stroud, and Margaret Harrell. *Life as a Private: A Study of the Motivations and Experiences of Junior Enlisted Personnel in the U.S. Army.* RAND Corporation, 2018. https://doi.org/10.7249/RR2252.

Hemingway, Ernest. *Green Hills of Africa.* New York: Charles Scribner's Sons, 1935.

———, ed. *Men at War: The Best War Stories of All Time.* New York: Bramhall House, 1955.

Herr, Michael. *Dispatches.* Reprint ed. New York: Vintage, 1991 [1977].

Hooker, Richard D. "Soldiers of the State: Reconsidering American Civil-Military Relations." *Parameters* 23, no. 4 (Winter 2003–2004): 4–17.

Huntington, Samuel P. *The Soldier and the State: The Theory and Politics of Civil-Military Relations.* Cambridge, MA: Harvard University Press, 1957.

Hutcheon, Linda. *A Poetics of Postmodernism: History, Theory, Fiction.* New York: Routledge, 1988.

Hutchinson, George. *Facing the Abyss: American Literature and Culture in the 1940s.* New York: Columbia University Press, 2018.

Hutchison, Hazel. *The War That Used Up Words: American Writers and the First World War.* New Haven, CT: Yale University Press, 2015.

Irr, Caren. *Toward the Geopolitical Novel: U.S. Fiction in the Twenty-First Century.* New York: Columbia University Press, 2013.

Bibliography

———. "Toward the World Novel: Genre Shifts in Twenty-First-Century Expatriate Fiction." *American Literary History* 23, no. 3 (September 1, 2011): 660–79. https://doi.org/10.1093/alh/ajr021.

Janowitz, Morris. "The All-Volunteer Military as a 'Sociopolitical' Problem." *Social Problems* 22, no. 3 (February 1975): 432–49.

———. *The Professional Soldier: A Social and Political Portrait*. New York: Free Press, 1960.

Johnson, Denis. *Tree of Smoke*. New York: Picador, 2007.

Johnston, Andrew James, and Kai Wiegandt. *The Return of the Historical Novel? Thinking about Fiction and History after Historiographic Metafiction*. Heidelberg: Universitätsverlag Winter, 2017.

Judt, Tony. *Reappraisals: Reflections on the Forgotten Twentieth Century*. New York: Penguin Books, 2008.

Junger, Sebastian. *Tribe: On Homecoming and Belonging*. New York: Twelve Books, 2016.

Just, Ward. *Military Men*. New York: Michael Joseph, 1970.

Kakutani, Michiko. "Novelists and Vietnam: The War Goes On." *New York Times Book Review*, April 15, 1984.

Kane, Tim. "Who Bears the Burden? Demographic Characteristics of U.S. Military Recruits before and after 9/11." Heritage Foundation, Center for Data Analysis, November 7, 2005.

Kennedy, David M., ed. *The Modern American Military*. New York: Oxford University Press, 2013.

———. *Over Here: The First World War and American Society*. New York: Oxford University Press, 1980.

Kilcullen, David. *Counterinsurgency*. Melbourne: Scribe, 2010.

Kirbach, Benjamin. "Institutional Itinerancy: Malcolm Cowley and the Domestication of Cosmopolitanism." In *After the Program Era: The Past, Present, and Future of Creative Writing in the University*, edited by Loren Glass. Iowa City: University of Iowa Press, 2016.

Klay, Phil. "After War, A Failure of the Imagination," *New York Times*, February 8, 2014.

Kleykamp, Meredith, and Crosby Hipes. "Coverage of Veterans of the Wars in Iraq and Afghanistan in the U.S. Media." *Sociological Forum* 30, no. 2 (June 2015): 348–68. https://doi.org/10.1111/socf.12166.

Kleykamp, Meredith, Crosby Hipes, and Alair MacLean. "Who Supports U.S. Veterans and Who Exaggerates Their Support?" *Armed Forces & Society* 44, no. 1 (January 2018): 92–115. https://doi.org/10.1177/0095327X16682786.

Krebs, Ronald R., and Robert Ralston. "Patriotism or Paychecks: Who Believes What about Why Soldiers Serve." *Armed Forces and Society*, April 15, 2020. https://doi.org/10.1177/0095327X20917166.

Krepinevich, Andrew F. *The Army and Vietnam*. Baltimore: Johns Hopkins University Press, 1988.

Bibliography

Kreps, Sarah. *Taxing Wars: The American Way of War Finance and the Decline of Democracy*. New York: Oxford University Press, 2018.

Landsberg, Melvin. *Dos Passos' Path to U.S.A.: A Political Biography, 1912–1936*. Colorado: Associated University Press, 1972.

Lembcke, Jerry. *The Spitting Image: Myth, Memory, and the Legacy of Vietnam*. New York: New York University Press, 1998.

Licursi, Kimberly J. Lamay. *Remembering World War I in America*. Lincoln: University of Nebraska Press, 2018.

Liebert, Hugh, and James Golby. "Midlife Crisis? The All-Volunteer Force at 40." *Armed Forces and Society* 43, no. 1 (January 2017): 115–38. https://doi.org/10.1177/0095327X16641430.

———. "National Service and the All-Volunteer Force: A Response to Hauser's 'Why America Should Restore the Draft.'" *Armed Forces and Society* 44, no. 1 (January 2018): 186–92. https://doi.org/10.1177/0095327X17715245.

Lomperis, Timothy J. *"Reading the Wind": The Literature of the Vietnam War*. Durham, NC: Duke University Press, 1987.

MacLean, Alair, and Kleykamp, Meredith. "Coming Home: Attitudes toward U.S. Veterans Returning from Iraq." *Social Problems* 61, no. 1 (February 2014): 131–54. https://doi.org/10.1525/sp.2013.12074.

Mailer, Norman. *Advertisements for Myself*. Cambridge, MA: Harvard University Press, 1992.

Maine, Barry, ed. *Dos Passos: The Critical Heritage*. London: Routledge, 1988.

Mann, Christopher T., and Hannah Fischer. "Recent Trends in Active-Duty Military Deaths." Congressional Research Service, May 20, 2019.

Margalit, Avishai. *The Ethics of Memory*. Cambridge, MA: Harvard University Press, 2002.

Marin, Peter. "Coming to Terms with Vietnam." *Harper's*, December 1980.

Marlantes, Karl. *What It Is Like to Go to War*. New York: Atlantic Monthly Press, 2011.

Mason, Bobbie Ann. *In Country*. New York: Harper Perennial, 1985.

Matsen, William E. *The Great War and the American Novel: Versions of Reality and the Writer's Craft in Selected Fiction of the First World War*. New York: Peter Lang Publishing, 1993.

Mattis, Jim, and Kori N. Schake, eds. *Warriors and Citizens: American Views of Our Military*. Stanford, CA: Hoover Institution Press, 2016.

Mazzeno, Laurence W. *The Critics and Hemingway, 1924–2014: Shaping an American Literary Icon*. Rochester, NY: Camden House, 2015.

McGrath, Laura. "Literary Agency." *American Literary History* 33, no. 2 (2021): 350–70.

McGregor, Ross. *A Terrible Irony: American Response to the Vietnam War in Fiction*. Trier: Wissenschaftlicher Verlag Trier, 1990.

McGurl, Mark. *The Program Era: Postwar Fiction and the Rise of Creative Writing*. Cambridge, MA: Harvard University Press, 2009.

Bibliography

McLoughlin, Kate. *Authoring War: The Literary Representation of War from the Iliad to Iraq.* Cambridge: Cambridge University Press, 2011.

Melling, Philip H. *Vietnam in American Literature.* Boston: Twayne, 1990.

Miller, Wayne Charles. *An Armed America, Its Face in Fiction: A History of the American Military Novel.* New York: New York University Press, 1970.

Morris, James McGrath. *The Ambulance Drivers: Hemingway, Dos Passos, and a Friendship Made and Lost in War.* Boston: Da Capo Press, 2017.

Musiał, Aleksandra. *Victimhood in American Narratives of the War in Vietnam.* New York: Routledge, 2020.

Myers, Thomas. *Walking Point: American Narratives of Vietnam.* New York: Oxford University Press, 1988.

Newman, John. *Vietnam War Literature: An Annotated Bibliography of Imaginative Works about Americans Fighting in Vietnam.* 3rd ed. Lanham, MD: Scarecrow Press, 1996.

Nguyen, Viet Thanh. *Nothing Ever Dies: Vietnam in the Memory of War: Vietnam and the Memory of War.* Cambridge, MA: Harvard University Press, 2016.

———. *The Sympathizer.* New York: Grove Press, 2016.

O'Brien, Tim. *The Things They Carried.* New York: Penguin, 1990.

O'Connell, Aaron B. "Review of Stacey Peebles, *Welcome to the Suck: Narrating the American Soldier's Experience in Iraq* (2011)." *Journal of American Studies* 47, no. 3 (2013). https://doi.org/10.1017/S0021875813001230.

O'Connor, Margaret Anne, ed. *Willa Cather: The Contemporary Reviews.* New York: Cambridge University Press, 2001.

Parker, Kim, Ruth Igielnik, Amanda Barroso, and Anthony Cilluffo. "The American Veteran Experience and the Post-911 Generation." Pew Research Center, September 2019.

Parrott, Scott, David L. Albright, Caitlin Dyche, and Hailey Grace Steele. "Hero, Charity Case, and Victim: How U.S. News Media Frame Military Veterans on Twitter." *Armed Forces and Society* 45, no. 4 (October 2019): 702–22. https://doi.org/10.1177/0095327X18784238.

Patell, Cyrus R. K. *Cosmopolitanism and the Literary Imagination.* New York: Palgrave Macmillan, 2015.

———. *Emergent U.S. Literatures: From Multiculturalism to Cosmopolitanism in the Late Twentieth Century.* New York: New York University Press, 2014.

Peebles, Stacey. *Welcome to the Suck: Narrating the American Soldier's Experience in Iraq.* Ithaca, NY: Cornell University Press, 2011.

Pew Research Center. "Public Trust in Government: 1958–2019." May 2017. https://www.pewresearch.org/politics/2019/04/11/public-trust-in-government-1958-2019/.

———. "Trust and Distrust in America." July 2019. https://www.pewresearch.org/politics/2019/07/22/trust-and-distrust-in-america/.

———. "War and Sacrifice in the Post-9/11 Era." October 5, 2011. https://www.pewsocialtrends.org/2011/10/05/war-and-sacrifice-in-the-post-911-era/.

Bibliography

Piehler, G. Kurt. *Remembering War the American Way*. Washington, DC: Smithsonian Books, 2004 [1995].

Pizer, Donald. "The Hemingway-Dos Passos Relationship." *Journal of Modern Literature* 13, no. 1 (March 1986): 111–28.

Pleeter, Saul, Alexander Gallo, Brandon Gould, Maggie Li, Shirley Liu, Curtis Simon, Carl Witschonke, and Stanley Horowitz. "Risk and Combat Compensation." Alexandria, VA: Institute for Defense Analyses, August 2011.

Prorokova, Tatiana. *Docu-Fictions of War: U.S. Interventionism in Film and Literature*. Lincoln: University of Nebraska Press, 2019.

Putnam, Robert D. *Bowling Alone: The Collapse and Revival of American Community*. New York: Simon & Schuster, 2000.

Rahbek-Clemmensen, Jon, Emerald M. Archer, John Barr, Aaron Belkin, Mario Guerrero, Cameron Hall, and Katie E. O. Swain. "Conceptualizing the Civil–Military Gap: A Research Note." *Armed Forces and Society* 38, no. 4 (2012): 669–78. https://doi.org/10.1177/0095327X12456509.

Rapp, Rebecca. "Bravo! Ben Fountain Scores a Touchdown on Reality." *Wrath-Bearing Tree*, August 2020. https://www.wrath-bearingtree.com/2020/08/bravo-fountain-scores-touchdown-on-reality/.

Ricks, Thomas E. "The Widening Gap between Military and Society." *The Atlantic*, July 1997. https://www.theatlantic.com/magazine/archive/1997/07/the-widening-gap-between-military-and-society/306158/.

Ringnalda, Donald. "Fighting and Writing: America's Vietnam War Literature." *Journal of American Studies* 22, no. 1 (April 1988): 25–42. https://doi.org/10.1017/S0021875800032990.

Robinson, Roxana. "The Right to Write." *New York Times*, June 28, 2014. https://opinionator.blogs.nytimes.com/2014/06/28/the-right-to-write/.

Rohrkemper, John. *John Dos Passos: A Reference Guide*. Boston: G. K. Hall, 1980.

———. "Mr. Dos Passos' War." *Modern Fiction Studies* 30, no. 1 (Spring 1984): 37–51.

Rostker, Bernard. *I Want You! The Evolution of the All-Volunteer Force*. Santa Monica, CA: RAND, 2006.

Rothstein, Bo, and Dietlind Stolle. "The State and Social Capital: An Institutional Theory of Generalized Trust." *Comparative Politics* 40, no. 4 (July 2008): 441–59. https://doi.org/10.2307/20434095.

Rowe, John Carlos. "Eye-Witness: Documentary Styles in the American Representations of Vietnam." *Cultural Critique*, no. 3 (Spring 1986): 126–50.

Ryan, Maureen. "Intraspecies Communication: Memory, Story-Telling, and Football in American Fiction of the Iraq and Afghanistan Wars." *War, Literature and the Arts* 28 (2016).

———. *The Other Side of Grief: The Home Front and the Aftermath in American Narratives of the Vietnam War*. Amherst: University of Massachusetts Press, 2008.

Bibliography

Sacks, Sam. "First-Person Shooters." *Harper's*, August 2015. https://harpers.org/archive/2015/08/first-person-shooters-2/.

Sanborn, Wallis R., III. *The American Novel of War: A Critical Analysis and Classification System.* Jefferson, NC: McFarland, 2012.

Sanders, David. "Lies and the System: Enduring Themes in Dos Passos's Early Novels." *South Atlantic Quarterly* 65 (Spring 1966): 215–28.

Saunders, George. *Tenth of December: Stories.* New York: Random House, 2013.

Scarborough, Elizabeth Ann. *The Healer's War: A Fantasy Novel of Vietnam.* Reissue ed. New York: Open Road Media Sci-Fi and Fantasy, 1988.

Schafer, Amy. "Generations of War: The Rise of the Warrior Caste and the All-Volunteer Force." Center for a New American Security, May 2017.

Schroeter, James Marvin, ed. *Willa Cather and Her Critics.* Ithaca, NY: Cornell University Press, 1967.

Schwind, Jean. "The 'Beautiful' War in *One of Ours.*" *Modern Fiction Studies* 30, no. 1 (1984): 53–71.

Scranton, Roy. *Total Mobilization: World War II and American Literature.* Chicago: University of Chicago Press, 2019.

———. "The Trauma Hero: From Wilfred Owen to 'Redeployment' and 'American Sniper.'" *Los Angeles Review of Books*, January 25, 2015. https://lareviewofbooks.org/article/trauma-hero-wilfred-owen-redeployment-american-sniper/.

Shay, Jonathan. *Achilles in Vietnam: Combat Trauma and the Undoing of Character.* New York: Simon & Schuster, 1994.

———. *Odysseus in America: Combat Trauma and the Trials of Homecoming.* New York: Scribner, 2002.

Soli, Tatjana. *The Lotus Eaters.* New York: St. Martin's Press, 2010.

Stegner, Wallace. "Writing as Graduate Study." *College English* 11, no. 8 (May 1950): 429–32. https://doi.org/10.2307/585943.

Summers, Harry G. *On Strategy: A Critical Analysis of the Vietnam War.* New York: Presidio Press, 1982.

Tal, Kalí. "The Mind at War: Images of Women in Vietnam Novels by Combat Veterans." *Contemporary Literature* 31, no. 1 (1990): 76. https://doi.org/10.2307/1208637.

Tallent, Elizabeth. "The Big X: Unravelling Mysteries in a Workshop for Fine Writing," *Stanford Today*, March/April 1996. http://stanford.edu/dept/news/stanfordtoday/ed/9603/9603bigx.html.

Tanielian, Terri L., and Lisa Jaycox. *Invisible Wounds of War: Psychological and Cognitive Injuries, Their Consequences, and Services to Assist Recovery.* Santa Monica, CA: RAND, 2008.

Taylor, Desmond. *The Novels of World War II: An Annotated Bibliography, Volumes 1 and 2.* New York: Garland Publishing, 1993.

Taylor, William A. *Military Service and American Democracy: From World War II to the Iraq and Afghanistan Wars.* Lawrence: University Press of Kansas, 2016.

Bibliography

Teachman, Jay. "A Note on Disappearing Veterans." *Armed Forces and Society* 39, no. 4 (October 2013): 740–50. https://doi.org/10.1177/0095327X12468731.

Thompson, John B. *Merchants of Culture.* Cambridge: Polity, 2010.

Trott, Vincent. *Publishers, Readers and the Great War: Literature and Memory since 1918.* London: Bloomsbury Academic, 2017.

Trout, Steven. *Memorial Fictions: Willa Cather and the First World War.* Lincoln: University of Nebraska Press, 2002.

———. *On the Battlefield of Memory: The First World War and American Remembrance, 1919–1941.* 1st ed. Tuscaloosa: University Alabama Press, 2010.

Twenge, Jean M., W. Keith Campbell, and Nathan T. Carter. "Declines in Trust in Others and Confidence in Institutions among American Adults and Late Adolescents, 1972–2012." *Psychological Science* 25, no. 10 (2014): 1914–23. https://doi.org/10.1177/0956797614545133.

US Congress, House. Subcommittee on Disability Assistance and Memorial Affairs of the House Committee on Veterans' Affairs. *The Nexus between Engaged in Combat with the Enemy and Post-Traumatic Stress Disorder in an Era of Changing Warfare Tactics.* 111th Cong., 1st sess., March 24, 2009.

US Department of State, Bureau of Political-Military Affairs. *United States Government Counterinsurgency Guide.* January 2009. https://2009-2017.state.gov/documents/organization/119629.pdf.

Vernon, Alex. *Soldiers Once and Still: Ernest Hemingway, James Salter, and Tim O'Brien.* Iowa City: University of Iowa Press, 2004.

Vlieg, Heather. "Were They Spat On? Understanding the Homecoming Experience of Vietnam Veterans." *Grand Valley Journal of History* 7, no. 1 (2019): 1–36.

Wachtell, Cynthia. "Introduction," in *The Backwash of War: An Extraordinary American Nurse in World War I*, by Ellen La Motte. Baltimore: Johns Hopkins University Press, 2019.

Wagner, Linda. *Dos Passos: Artist as American.* Austin: University of Texas Press, 1979.

Wagner-Martin, Linda. *A History of American Literature, 1950 to the Present.* Malden, MA: Wiley-Blackwell, 2015.

Walsh, Jeffrey. *American War Literature, 1914 to Vietnam.* London: Macmillan, 1982.

Wenger, Jennie W., Caolionn O'Connell, and Linda Cottrell. "Examination of Recent Deployment Experience across the Services and Components." Santa Monica, CA: RAND Corporation, 2018. https://www.rand.org/pubs/research_reports/RR1928.html.

White, Hayden. *Metahistory: The Historical Imagination in Nineteenth-Century Europe.* Baltimore: Johns Hopkins University Press, 1973.

———. *The Practical Past.* Evanston, IL: Northwestern University Press, 2014.

Williams, Brian J. "The Desert of Anatopism: War in the Age of Globalization." *American Literature* 87, no. 2 (January 1, 2015): 359–85. https://doi.org/10.1215/00029831-2886163.

Bibliography

Williams, John. "Writing Differently about the War, but Drawing from the Same Rich Vein," *New York Times*, November 13, 2012.

Wood, David. *What Have We Done?: The Moral Injury of Our Longest Wars*. New York: Little, Brown and Company, 2016.

Wood, John A. *Veteran Narratives and the Collective Memory of the Vietnam War*. Athens: Ohio University Press, 2016.

Wright, James. *Those Who Have Borne the Battle: A History of America's Wars and Those Who Fought Them*. New York: Public Affairs, 2012.

Wright, Robert A. "'History's Heavy Attrition': Literature, Historical Consciousness and the Impact of Vietnam." *Canadian Review of American Studies* 17, no. 3 (Fall 1986): 301–16. https://doi.org/10.3138/CRAS-017-03-03.

Wunderle, William D. *Through the Lens of Cultural Awareness: A Primer for US Armed Forces Deploying to Arab and Middle Eastern Countries*. Fort Leavenworth, KS: Combat Studies Institute Press, 2006.

Young, Lance Brendan. "'Thank a Veteran': The Elevation and Instrumentation of U.S. Military Veterans." *Journal of Veterans Studies* 2, no. 2 (September 18, 2017): 58. https://doi.org/10.21061/jvs.16.

INDEX

Abrams, David, 177–78

Ackerman, Elliot, 18, 127, 152–56, 161, 162

Afghanistan War: consequences of, 5, 110–11, 161–62; justifications for, 175; public attitudes toward, 133, 168; rules of engagement in, 111–13, 138, 145–48. *See also* contemporary war fiction

alienation, 65–67, 74, 115–17, 119–25

all-volunteer military: and civil-military gap, 96–102, 166–69, 175; demographics of, 163–65; enlistment motivations, 168–79; ethical/moral issues in, 5, 134, 174–79; in fiction, 83–85, 169; literary paradox of, 18, 101, 163, 165, 174. *See also* draft

"The American Couple" (Butler), 144

American Literature and the Experience of Vietnam (Beidler), 70–71, 73–75

The American Novel of War (Sanborn), 22, 113

American public: disengagement of, 99–101, 118, 122, 124–25, 126–32, 179–83; ethical/moral issues for, 179–83; as readers, 65–67, 148–49; relationship with military, 1–6, 164–69, 174, 179–83, 185–86, 214–15n2; support of war, 118, 148–49; trust of government, 76, 167

Amos, James, 145–48

anatopisms, 139–40

Andrews, Mary Shipman, 26

antiwar sentiments, 67, 77–78, 115, 168–69

apathy. *See* disengagement

appropriation, cultural, 12, 14–15

Asia Society, 1985 conference, 67, 86–87, 137

Asymmetry (Halliday), 141

authenticity: as aesthetic theme, 23; of characters, 140–41; critiques of, 34, 37–38, 50, 55, 88, 92–96; cultural, 53–54, 60–62, 79–80, 83–85, 101–2; and memory, 43, 85–93; of narrators, 8–9, 21, 84–96, 101–2; sources of, 2, 34, 41–44, 49–51, 88, 90, 101–2. *See also* combat gnosticism

Authoring War (McLoughlin), 9, 22

authority: critiques of, 55, 68–75, 149–62; dispersion of, 13, 83–85, 96–108, 140–42, 151; of flesh-witnesses, 78–79; to interpret, 179–83; and memory, 85–93; of narrator, 1–3, 5, 12, 38–42, 105–6, 140–41, 174–79; sources of, 14–15, 43–44, 101–2. *See also* experiential authority, in fiction

autopoetics, 50

"baby killer" stereotype, 116, 118–19, 124, 182

Bacevich, Andrew J., 7

Backwash of War (La Motte), 26

Bailey, Temple, 27–28

Baker, Mark, 70, 72

Baky, John S., 78

Barbusse, Henri, 57

Barth, John, 60

Batiste, John, 145–51

Be Safe I Love You (Hoffman), 121, 127–32, 171–73

Beidler, Philip D., 70–71, 73–75, 107

Benedict, Helen, 44, 95–96, 141, 172–73

Bennett, Eric, 7, 60

243

Index

Bierce, Ambrose, 23
A Big Enough Lie (Bennett), 7
The Big V (Pelfrey), 115
"The Big X" (Tallent), 47–48, 54
Billy Lynn's Long Halftime Walk (Fountain), 103–6, 118–19, 123–25, 181–82
Blair, Edward, 52
blurbs, 95, 103. *See also* literary criticism and scholarship; publishing industry
Bowling Alone (Putnam), 99–100
Brave Deeds (Abrams), 177–78
Bring out the Dog (Mackin), 177
Broun, Heywood, 34, 38
Brown, Jeffrey, 104
Broyles, William, Jr., 75, 78
Bruccoli, Matthew J., 55
Buchanan, David, 22, 102, 107, 213–14n56
Buchholz, Benjamin, 18, 152–53, 161
Burdick, Eugene, 47–48
Burk, James, 167
Butler, Robert Olen, 11, 95, 144

Cage, Caleb, 107, 179
Campbell, James, 10, 21
Canby, Henry Seidel, 34, 38
"The Case against Willa Cather" (Hicks), 41–42
Cassill, Ronald, 52
casualty statistics, 112–13, 215–16n11, 222n27
Cather, Willa, 2, 23, 29, 36–42, 88–89, 200n72
censorship, 24, 26, 30–31
characters, 13–15, 18, 138–45, 149–50, 151–62, 221n19
Cherry (Walker), 126, 127
Childress, Clayton, 93–96
Chopan, Jon, 105, 126, 170–71
civic responsibility, 5–7, 99, 101, 118, 175. *See also* disengagement

Civil War, 16, 23, 46
civilians, 123–25, 137, 142–45, 222n27. *See also* American public; noncombatants
civil-military gap: and all-volunteer military, 96–102, 108–10, 118–25, 166–69, 175; critiques of, 6, 212–13n41; in fiction, 104–6, 109–10, 126–32, 140–42, 173, 177–79; origins of, 3–6, 163–65; significance of, 5–6, 83–84, 96–97, 169, 179–84. *See also* American public; military
Close Quarters (Heinemann), 72
COIN. *See* counterinsurgency
Cold War, 88, 115–16, 166
collective memory, 87, 89–93, 98–99
combat: conflicts compared, 112–13; vs. counterinsurgency, 111–13; definitions of, 110–11; distanced from home front, 1–2, 140; as real world, 121–22; trauma from, 125–26; and war fiction, 24, 32, 71–72, 76, 113–14, 124, 143
combat gnosticism: and all-volunteer military, 83–84; origins of, 10, 21–23, 43–44; rejection of, 102–3, 105–8, 111; and war fiction, 33, 61–62
"Combat Gnosticism" (Campbell), 10, 21
Combat Studies Institute, 147–48
combatants. *See* soldiers; veterans, generally
coming home: alienation/isolation of, 73–75, 114–15, 118–32, 207n24, 216n16, 217–18n31; for professional soldiers, 17, 174–79; as reverse culture shock, 109–10
Committee on Public Information, 24, 30–31
conscription, in US history, 4, 83, 98–99, 116. *See also* draft

244

Index

conservative politics, 77, 167, 181–83, 185

consumerism, 100, 118

contemporary war fiction: authors of, 3, 11–13, 84; civil-military gap in, 163–65, 183–86; critical assessment of, 138–40; ethical/moral issues in, 13, 14, 44, 174–79; as historical fiction, 11–12, 44, 92, 96; homecoming in, 118–25; key themes, 125–32, 138, 170–74, 176–79; non-American characters in, 151–62; quantity of, 96; stereotypes in, 165; titles listed, 187–89, 211n34, 211n35; trauma hero in, 103–6, 139, 148, 159

Cooperman, Stanley, 42

Corley, Liam, 175

cosmopolitanism, 137, 139–40, 148. See also cultural awareness

counterinsurgency, 111, 113, 137–51

Cowley, Malcolm, 58, 59, 61–62

craft. See literary merit

Crane, Stephen, 23, 29, 35, 43, 106, 170

creative writing programs: and experiential authority, 51, 60–61; influence of, 2–3, 12–13, 45–47, 51–54, 62, 149; Iowa, 2–3, 45, 48–50, 51–54; standards of, 50, 138–39; Stanford, 2–3, 46–49, 51–54

critics. See literary criticism and scholarship

cultural authority, 51, 53–54, 60–62, 77–80, 83–85, 101–2

cultural awareness, 112, 138, 142–51

cultural identity, 12, 51

"cut-and-runners," 105, 182

Daddis, Gregory A., 77–78

Darda, Joseph, 13, 138–39, 148–49

Däwes, Birgit, 16–17

Dawes, James, 42

Dawson, Coningsby, 30–31, 34, 41

dehumanization, 14, 30, 138. See also "Other"

Del Vecchio, John M., 65–67, 72, 74, 169

democracy, 91–92, 158, 160, 183–84

Denny, Harold Norman, 31–33, 41

Department of Defense, 111, 146, 163

disability, 17–18, 110–11, 129

disengagement, 99–101, 118, 122, 124–32, 179–83

disillusionment: in fiction, 29–34, 43, 55, 170, 173–74; with home front, 70, 73–75, 100, 118, 121; vs. noble cause, 36; vs. romanticism, 86

Dispatches (Herr), 69, 101

Docu-fictions of War (Prorokova), 85

Doner, Dean, 52

Dos Passos, John: background, 29; experiential authority of, 2, 31; reputation of, 40, 44, 53; *Three Soldiers*, 23, 29–36, 39, 57, 85–86, 156

Dos Passos (Maine), 29–30

draft: abolishment of, 4–5, 83, 99, 163–65; citizenship-service link, 99; effects of, 116, 165–69; in fiction, 72; morality of, 134, 169, 179. See also all-volunteer military

Dudziak, Mary L., 4

editors, influence of, 93–96

education. See creative writing programs; GI Bill

empathy, 140, 143–44, 148–49, 162

Empire of Defense (Darda), 138–39, 148–49

engagement, protest as, 168–69. See also disengagement

enlistment, motivations for, 165, 169–79, 227n29, 228n46

Erll, Astrid, 7, 50, 87, 89–90, 91–92

ethics: of conscience, 198n36; of representation, 13–15, 137–42, 149–51

245

Index

ethnic identity, 12, 51
evangelical movement, 77
experiential authority, in fiction:
combat as source of, 67, 74, 111, 138;
critics' emphasis on, 38–39, 43–44,
55; vs. cultural authority, 101–2; flesh
vs. eyewitness, 78–79, 91–92; and historical memory, 68–70, 79, 85–93; vs.
literary merit, 45, 105; media access
effects, 17, 89; and writing programs,
45–51. *See also* personal experience
eyewitness accounts, 69, 78–79, 86–87,
91–92, 107, 208n40

Fallon, Siobhan, 119–20
family relationships, 98–99, 168, 170,
178–79, 227n29
fantasy, home front as, 70, 100, 121
A Farewell to Arms (Hemingway), 37, 54,
55
Ferrone, John, 52
fiction, generally, 1, 68–75. *See also*
genre fiction; war fiction
Field Manual 3-24: counterinsurgency
field manual, 145–48
Fields of Fire (Webb), 72, 156
figurative language, 73–75
financial motivations, for enlistment,
170, 171–72
First Encounter (Dos Passos), 29
First World War. *See* World War I
Fisher, Dorothy Canfield, 36–37
Fives and Twenty-Fives (Pitre), 18, 122–23,
126, 152, 156–57, 161
Flashes of War (Schultz), 100, 141
flesh-witnessing ideology, 10, 78–79,
83–84, 102–3, 108, 212n37
For Whom the Bell Tolls (Hemingway),
54, 55
foreign policy, 5, 99, 151, 152, 156,
160–61

The Forever War (Haldeman), 74
Fountain, Ben: *Billy Lynn's Long Halftime
Walk*, 103–6, 118–19, 123–25, 181–82;
"Soldiers on the Fault Line," 89, 100;
on war fiction, 44, 89, 100
freedom, rhetoric of, 158, 175–76
Fussell, Paul, 9–10, 21, 22–23, 92, 107,
135

Gallagher, Matt, 1, 3, 105, 149
Gates Commission, 163–64
gender, authority and, 38–42. *See also*
women authors
genre fiction, 24, 26, 28, 34–36, 38, 74.
See also historical fiction
GI Bill, 48, 53–54, 203n21
Gilman, Owen W., Jr., 30, 100, 118, 119,
121
global storytelling, 139–40
Going After Cacciato (O'Brien), 72, 169
Going Scapegoat (Buchanan), 22, 102, 107
Golby, Jim, 184
A Good Scent from a Strange Mountain
(Butler), 144
Goolsby, Jesse, 126, 127, 177, 178
government, public attitude toward,
76, 167, 174. *See also* military
The Great War and Modern Memory (Fus-
sell), 9–10, 21, 92, 107
Green on Blue (Ackerman), 18, 152–56,
161, 162
Green on Blue incidents, 112, 153–54
Ground Zero Fiction (Däwes), 16–17
guerrilla tactics, 113, 142–43, 215n10
guilt, 124–25, 130, 134
Gwyn, Aaron, 176

Hager, Philip, 43
Hailperin, Bernard, 53
Haldeman, Joe, 74
Hall, James Byron, 45–47, 52

Index

Hall, John J., 110

Halliday, Lisa, 141

Hamilton, Masha, 141, 178

Hannah, Kristin, 126, 130–31, 176, 178–79

"happening," vs. history, 16, 84, 85–91, 96

Harari, Yuval Noah, 10, 78–79

A Hard and Heavy Thing (Hefti), 126–27

Harvard Institute of Politics report, 99

Hasford, Gustav, 72, 74, 115

Haytock, Jennifer, 8–9, 22, 35, 42, 138, 139

The Healer's War (Scarborough), 144

Hefti, Matthew J., 126–27

Heinemann, Larry, 11, 72, 126, 169

The Hell of War Comes Home (Gilman), 100, 118, 119

Hemingway, Ernest: criticism of Cather, 38, 200n72; and experiential authority, 2, 55, 201n92; influence of, 40, 54–62; *Men at War*, 56–58; novels of, 37, 54, 55; short stories, 45, 54

hero narratives, 61, 104, 116–17, 229n73. *See also* trauma hero concept

Herr, Michael, 11, 69, 101

Hicks, Granville, 41–42

Hinwood, Robert Waring, 53

Hipes, Crosby, 184

historical fiction, 62, 84–85, 88–92, 96–102, 105

history and historiography: authority of, 71, 79; and disengagement, 100–102; vs. "happening," 16, 84, 85–91, 96; rejection of, 67–75; temporal distancing effects in, 85–93; writing and, 61–62, 86–87, 89–91, 105–6

Hoffman, Cara, 44, 121, 127–32, 171–73

Holocaust, as collective memory, 91

"Home" (Saunders), 180–81

home front: distanced from combat, 1–2, 140; sacrifice on, 13, 98, 184; tensions of, 116–17, 132–36; in war fiction, 104–6, 109–10, 148–49, 165. *See also* coming home

Home Front (Hannah), 126, 130–31, 176, 178–79

Homer, 92

"How to Tell a True War Story" (O'Brien), 68

Howard, Sidney, 33–34, 38, 39–41

Huard, Frances Wilson, 25

human rights, fight for, 91–92

Huntington, Samuel, 5–6, 164, 169

Hutcheon, Linda, 68

Hynes, Samuel, 22, 107

I'd Walk with My Friends If I Could Find Them (Goolsby), 126, 127, 177, 178

idealism, 42, 173–74

identity considerations, 4, 12, 51

IEDs, 112

imagination: vs. history, 70–71, 85–86, 89–91; in war fiction, 1, 8, 61

improvised explosive devices (IEDs), 112

In Country (Mason), 11–12, 92, 126

injuries, 17–18, 110–11, 129

insurgency, 149, 159. *See also* counterinsurgency

interpretation, 5, 85, 88, 102–8

Introduction to American War Literature (Haytock), 22

Iowa Writers' Workshop, 2–3, 45, 48–50, 51–54

Iraq War: and all-volunteer military, 5; counterinsurgency in, 111–12, 138, 145–48; fictional critique of, 156–59, 161–62; and historical memory, 96; nonphysical injuries from, 110–11; political aspects, 152, 175; public attitude toward, 133, 168. *See also* contemporary war fiction

247

Index

Irr, Caren, 137
Islamic State in Iraq and Syria (ISIS), 99

Janowitz, Morris, 5–6, 164, 166
Johnny Got His Gun (Trumbo), 87, 91
Judt, Tony, 4
Junger, Sebastian, 99, 125–26, 167, 210n23
Just, Ward, 166
just war theory, 175–76, 181–83

Kakutani, Michiko, 71
Kane, Tim, 165
Kesey, Ken, 45
killing, morality and, 130–31, 138
Kirbach, Benjamin, 59
Klay, Phil, 89, 106, 118, 127, 130, 149
Kleykamp, Meredith, 184
Komatsu, Matthew, 106
Korean War, 101, 114
Kulish, Nicholas, 175–76

La Motte, Ellen, 26
The Language of War (Dawes), 42
Last One In (Kulish), 175–76
Lewis, Sinclair, 38
liberation narratives, subversion of, 151–52
Licursi, Kimberly J., 42–43
Liebert, Hugh, 184
literary agents, 94, 96, 210–11n25
literary criticism and scholarship: of contemporary war fiction, 84–85, 95–102, 105–8; cultural authority in, 53–54; and historical memory, 85–86, 89–91; and publishing, 93–96; veterans' influence on, 47–54; of WWI fiction, 21–28, 31–44, 54–59; of WWII fiction, 61–63

literary merit: and combat gnosticism, 45, 49–51, 60–63, 205n47; content vs. style in, 57, 73–75, 105–6
Lomperis, Timothy J., 86–87, 101
The Lotus Eaters (Soli), 92–93

Mackin, Will, 177
Mailer, Norman, 7, 169
Maine, Barry, 29–30
Manning, Frederic, 57
Markley, Stephen, 120, 126, 133–35, 176
Marlantes, Karl, 92, 117, 210n23
The Marne (Wharton), 27
Mason, Bobbie Ann, 11–12, 44, 92, 106, 126
Matsen, William, 35
Matterhorn (Marlantes), 92, 210n23
Mattis, James, 6
McGregor, Ross, 143–44
McGurl, Mark, 12, 48–51, 140
McLoughlin, Kate, 9, 22
media and media effects, 89, 116, 120, 129–30, 184–85
Melling, Philip H., 76, 77
memory, 72, 85–93, 98–99, 103, 117–18, 136
Memory in Culture (Erll), 7, 87, 89–90
Men at War (Hemingway), 56–58
Mencken, H. L., 31, 34, 38–39
mental health issues, 126–32, 219n61, 220n75. *See also* post-traumatic stress disorder
mercenaries, 177
Metahistory (White), 68
MFA programs. *See* creative writing programs
military: conformity in, 48–49; demographics of, 98–100, 164; professional, 99, 163–65, 177, 185; public attitude toward, 3–6, 164–69, 179–86;

248

Index

stereotypes about, 13, 30, 138–39, 143–44, 185. *See also* all-volunteer military
Miller, Wayne, 35, 43
"Miss Cather Goes to War" (Howard), 33–34, 39–41
morality: civil disobedience as, 198n36; of counterinsurgency, 138; for democracy, 183–84; in fiction, 13–14, 18, 76, 77; of killing, 130–31, 138; moral authority, 76–77, 169, 174–83; moral injury, 17–18, 129, 130, 132–36
multiculturalism, 137, 139–40, 148. *See also* cultural awareness
Muslim characters, 149, 160, 224n60
My Lai massacre, 116
Myers, Thomas, 143

The Naked and the Dead (Mailer), 7, 156, 169
Nam (Baker), 70, 72
narrative authenticity, 84–93, 101–2
narrative authority, 1–3, 5, 12, 38–42, 105–6, 140–41, 174–79. *See also* experiential authority, in fiction
nationalism: ethical modes of, 150–51; in fiction, 13–14, 31, 34, 42, 46, 76–77, 170, 172; and military, 150, 164, 167–68, 170, 172, 175; in moral injury, 133–36; public expressions of, 118, 150, 168
"Neverneverland" metaphor, 70
Nguyen, Viet Thanh, 14, 92, 148–50
9/11. *See* September 11, 2001 attacks
Nipson, Herbert, 52
Nixon, Richard, 76, 80, 163–64, 166
noble cause, war as, 29, 36, 41–43
noncombatants, 8–9, 13–15, 32, 96–97, 111–12, 145–51. *See also* civilians
nonveteran authors: of contemporary war fiction, 11, 13, 15, 127, 132, 172,

183; and narrative authenticity, 2, 8–12, 21, 63, 93–96
Nothing Ever Dies (Nguyen), 14, 148–50
nurses, 8, 26, 134–35, 144

O'Brien, Tim: *Going After Cacciato*, 72, 169; "How to Tell a True War Story," 68; influence of, 11; on limit of facts, 93; *The Things They Carried*, 74, 96
objectivity, in history, 68–69
"obligation," to write, 50
Ohio (Markley), 120, 126, 133–35, 176
The Old Blood (Palmer), 25, 34–35
One Hundred and One Nights (Buchholz), 18, 152–53, 161
One Man's Initiation—1917 (Dos Passos), 29
One of Ours (Cather), 23, 29, 38–42, 88–89
"Operation Battle Mountain" (Cage), 179
"Other," 14–15, 138–42, 149–52, 217n25

Packer, George, 22
Palmer, Frederick, 25, 34–35
Patell, Cyrus, 137
patriotism. *See* nationalism
Pearl Harbor, 175–76
Peebles, Stacey, 9
Pelfrey, William, 86–87, 115
personal experience: and authenticity, 2, 23, 138; authority from, 8, 9, 17, 179–83; critiques of, 31, 103–6; and society, 68–75, 138, 168; in writing, 50. *See also* combat gnosticism
pessimism. *See* disillusionment
Petraeus, David, 145–48
Pew Research Center, 2011 survey, 168
Pitre, Michael, 18, 122–23, 126, 152, 156–57, 161

249

Index

politics and political institutions: conservatism, 77, 167, 181–83, 185; and draft, 99, 166–67; in fiction, 105, 181–83; homecoming and, 114–18; leadership in, 184; polarization in, 185, 229n73; and Vietnam war, 76

The Portable Hemingway (Cowley), 58–59

postmodernism, 68

post-traumatic stress disorder (PTSD), 17–18, 110–11, 125, 132–36, 174–79, 185, 219n61

Powers, Kevin, 103–6, 133–34, 149

Pratt, John Clark, 67–68

professional military, 99, 163–65, 177, 185. *See also* all-volunteer military

The Professional Soldier (Janowitz), 5–6, 166

propaganda, 56–57. *See also* nationalism

Prorokova, Tatiana, 85

protagonists, selection of, 149–50

protest literature, 46. *See also* antiwar sentiments

"Proxy War" (Cage), 179

PTSD. *See* post-traumatic stress disorder

public opinion. *See* American public

publishing industry: influence of, 44, 58–59, 92–96, 101–2, 209n4; representation in, 195n35; trends in, 11–12, 16; writing programs graduates in, 52. *See also* literary criticism and scholarship

Putnam, Robert, 99–100

racial issues: vs. identity, 51; racism, 142–45, 203n21, 224n60; representation, 138–39, 149, 164, 185–86, 195n35

RAND Corporation, 2018 study, 170

"*Reading the Wind*" (Lomperis), 101

realism, 41–44, 49–51, 61–62, 89

redeployment, 114–18, 125–32. *See also* coming home

Redeployment (Klay), 106, 118, 127

"Reframing War Stories" (Haytock), 138, 139

representation: ethics of, 13–15, 149–51; failure of, 66–67, 86–87, 117; in publishing, 195n35

"Rest Camp on Maui" (Burdick), 47–48

reviews. *See* literary criticism and scholarship

Ricks, Thomas E., 6

the right to write, 7–8. *See also* narrative authority

roadside bombs, 112

Robinson, Roxana, 7–8, 44, 121–22, 127, 171–73

romanticism, about war, 78, 86

The Routledge Introduction to American War Literature (Haytock), 8–9, 35, 42

Rowe, John Carlos, 69

Roy-Bhattacharya, Joydeep, 141

Ryan, Maureen, 116–17, 139

Sacks, Sam, 13, 138

sacrifice: by foreign civilians, 98, 143–45; public's lack of, 5, 101, 148–49, 184; as theme, 13, 28, 31, 40

Sanborn, Wallis, 22, 113

Sand Queen (Benedict), 95–96, 141, 172–73

Saunders, George, 180–81

scapegoats, 76, 86, 115, 217n20, 217n25, 224n60

Scarborough, Elizabeth, 144

Schafer, Amy, 98–99

Schake, Kori, 6

Schultz, Katey, 100, 141

Scranton, Roy: *Total Mobilization*, 107, 148; "The Trauma Hero," 55, 139;

Index

War Porn, 18, 120–21, 152, 156–57, 160–61, 178, 180

Second World War. *See* World War II

secondary texts, 95

security contractors, private, 100

Selective Service System, 166, 167, 226n18

self-publishing, 96

sentimentality, 24, 28

September 11, 2001 attacks, 16–17, 104, 134, 160, 168–70

service, concept of, 164, 170, 183

Sherwood, Margaret Pollock, 26

The Short-Timers (Hasford), 72, 74, 115

The Soldier and the State (Huntington), 5–6, 169

"Soldier's Cross" (Cage), 179

"Soldier's Handbook to Iraq" (1st Infantry Division), 145–47

"Soldier's Home" (Hemingway), 45, 54, 55

soldiers, 12, 65–66, 145–51, 165, 169–79. *See also* all-volunteer military; draft; veterans

"Soldiers on the Fault Line" (Fountain), 89, 100

Soldiers Once and Still (Vernon), 50, 54–55

Soli, Tatjana, 92–93

A Son at the Front (Wharton), 43

"Song of Myself" (Whitman), 75

Sparta (Robinson), 7–8, 121–22, 127, 132, 171–72, 173

Spoils (Van Reet), 18, 152, 156, 159–61, 182–83

Stanford University creative writing program, 2–3, 46–49, 51–54

"status economy," for veteran-authors, 94–96

Stegner, Wallace, 2, 45, 46–49, 54

stereotypes: about military/veterans, 19, 116, 137, 165, 183–86, 206n15; avoidance of, 161; based on class,

169–74; of opponents, 145, 160, 224n60

storytelling, as medium of memory, 92

Stouck, David, 42

substance use, 126–32, 170

suicide, 125, 126–32, 174, 218–19n58

surrealism, 70–75, 173

Tal, Kalí, 144

Tallent, Elizabeth, 46, 48, 54

Taper, Bernard, 53

Taylor, Desmond, 43

Taylor, William, 164

"tell it like it was," 51. *See also* experiential authority, in fiction

temporal distance effects, 16, 84, 85–93, 96–102

terrorism, 16–17, 104, 134, 160, 168–70

testimony, fiction as, 35, 50, 65, 76–77

Thank God for the Atom Bomb (Fussell), 135

The Things They Carried (O'Brien), 68, 74, 169

The 13th Valley (Del Vecchio), 65–67, 72, 74, 156

Those Who Have Borne the Battle (Wright), 114–15, 168

Three Soldiers (Dos Passos), 23, 29–36, 39, 57, 85–86, 156

Through the Lens of Cultural Awareness (Wunderle), 147–48

The Tin Soldier (Bailey), 27–28

Total Mobilization (Scranton), 107, 148

Trail of Tears, 69

trauma, 75–81, 103–5, 125–32, 219n61

"The Trauma Hero" (Scranton), 55, 139

trauma hero concept, 107, 139, 148, 159, 184, 208n41, 208n42

Tribe (Junger), 99, 125–26, 167

Trumbo, Dalton, 87, 91

trust, 76, 77, 107, 165–69

truth, 55, 57, 61, 67–75, 89, 107

251

Index

United States, violent history of, 4, 69. *See also* politics and political institutions

university writing programs. *See* creative writing programs

"Unless It's a Sucking Wound" (Klay), 89, 130

Van Reet, Brian, 18, 106, 152, 156, 159–61, 182–83

Vernon, Alex, 50, 54–55

veteran-authors: and autobiography, 49; vs. civilian readers, 65–67, 75, 78–81; of contemporary war fiction, 96–97; cultural authority of, 61–62, 83–85; history of, 23; narrative authority of, 1–3, 7–15, 102–8, 152; vs. non-combatant authors, 8–9; in post–WWII era, 51–54; "status economy" for, 94–96; and trauma, 78–81, 103–5; in writing programs, 47–48, 51–54

veterans, generally, 19, 99, 168, 174, 184–85, 229n70. *See also* veteran-authors

Veterans Crisis Hotline (Chopan), 105, 126, 170–71

victim narrative, 208n41, 229n73

victory, 46, 86, 91, 111, 217n25

Vietnam in American Literature (Melling), 76, 77

Vietnam War: casualty statistics, 222n27; and civil-military gap, 4–5; draft and, 98, 166–67; as history, 92; public attitude toward, 67, 77–78, 168, 173; rhetoric of uniqueness around, 75, 207n24; rules of engagement in, 112–13; and veteran alienation, 114–18, 133

Vietnam War fiction: American perspective in, 142–45; antagonism toward government in, 174; authors of, 3, 10–11, 65–75; characteristics of, 13, 79, 143, 169, 206n15; dehumanization in, 14; historical perspectives in, 68–75, 92; homecoming in, 126; legacy of, 76, 78, 92; objectives, 75–76; rhetoric of uniqueness around, 70–71; and trauma, 75–81

Vietnamese people, 137, 142–45

violence: and ethics/morals, 130–31, 138, 150; in fiction, 24, 113–14; soldiers as agents of, 14, 175; in US history, 4, 69

volunteering, as theme, 174. *See also* all-volunteer military

Walker, Nico, 126, 127

Walsh, Jeffrey, 35

war, generally, 5, 75, 91, 100–101, 161–62, 184. *See also* Afghanistan War; Iraq War; Vietnam War; World War I; World War II

war crimes, 135–36

war fiction: conventions and traditions of, 17, 21–23, 56–58, 137–38; as cultural object, 7, 149; definitions of, 49, 105, 113; as genre, 34–36; purpose of, 207–8n17. *See also* contemporary war fiction; Vietnam War fiction; World War I fiction; World War II fiction

War Narratives (Cage), 107

"War Novels" (Cowley), 61

War Porn (Scranton), 18, 120–21, 152, 156–57, 160–61, 178, 180

warrior caste, 98–99

Wartime (Fussell), 92

The Watch (Roy-Bhattacharya), 141

Webb, Jim, 11, 72

Welcome to the Suck (Peebles), 9

Wharton, Edith, 27, 43

Index

What Changes Everything (Hamilton), 141, 178

What It Is Like to Go to War (Marlantes), 117

White, Hayden, 68, 90, 105–6

Whitman, Walt, 75

"Why Men Love War" (Broyles), 75

"The Widening Gap between the Military and Society" (Ricks), 6

Willa Cather's Imagination (Stouck), 42

Williams, Brian J., 139–40

Winn, Howard, 53

witness, fiction as bearing of, 35. *See also* eyewitness accounts

Wolfe, Tom, 103

women: fictional depictions of, 13–14, 144; in military, 164, 226n18. *See also* women authors

women authors: of contemporary war fiction, 92, 96–97; critiques of, 11, 38–42, 201n80; and Fussell, 21; scholarship regarding, 43; of WWI fiction, 23, 26, 38–42, 41

Workshops of Empire (Bennett), 60

"World," in Vietnam war fiction, 73–75

World War I, 101, 114

World War I and the American Novel (Cooperman), 42

World War I fiction: audience for, 28; authors of, 21, 23, 26, 38–42, 41; characteristics of, 13, 24–28, 25, 34; and

combat gnosticism, 21–23; critical response to, 9–10, 25–28, 61; and historical memory, 88, 91; legacy of, 43, 48, 55–57; objectives, 75–76. *See also One of Ours; Three Soldiers*

World War II, 45–47, 91, 101, 114–16, 122, 206n14

World War II fiction: authors of, 45–47, 61–62; characteristics of, 13, 46, 169, 202n3; and historical memory, 91; objectives, 75–76; reportorial realism in, 46

The Worn Doorstep (Sherwood), 26

Wright, James, 114–15, 168

"write what you know," 49, 50, 60, 61–62

writing programs. *See* creative writing programs

Wunderle, William D., 147–48

The Yellow Birds (Powers), 103–6, 133–34

"You Don't Have to Be a Veteran to Write about War" (Gallagher), 1, 3, 105

"you had to be there" sentiment, 3, 17, 66–67, 81, 86–87, 106, 117

You Know When the Men Are Gone (Fallon), 119–20

"you volunteered to get screwed" sentiment, 176–79

THE NEW AMERICAN CANON

Half a Million Strong:
Crowds and Power from Woodstock
to Coachella
by Gina Arnold

Violet America:
Regional Cosmopolitanism in U.S. Fiction
since the Great Depression
by Jason Arthur

The Meanings of J. Robert Oppenheimer
by Lindsey Michael Banco

Neocolonial Fictions of the Global Cold War
edited by Steven Belletto and
Joseph Keith

Workshops of Empire: Stegner, Engle,
and American Creative Writing during
the Cold War
by Eric Bennett

Places in the Making:
A Cultural Geography of American Poetry
by Jim Cocola

The Legacy of David Foster Wallace
edited by Samuel Cohen and
Lee Konstantinou

Writing Wars: Authorship and American
War Fiction, WWI to Present
by David F. Eisler

Race Sounds:
The Art of Listening in
African American Literature
by Nicole Brittingham Furlonge

Postmodern/Postwar — and After:
Rethinking American Literature
edited by Jason Gladstone,
Andrew Hoberek, and Daniel Worden

After the Program Era:
The Past, Present, and Future of
Creative Writing in the University
edited by Loren Glass

Hope Isn't Stupid:
Utopian Affects in Contemporary
American Literature
by Sean Austin Grattan

It's Just the Normal Noises:
Marcus, Guralnick, No Depression,
and the Mystery of Americana Music
by Timothy Gray

Wrong:
A Critical Biography of Dennis Cooper
by Diarmuid Hester

Reverse Colonization:
Science Fiction, Imperial Fantasy,
and Alt-victimhood
by David M. Higgins

Art Essays:
A Collection
edited by Alexandra Kingston-Reese

Contemporary Novelists and the Aesthetics
of Twenty-First Century American Life
by Alexandra Kingston-Reese

American Unexceptionalism:
The Everyman and the Suburban Novel
after 9/11
by Kathy Knapp

Visible Dissent:
Latin American Writers, Small U.S. Presses,
and Progressive Social Change
by Teresa V. Longo

Pynchon's California
edited by Scott McClintock and
John Miller

Richard Ford and the Ends of Realism
by Ian McGuire

Novel Subjects:
Authorship as Radical Self-Care in
Multiethnic American Narratives
by Leah A. Milnes

William Gibson and the Futures
of Contemporary Culture
edited by Mitch R. Murray and
Mathias Nilges
Poems of the American Empire:
The Lyric Form in the Long
Twentieth Century
by Jen Hedler Phillis

Reading Capitalist Realism
edited by Alison Shonkwiler and
Leigh Claire La Berge

Technomodern Poetics:
The American Literary Avant-Garde
at the Start of the Information Age
by Todd F. Tietchen

Contested Terrain
by Keith Wilhite

Ecospatiality:
A Place-Based Approach to
American Literature
by Lowell Wyse

How to Revise a True War Story:
Tim O'Brien's Process of Textual Production
by John K. Young